1981

A READING OF
DANTE'S *INFERNO*

Wallace Fowlie

A READING OF

DANTE'S
INFERNO

The University of Chicago Press

Chicago and London

The University of Chicago Press, Chicago 60637
The University of Chicago Press, Ltd., London

The illustrations are reproduced from
Illustrations to the Divine Comedy of Dante
by William Blake (New York: Da Capo Press, 1968).

Library of Congress Cataloging in Publication Data

Fowlie, Wallace, 1908–
  A reading of Dante's Inferno.

  Bibliography: p.
  Includes index.
  1. Dante Alighieri, 1265–1321. Divina commedia.
Inferno. I. Dante Alighieri, 1265–1321. Divina com-
media. Inferno. II. Title.
PQ4443.F68   851'.1   80–19025
ISBN 0-226-25887-4
ISBN 0-226-25888-2 (pbk.)

WALLACE FOWLIE is the translator of *The Complete Works
of Rimbaud with Selected Letters* and author of *Rimbaud,
A Reading of Proust,* and *Mallarmé,* all published by the
University of Chicago Press.

To Austin Warren

Contents

Introduction

Personal Thoughts on Reading the Inferno

EACH TIME the Dante semester returns in my teaching schedule—
Monday, Wednesday, and Friday, for fifteen weeks—with all
those class hours to be given to the thirty-four cantos of the first
cantica, I plot and replot the purpose of the course, trying to
decide what to emphasize and how to emphasize it. Every two
or three years these preparations vary because of the historical
moment in the literary criticism, in religion, in the preoccupa-
tions of students. The spring of 1970, when I first taught Dante
at Duke University, was different in all those respects from the
spring of 1979, when I taught the *Inferno* for the first time as a
professor emeritus.

During some of the semesters I plan to accentuate the psychic
aspects over the moral and religious. I plan to consider Dante's
descent into Hell as a descent into his subconscious, into his
past, in order to understand why he is lost, why he is estranged. I
argue with myself and my students that to justify and understand
himself, a man has to know the worst about himself. By "worst" I
mean those experiences, often forgotten or concealed, that have
alienated him from the order of the world.

The guiding thought of the course would therefore be that
Dante *has* to descend into Hell. Virgil tells him in canto 1 that
there is no other way out of his dilemma. *Cammino*, "the way,"
is in the first line and in the seventh from the last line of canto 34.
The "way" leads to the worst that has to be known before the best
can be reached in a man's life. And it certainly is the worst: Dante

1

avoids nothing that is bad and corrupt and malicious. Hell is the world reinvented. It is the world written in Italian verse. It is composed of one fantasy-picture after another, and each one is a form of obsession which, if allowed to remain in the form of an obsession, would cause serious suffering in a man's being, would impede him from self-realization and ultimate salvation, even salvation in the purely human sense.

A *Reading of Dante's "Inferno"* was undertaken to complement and offset an earlier book, *A Reading of Proust*. I taught the *Divine Comedy* three times at Bennington College, and the *Paradiso* once at the University of Chicago (as a graduate course) at the invitation of Professor Borgese who framed his invitation with the words: "It will be interesting to see what a specialist in French Symbolism will have to say about Dante!" Then, every other spring during the 70s I taught the *Inferno* at Duke.

Each time I resume the teaching of the *Inferno*, it is with the same self-acknowledged confession: Dante is the fountainhead of literature for me, the source. I have never felt the need of going before him to a detailed study of earlier writers: to the *chansons de geste* or Chrétien, to the Greek or Latin poets. They are all there in Dante, in places where I can see them, not analyzed but used and illuminated, assigned to some niche in a vast reproduction of the world and the apocalyptic life of the world beyond the world.

More than any other single work, the *Inferno* has given me the fullest realization of what literature is. Dante is the supreme example of an artist who seizes everything around him, and uses everything within him: his mind, his heart, his sex. Everything is to be utilized and conquered. And because he is satisfied with nothing less than everything, his work abounds with enigmas and inconsistencies. They are countless, there in his texts, even in his early work, the *Vita nuova*, and he wanted them as enigmas, and left them as such.

I always felt more secure in teaching my courses in French literature: Proust or the symbolist poets, for example; but Dante exalts and excites me more. I have to plan the lessons on each canto more carefully, and choose the words I want to emphasize, the lines I want to make as memorable as possible, the characters and scenes I want the students to remember for life. As I prepare the lessons, I often think back to the course I took at Harvard with Professor Grandgent when we read *The Divine Comedy* in his edition: the Italian text only, with voluminous notes on each page along with a brief outline-introduction to each canto.

It was the last time he gave his famous course, and we were awed by his scholarly edition of the poem, by his age and his quiet manner. We were, I must confess, disappointed that all he did in class—throughout the entire year—was to have us translate the Italian text as it appeared in his edition. From time to time he read aloud a passage in Italian and then asked one of us to translate it. But the hour was largely filled with our own awkward, hesitating translations. Grandgent offered no commentary on the text, as if all he had to say had been consigned to the footnotes of his book. If once every two or three weeks one of us dared ask a question he would answer in a most complete and satisfactory way. Thus we realized he had not put everything he knew into his edition.

A few eminent American Dante scholars have succeeded the famous Harvard teachers and translators: Longfellow, Charles Eliot Norton, Santayana, Grandgent; I have in mind particularly Singleton, Burgin, Fergusson, Freccero, Musa. Professor Singleton, surely the best Dante scholar in the world today, has now revised Grandgent's edition of *The Divine Comedy*. Many teachers today use a bilingual edition, and many of them, like me, prepare a lecture-discussion class. That was not Mr. Grandgent's method! He listened to our translation in class and corrected us gently. No paper to write, no quiz to take, only a final exam, largely made up of long passages to translate! I doubt if any class in an American university today would tolerate such an absence of pedagogy and stimulation. We learned some Italian from Grandgent, but we had to learn by ourselves, outside of class, elements of what today we would call a critical-interpretive approach to Dante.

Nothing exists by itself in the poem, no figure, no landscape, no metaphor, no sin. Not even the poet himself. Everything is illuminated by everything else. His art is a close network of relationships: secret, invisible and visible relationships between things, between things and men, between their aspirations and their faults, between God and his creatures. Because of this complexity, the *Commedia* demands of its reader a full concentration and a willingness to subordinate to it, temporarily, the rest of life. Before it gives itself to the reader, the *Inferno* has to be examined over and over again. Then, one day, like a piece of music that has been listened to many times, it is there intact in the life of the reader, as part of his knowledge and being. This phenomenon of knowledge comes about not through "research" in the modern sense, but through the penetration of a world, through the seeing of a world that exists in words, in images and characters created by words.

More than device in teaching, the relating of Dante to contemporary literature is an obligation. The modern world has no purely poetic work comparable to the *Commedia,* but there are two works of prose that have the linguistic tenseness of poetry and that reveal in their power of imagery what poetry is able to reveal: the works of Proust and Joyce. In fact, the word *inferno* would not be a misnomer in designating *A la recherche du temps perdu* and *Ulysses.* Each is a world in itself organized into scenes of tests and punishments. Each of the three works offers as protagonist a writer (Dante, Marcel, and Stephen) who narrates his voyage throughout the episodes and who also participates in them to some degree. All three protagonist-writers are voyeurs and actors. In each case, their principal adventure is preceded by a form of prelude, a mysterious early work in which the writer tests himself and announces the greater work to come. It is the *Vita nuova* for Dante, a secretive and almost esoteric introduction to the *Divina commedia.* For Proust, it is *Un amour de Swann,* a prefiguration of Marcel's love for Gilberte and Albertine, and of his desire to know the two worlds, the two "ways" of Swann and Guermantes. Then, finally, for Joyce, the story of Stephen Dedalus is first told in *Portrait of the Artist as a Young Man* before being continued in *Ulysses.*

Is the world outside of time a stumbling block for students today? The finite story of man, in his life and in the history of his day, is carried over by Dante into the eternal world, and yet the finite form of his first life never disappears. A transformation has taken place, through which, however, one can see the finiteness of the earlier life. The miracle of Dante's creation is this power of giving to each scene a realistic contour and precision, and, at the same time, of giving to the reader the impression that he is watching a scene belonging to another world, the world beyond death, or at least the fantasy world of obsessions and nightmares.

Dante's poem is about what had been contemplated by him. He keeps telling us: I was there and I saw. The poem is the picture of a visionary, a picture provoked and sustained by a tremendous experience. The religious experience, at the heart of the poem, is continually overflowing into some historical or even some political action. Dante's feelings are continually turning into rational and intellectual thoughts, as his mind is always infused with the pulsations of his blood. In other words, the *Inferno* is a work of such plenitude and totality that it is capable of reflecting and absorbing experiences that come to his readers today or at any time.

Like every major artist, Dante was concerned with leaving after him a work that would never turn traitor. The face of such a work is always partially in a shadow. This is the inevitable result of every "lesson" (reading and discussion) on a canto. The luminous and shadowy parts of any work complex as Dante's poem come from the world's celebration of it. Literary fame comes on and goes off like the flashing light of a beacon, like the inevitable sequence of day and night, of comprehension and misunderstanding. It takes time for a work of this magnitude to rediscover its order and to reinvent its reality. The wisdom of Dante and Shakespeare, of Proust and Joyce, is so covered with scars, with all the imperfections of words, whether they be Italian or English or French, that we often read them and believe we see what we actually do not.

Dante's voyage to God goes through the world first. The circles of Hell, as conceived by the poet, are the scenes of human existence, but as they will be forever. The horrors of the world have to be experienced before one can move beyond them to the non-worldly joys of Purgatory and Paradise. All the forms of incontinence and malice have to be known in their terrestrial settings before the voyager can move to the world beyond them.

At the very beginning of the poem, Dante is in distress; a messenger, Virgil, comes to help him. But we learn in the second canto that this is no chance encounter. Virgil has been sent by Beatrice, who is among the blessed. Beatrice had been sent by Lucia, Dante's patron saint, who in turn had been spoken to by Mary, the queen of Heaven. Four intermediaries have been solicited to help Dante, since he could no longer help himself. His voyage, taking its point of departure on earth and going first through Hell, has therefore an absolute beginning in Heaven, where Mary, not named as such, but called a noble lady (*Donna è gentil nel ciel*), is the link with the divine mystery that sets everything in motion.

Dante will never be left alone, from the moment of the appearance of Virgil, who will lead him through all the phases and all the experiences of sin. These experiences are never cut off from the world. A historical reality surrounds them, which at the same time is depicted so as to appear eternal. The words *eterno* and *eternità* resound throughout the eternal regions. Everywhere on this voyage one is sensitive to a great change, the mutation of men passing from time into eternity. All the spirits, either historical or legendary, whom Dante meets and talks with, once walked on the earth.

Dante was not obsessed by time as Proust was. His power as a poet is in seizing time and inventing for it a pulsation that beats in the present. He puts together a structure for time. Proust, on the other hand, is time's victim. The descent in *A la recherche du temps perdu* is not into Hell—Proust is there already—but a universal descent into the void. Because of life's fluidity and ephemeral nature, death is real for Proust. The metamorphosis that death will bring is simply a mask for the degradation of life. Dante, who has no dread of time, no obsession with it, would call it that force that assassinates and, ironically, sustains life and promotes it.

Dante's motif is one of the oldest in literature: a voyage through the world beyond the world. Homer narrates one in the eleventh book of the *Odyssey*, in which Odysseus descends to the underworld in order to learn from Tiresias whether it will be granted to him to return to his wife and native land. Virgil, too, narrates one in the sixth book of the *Aeneid*, where we see Aeneas going to the underworld so that the ghost of his father Anchises will reveal to him his destiny. These two voyages of antiquity, both of which were known to Dante, demonstrate the belief that the dead know more about life than the living. The dead, in a word, are more powerful than the living

Between the fourteenth and twentieth centuries, how, if at all, has man's history changed? In a general sense, it is not difficult to make the transition from the dead in the underworld regions of Homer and Virgil, and the damned souls in Dante's *Inferno*, to the descent into the subterranean cosmos of personality which one can achieve today, especially at moments of great life crisis when we need to consult the dead of our race who still live in us, and the dead figures of our own personality who desire to return to the living self and resume an interrupted existence.

The subconscious is endless and as deep as Dante makes his Hell. It is filled with as many grimacing and sad and violent figures as those that we encounter in the Italian poem. The speech of the lost figures in our own life is as enigmatical, dramatic, and elliptical as the speech of Filippo Argenti, Farinata, and Cavalcante, father of Guido Cavalcanti. In the circles of his Hell, Dante encounters ghosts of the past who bear some relation to his own moral scruples and defects, as today an individual encounters, in successive medical consultations and self-analyses, the origins of his conflicts.

Dante's spirits and the realms they inhabit are graphically portrayed. Only the size of these realms is incommensurable with the earth and hard for the reader to grasp. It is the difference between earth and eternity, and yet Dante keeps reminding his readers that it is on earth that man's eternal existence is determined. Everything on the earth is eternalized once life ends. This is in keeping with the defects and trials and devastations that are prolonged and eternalized for us through our very distant and very immediate pasts. The funnel of Dante's Hell constitutes a landscape of sin, which today in our more tentative and more evasive language we call "obsessions."

The map of Hell, both that which precedes and that which makes up the city of Dis, is the map of the heart turned against itself, which in its freedom has turned away from freedom's source, namely, the love of God. The reader is bewildered and even depressed by the number of sins that Dante shows us in action, each sin undoing itself. But Dante never meant us to believe that a single soul commits all of the sins. However, since the poet's focus is on the city, the *città dolente*, on a society affected by all individual sins, he has to show all of them within a single image. Dis is therefore the image of the city perverted. At the summit of Paradise, it will appear in the form of a yellow rose.

First, the voyager has to move downward. Hell is a funnel sucking him in, and it can begin anywhere, in a dark forest, for example. Before one knows it, one is sucked into all the possibilities of depravity. The slightest turning away from the good, the slightest indulgence in self-knowledge, will lead to a more deliberate, serious turning away. This is the story of Dante's *Inferno*, and the story behind most individual lives.

The source of the fourfold interpretation of the *Commedia* is to be found with Dante himself, in his letter to Can Grande (letter eleven in the collected letters). To interpret the literal meaning of a line (or a passage) on three levels—allegorical, moral, and anagogical—was an accepted method of interpreting the Bible and goes back to the early Church Fathers. In the *Summa theologica*, Saint Thomas Aquinas speaks of the literal or historical meaning of a passage and of the old law signifying the new; the moral or tropological meanings would be the acts of Christ which are signs of what we should do; and the anagogical meanings are acts of Christ that refer to eternal glory.

After reading the thirty-four cantos of the *Inferno*, the reader begins another experience, that of remembering Dante's voyage through Hell. Even after a brief interval, the experience of the reading tends to disintegrate. Memory of the voyage grows fainter and fainter, and most readers realize that they have not been profound readers but merely tourists, and rather than a voyage, built on progress and development, the *Inferno* has been for them a series of pictures, whose brilliance and drama and horror fade into time, until only a few episodes are remembered.

The seemingly separate drama of a canto is connected with all the rest. If the sense of development is lost, the work is lost, too. A single reading will serve little purpose. A long, intimate acquaintance is indispensable for an appreciation of Dante. All the connections have to be remembered. That is why Dante so persistently uses chronology during his journey, as well as astronomy, geography, history, and moral philosophy. Recollection of the *Inferno* is a willed intellectual activity. Such activity, however, is not over-arduous. What helps us the most in understanding and remembering Dante is our sympathy for all we see, a sympathy that grows inwardly without our daring to use such a term as sympathy. The sins we observe being punished, if not our own, are at the least their close relatives.

Background for the Reading

Is it possible to explain the power Dante has exerted over so many readers for so long a time? The efforts of the present study are centered quite deliberately on this question. The mark of a major work of art would seem precisely to be its ability to awaken in the sensibility of every generation awareness, elations, recognitions, and new ways of understanding human life. By means of his art, a poet sees men more clearly than they see themselves and reveals to them fresh illuminations about the world in which they live.

Readers of Dante today come to him with knowledge, manners, and beliefs vastly different from those in all the centuries between the fourteenth and the twentieth. What has not changed in the world is human nature—and that is the subject matter of *The Divine Comedy*. The unchangeableness of human nature gives to the art of such major poets as Homer, Dante, and Shakespeare their permanent relevance. The degrees of relevance, even for these three poets of the very distant past, vary today in the lives of living readers, as they have varied in the centuries preceding ours. It is perhaps trite to say that the great poet is perpetually modern, but that is the miracle of art, the cause of our wonderment, and in many ways, the most arduous task of the critic to encompass.

The poet, and surely this is the case for the three poets just named, is the interpreter of his age, and then the interpreter of human life to other persons in all ages. Each of these poets presents a view of life, but in each case this view is projected by the faculty of the imagination. Each is an image-maker. The supreme sources of literary art are language and imagination: the use of words, in their meaning and rhythm, and the power of words to paint pictures. The characters of Homer are clearly defined amd the motives for their behavior are simple. Shakespeare's characters, too, are clearly drawn, but the motives for their actions are complex and unclear even to themselves. The paradoxes and dilemmas of life form a large part of Shakespeare's art. Midway between Homer and Shakespeare, Dante wrote his *Divina commedia*, wherein again there is clearly delineated a large number of characters whose motives are analyzed from a very special viewpoint: that of the Christian principles of right and wrong. Dante is more rigorously the poet and moralist than Homer or Shakespeare, but he is their equal in his use of strongly rhythmical language and in the creating of images.

Whereas Homer and Shakespeare never intervene in their writings, never clearly stamp a passage with their own opinion, Dante's writings are primarily autobiographical. There is no direct comment on the Trojan War by Homer, no comment by Shakespeare on the mysterious relationship between Othello and Iago. But Dante Alighieri is present in every line of the *Divine Comedy*, telling the reader what he thinks and feels and knows. In his art Dante not only testifies to, but is, the variousness of the human soul, and enacts a search, which he calls a "comedy," both deeply personal and universal.

Far more than the art of Homer and Shakespeare, Dante's art is a lesson on righteousness. He is, beyond any doubt, still today the chief moralist poet of the world. Homer is Greece, classical antiquity, the eternal story of war, and the warrior's return after war. Shakespeare is England, the emergence of the modern world from the Middle Ages, with the endless torment of knowledge, of conflicting drives and ambitions, of forms of love so hard to sustain that survival is impossible. Dante is, of course, Italy, and all of Italy, the dream of man's secular life that once was Rome; but he is also the promise of the Christian faith, and especially the belief of that faith and of all religions, that the spirit of each person who has lived is immortal.

Before he can become the poet of every age, a poet of Dante's dimension, must be the poet of is own age. By far, Dante is the representative artist, the leading poet of what historians like to call the medieval millenium, the thousand years between A.D. 500 and 1500. This era began with the collapse of the Roman Empire in 476, and ended with the discovery of the western hemisphere in 1492. Among the creations of the medieval world we might list romanesque and gothic architecture; new literary forms such as the chanson de geste, the courtly romance, the dolce stil nuovo; the scholastic philosophy unified and strengthened by Saint Thomas Aquinas; a newly formed social order composed of nobility, gentry, and bourgeoisie; and the founding of the universities at Paris, Bologna, and elsewhere. But of all medieval creations, the most powerful and the most perfected was the Church.

Immediately after the fall of Rome, all forms of art, language, literature, and institutions were vague and confused. Centuries were necessary for the establishment of geographical boundaries of monarchical states and for the development of languages. By the end of the eleventh century there were clear signs that such changes were coming about. The Song of Roland, probably dating from the beginning of the twelfth century, was a form of literature celebrating a new heroic age in Europe, represented by a fighting emperor (Charlemagne), a fighting leader (Roland), and even by a fighting priest (Archbishop Turpin). The heroic age of the twelfth century, with its fusion of Greco-Roman culture and Christian religion, became in the thirteenth century an age characterized primarily by theological unity and ecclesiastical authority. Saint Thomas Aquinas, in his defense of Christianity against the pagans (*Summa contra gentiles*) and in his *Summa theologica*, which still today is the basis of Catholic philosophy, helped to establish a church-dominated world unmatched before or after the Middle Ages.

In Rome, at the height of its power, there had been political unity, but moral and spiritual problems had been, on the whole, left to the individual. The reverse was true in the Middle Ages, when political disunity was rampant but when there was a strong unity of spiritual attitudes and ideals. Latin was the standard language; most intellectuals were clerics; Christianity had provided painters and sculptors with a common subject matter. In the domain of literature, the medieval stories of Charlemagne, Roland, and Arthur, along with the Latin epic of Aeneas and the Greek myths of Troy and Thebes were common European property.

The human values in which medieval man believed and by which he lived were wholly Christian. If these values were stated in their most basic form, they would read something like this: Man is a creature created by God and belonging to God; man is separated from God by the world in which he has to live out his mortal life; the world and its civilization are so designed as to assist man in his return to union with God; man has both a worldly and a spiritual side to his nature, and the spiritual always transcends the worldly or the material; the ideal man or the ideal woman is the saint, and the saint may take many forms: a philosopher like Aquinas, a humble peasant, a king like Louis IX of France, or a housewife.

Although there was no national unity in Dante's century, there were papal states from the beginning of the thirteenth century, which were indepedent city-republics. Pride in the authority of the Roman Church was a sentiment shared by all Italians. The supremacy of the pope had been established by the end of the eleventh century, and at the beginning of the thirteenth century, Innocent III defined the pope as the vicar of God on the earth, thus making Catholicism into a theocracy, that is, a religious government deriving its authority from God. The medieval church, even with its obvious elements of corruption, was looked upon as the ark of civilization. By the middle of the thirteenth century, just prior to Dante's birth, the new monastic orders of Saint Francis and Saint Dominic, as well as the much older order of Saint Benedict, boasted large numbers of monks, and were admirable in the degree of religious ardor they manifested. These orders began admitting tertiary members, men who continued to live in the world but who helped the poor and who, by refusing to take arms, helped break the feudal system in Italy.

Dante, for most of us today, represents the culmination of medievalism, a philosophy which in its most succinct form stated that man is an immortal being for whom this planet is but the first stage.

If Dante was primarily a religious poet, he was at the same time a political thinker. Our immortal life is dependent upon our moral life. We are creatures of God, desired by God, but we are also human beings living in a society, a city, an empire, and our relationship with our fellows is almost as significant as our relationship with God.

The ideological conflict between the Guelfs and Ghibellines raged in Italy throughout Dante's lifetime and long after his death. It is hard to read *The Divine Comedy*, and especially the *Inferno*, without some knowledge of this political conflict, which has analogies to the more familiar problems of class struggles, racism, party politics, power drive, and civic corruption. The Ghibellines represented aristocracy, upholding the emperor while opposing papal territorial power. The Guelfs, to whose party Dante belonged, represented a more "democratic" attitude, desiring a constitutional government. The Guelfs looked upon themselves as representing an indigenous Italian stock, individuals who looked to the pope for support against the Ghibelline clan. They were part merchant middle class and part minor nobility. The other European powers took sides with the Ghibellines and Guelfs. Since the Germanic states made strong claims for a Germanic emperor, they naturally sided with the Ghibellines. But France, closer to the pope, lent support to the Guelfs.

At the same time that this political division was felt in Italy, wealth and culture were developing rapidly. The Dark Ages were over, and signs of what historians now call the early Renaissance were in evidence. Guilds of craftsmen and merchants were multiplying at the same time that classical learning was being rediscovered. Although a few Ghibelline leaders in Dante's time were suspected of heresy and even of atheism, there was no real schism in the western Church—the dualist heresy, under its various forms of gnosticism or Manichaeanism, had been put down, and the Church's unity was still strong: the pope's activist and the emperor's activist both received communion at the same altar from the same priest.

In the middle of the thirteenth century, there was a brief chance for political unity, due to the eccentric although versatile brilliance of Frederick II, king of Sicily. He was emperor of the Hohenstaufen dynasty and almost brought about again an effective Roman Empire. This would have brought about an Italian unity that was not actually achieved until centuries later. The pope, however, was hostile to Frederick, and the pope won.

Fifteen years later, at the battle of Benevento, Frederick's bastard son Manfred was slain by Charles d'Anjou. That year was 1265.

In that year Dante Alighieri was born in Florence. What we know of Dante comes from his own published works and from two early biographers. The first of these was the historian Giovanni Villani who came to Rome in the jubilee year 1300 and made brief mention of Dante in his chronicles. The second was Boccaccio, a contemporary who did not know the poet personally. His *Vita di Dante* is a little over forty pages long.

Dante's well-to-do family was Guelf, and of Florentine descent. His mother died when he was five, and his father when he was twelve. He was brought up by his stepmother. At the age of nine, the boy attended a May Day party at the home of Folco Portinari where he met the host's daughter Beatrice, a year younger than himself. She was wearing a red dress. Dante fell in love with her, and twenty years later told the story of his love. The truthfulness of this story, in its essence at least, is believed by most commentators. The poet tells us his love was chaste, and this also is usually accepted. In 1287, Beatrice Portinari married the banker Simone dei Bardi. This event was not mentioned by Dante.

When he was eighteen, Beatrice first spoke to him. This *saluto* was for the young man an experience of ectasy. But then, on hearing some semi-scandalous rumors about Dante, Beatrice refused to speak to him. This refusal of a salutation caused Dante deep suffering. On seeing her at a party, for example, Dante was so overcome that friends believed him ill. In 1289 Folco Portinari died, and Dante grieved because of Beatrice's grief. The following year, 1290, Beatrice herself died.

During the next ten years, the last decade of the thirteenth century, Dante studied philosophy, science, and theology. He read Latin literature and Provençal, and was probably guided in these matters by the teacher-writer Brunetto Latini. His family arranged his marriage to the daughter of an ancient Guelf family, Gemma Donati, who bore him at least four children. There is no reliable proof concerning either the happiness or unhappiness in this marriage.

At the turn of the new century Dante became increasingly involved in politics. He also belonged to the guild of physicians and apothecaries. Apothecary shops in the Florence of 1300 sold not only drugs, but also books, paintings, and jewels. In that first year of the century, Dante Alighieri was elected to the priorate of Florence. The Florentine Guelfs were at that time powerful, but a feud between two families, over the murder of a youth, caused a serious party split. The Cerchi family and their Florentine supporters were called the "Whites" (i Bianchi); the Donati family and their supporters were called the "Blacks" (i Neri). The priors, in order to bring back peace to Florence, banished the leaders of both Bianchi and Neri, and Dante, a "white" in his role of prior, was responsible for banishing his friend Guido Cavalcanti, as well as Corso Donati, a member of his wife's family.

Pope Boniface VIII intervened in this city strife in 1301. Charles de Valois, brother of the French king, and an army leader on the side of the Blacks, came to Florence to put down the strife, Dante was sentenced to exile in 1302. At that time, however, he was not yet the profound political thinker he was to become in later years. He was a White Guelf, which meant he had a liberal political outlook but favored the Ghibelline tradition of supporting art and learning. He disliked especially the Ghibelline lack of respect for religion.

Between 1302 and the year of his death, 1321, Dante led a twenty year period of exile, during a large part of which he wrote his Commedia. His family remained in Florence. There is no evidence that his wife Gemma ever joined him. There are indications that he stayed briefly as the guest of great families in several of the cities of Italy. He may have taught part of the time; indeed, his book, Il convivio, would seem to be a set of lectures. It is probably true that he spent some time in Paris, but doubtful that he ever reached Oxford.

He wrote in Latin a treatise on "writing in the common tongue" (De vulgari eloquentia), and a treatise on government

(*De monarchia*) in which he makes a case for world government, a concept he derived from Virgil's epic on the founding of Rome. Dante's thesis stated that world monarchy should be holy, imperial, and Roman. He looked upon both the Jews and the Romans as chosen peoples, seeing in Jews the source of the Church, and in the Romans the source of the Empire.

It is not known when Dante began writing the *Commedia*. Just a few facts concerning the end of his life can be authenticated. He was in Ravenna in 1317, a guest in the castle of the Count of Polenta. There he was joined by his sons Jacopo and Pietro and by his daughter Beatrice. He was sent on a mission in 1321 to Venice, where he contracted a fever. He died shortly after returning to Ravenna, at the age of fifty-six, and was buried in the convent of the Franciscan Friars. Although the city of Florence wished to have his body buried there, it is believed his remains are still in Ravenna. Except for a death mask, claimed to be Dante's, and a sensitive, youthful face painted by Giotto, Dante's contemporary, in a fresco in the Bargello (the thirteenth-century palace of the magistrates, today a national museum), there is no authentic portrait of the poet.

But the principal traits of the man's character are decipherable in his writings. His emotions were strong and deeply felt. Despite a tendency to cruelty and fierce vindictiveness, his nature was primarily compassionate and sympathetic. He was far more the sensualist than a scourger of sinners and demons. His sense of justice, as deeply felt as his sympathy, forced him to allocate men he admired, such as Farinata, to positions in Hell that corresponded to the known facts of their moral lives. Like a judge, Dante in his *Inferno* invaded the private life of countless men and women, and labeled them as offenders.

Dante was not a man of action, not a party leader. His brief career as prior seems inconsequential when compared to that other kind of action: the writing of such a work as *The Divine Comedy*. Dante was primarily the kind of poet in whom the world of the imagination endured throughout his lifetime. He knew, with all passionate men, moments of love and hate, of wrath and tenderness. Learned in all the fields of knowledge of his time—theology, jurisprudence, history, philosophy, physics, astronomy, mathematics, and poetics—Dante felt no basic conflict between philosophy and the teachings of the Church, between Aristotle and Saint Thomas Aquinas.

As a thinker, he maintained his basic belief in the two suns destined to guide humanity: the pope and the emperor, both responsible to God, both equal, provided the emperor expressed due reverence for the pope, for the spirit of man is superior to the body, and in this sense the pope is above the emperor. Dante's utopia, that of attaining and preserving peace for all of humanity, is still today the dream of mankind. It is a simple, logical dream, with the individual a member of a commune, the commune a part of the nation, and the nation a part of humanity. Yet Dante certainly believed the communes should submit to the emperor provided their liberties were respected.

In Dante's personal life, reference is made to a moral aberration or waywardness that followed the death of Beatrice. There is reference in the *canzoniere*, a group of his separate poems, to the strong sensuousness of his nature. But more than this fact, in the sense of specific misbehavior, is not known.

Dante's deep love for Florence was a strong part of his nature. And he seemed to love the two conflicting elements in the city's history: both the aristocratic splendor associated with the Ghibelline faction, and the more democratic manners represented by the Guelf ideals. But in Dante's mind, Florence is especially associated with Beatrice. They are the two souls of his poem: the woman and the city, birthplace and mothering figure sheltering all the children, expressive of love and yet rigorous in the teaching of duty and the virtue of loyalty.

Dante, in his love for his city, had no need to look toward Rome, because Florence was the daughter of Rome. It had been created by Romans who settled on the banks of the Arno, and who had fashioned Florence in the image of Rome. Dante thus looked upon himself as both Florentine and Roman.

At variance, perhaps, but miraculously joined in Dante's temperament, two traits in particular marked the man and the poet as he expressed himself in the one hundred cantos of the *Commedia*. His high moral ideals would seem to come from the stoics of antiquity. These were sustained through the strength of his nature, a fortitude that inevitably brought with it a trace of pride. Dante was admittedly aware of his pride. But his nature, in its sense of humility and practice of devotion, contained the antidote to pride. Franciscan in its essence, Dante's humility quieted the outbursts of vindictiveness and the element of pride in his stoical strength.

CANTO

1

The Dark Wood

THIS FIRST CANTO introduces the entire *Divine Comedy*. It defines each of the three realms that Dante the traveler has to visit in order to escape from the "dark wood" referred to in the opening tercet. *Una selva oscura* is the opening setting where the Florentine poet Dante Alighieri finds himself on the morning of Good Friday in the year 1300, in the thirty-fifth year of his life. He has lost his way and is frightened by the wildness of the wood.

The first tercet provides the motif and the motivation of the entire work. The motif is the journey of the poet who must find his way out of the dark wood. The motivation is the need to recover. Recover from what? What is the meaning of the dark wood and what has caused Dante's fear (the word *paura* is used twice in ten lines)? No precise answer is ever given to these questions. Today, some 680 years after the date of the poem's action, we would call the poet's condition that of alienation. And today we also know, or at least we believe, that the experience of alienation cannot be defined in any simple terms, that it is a complete situation formed by many causes.

Dante was indeed wise not to have attempted any strict analysis of his estrangement. If no specificity is possible in his case, we can be sure of the general cause which is always present, and often invisible, with every specific illness. Dante is estranged from the order of the world. This experience is a bitterness, comparable almost to death, in the sense that it has cut him off from the world. The real clue to this entire opening

passage is Dante's confession that he cannot explain how he has
come to this impasse: he was not conscious of losing his way. The
reasons for his estrangement are as dark as the wood itself.

This bewildered man comes to the foot of a hill, and sees at its
top the rays of the sun which he feels instinctively will guide him
out of the darkness. But when he begins to climb, three animals,
one after the other, impede his way, and again he loses hope, this
time of reaching the summit:

> io perdei la speranza de l'altezza. [1:54]
> [I lost hope of the height.]

By this line, and the reader has already followed an experience of
helplessness, frustration, and hopelessness. And already the
reader's mind is perhaps moving beyond the literalness of this
brief passage. The rays of light on the mountain top must be
something more that the physical sun. The leopard, the lion, and
the she-wolf, with their respective characteristics of litheness,
fury, and leanness, must be more than the three beasts named in
Jeremiah 5:6.

The wood, the hill, and the beasts appear to be outside of
Dante, thanks to the poet's art, but we begin to realize that they
are also within him, that they depict familiar fantasies we can easily recognize, fantasies created in the subconscious when one is
"out of joint" with the world, when, like Dante and Hamlet, one
is exiled, and relives, in some minor way which may yet be
stupendous in a single life, the drama of man's fall from God's
grace. Adam's dire experience is the archetype of innumerable
kinds of experience that cause an individual to feel abandoned.

Until the sudden unexpected appearance of Virgil, the atmosphere of this opening canto is decidedly Hebraic. The lost way,
the dark wood, the sense of bewilderment and estrangement are
reminiscent of the fall of man in Genesis and the chosen people's
intermittent separations from God. The three beasts of Jeremiah
were interpreted by Saint Jerome as representing sensuality (the
leopard), pride (the lion), and greed (the she-wolf), and this
moral interpretation seems as sound for Dante's passage as the
political interpretations offered by some scholars.

When Virgil's figure emerges from the darkness, a new atmosphere develops. Virgil is a clearly delineated character from the
classical world, explicit in his directions, the counterpart of
Dante's muddled mind, which is half asleep, half terrorized. Virgil died nineteen years before the birth of Christ, and therefore

stands at the end of the old world and at the beginning of the new. Appropriately, he will be the one to rescue Dante from the dark wood (he had already served as a guiding poet in Dante's development as a writer). *Poeta fui* (1:73), "I was a poet," he says, and Dante immediately acknowledges Virgil's rich inspiration for Italian verse (*quella fonte*, 1:79, "that fountain"). His recognition of Virgil is a moving moment in the action:

> Or se' tu quel Virgilio [1:79]
> [Are you then that Virgil?]

In total simplicity, Dante states Virgil's prevenience: the Latin poet was his master:

> Tu se' lo mio maestro [1:85]
> [you are my master]

In the form of a command, he asks for help: *aiutami* 1:89)—help me.

Before Virgil speaks of a way out from the predicament, we are reminded of the descent into Hades in the *Aeneid*, which was doubtless inspired by the same kind of descent narrated in Homer. We are reminded, too, of that passage in Virgil's fourth ecologue often interpreted as being a prophecy of the coming of Christ. Virgil is indeed the spiritual and historical and literary counterpart of Dante. From the very start, Dante accepts him as a doctor who prescribes.

Virgil's role as leader is clear in line 91:

> A te convien tenere altro vïaggio
> [you must take another way]

and with this statement we have a first insight into the entire scheme of the *Commedia*. The third beast, the *lupa*, has to be avoided at all costs because she will reign until a savior comes. She will finally be routed by a greyhound (*Veltro*, 1:101), but the time is not yet at hand. The history of political parties and political power does indeed count in the life history of the individual. Meanwhile, Virgil will serve as guide:

> e io sarò tua guida [1:113]
> [and I will be guide]

Virgil then briefly describes the three realms that Dante must go through in order to escape not only the *lupa* impeding his way, but also the beast within him.

The first is an eternal place (*loco etterno*, 1:114) of suffering spirits (*spiriti dolenti*, 1:116) and cries. Such is the torment there that the spirits call out for a second death. The second realm is that place where there is suffering, but the sufferers are happy in the fire (*son contenti / nel foco*, 1:118–19) because they know it is for a reason and that they will eventually move out of Purgatory into the third realm. Purgatory is a discipline for the higher life, for that place where the blessed live (*beate genti*, 1:120).

Dante gratefully consents to go wherever Virgil will take him. Virgil moves ahead, and Dante follows. It is the last line of the canto:

Allor si mosse, e io li tenni dietro.
[Then he moved on and I kept on behind him.]

The Latin poet Virgil, who had sung of Aeneas, founder of Rome, the eternal city where Christendom was to find its center, makes three promises to Dante before the beginning of the journey. These promises would seem to represent three kinds of salvation, and they embrace the entire poem. Virgil promises first a way of escape from the dark wood. This is the immediate, personal salvation of man who has reached an impasse in his thoughts and in his life. The man believes in God. He can see the rays of the sun on the distant hill and knows that God is the source of light and life, but he cannot, by himself, go to God. He is alienated in a mysterious psychic way and in such a state of confusion that he needs a slow, careful, documented picture of the ways in which transgressions against men and the cities of men result in blindness. All that Dante knows at this moment is that he is lost and impotent. This promise of a personal cure is made to him by a fellow poet of another age, his literary master, who, although not saved in the full Christian sense, lives eternally just outside of the realm inhabited by those spirits who, when they were on earth, willfully turned against the good and did not repent.

The second promise concerns Italy. Dante himself at this moment in his life is in exile from his beloved Florence. He has been forced by politics into the role of pilgrim and wayfarer. Virgil mysteriously names the one who is to save Italy *il Veltro* (the greyhound). Through the exercise of wisdom, love, and virile power (*sapïenza, amore e virtute*, 1:104), he will restore Italy. In giving Virgil these words, Dante may have had in mind Can Grande della Scala, whose birthplace was Verona, a city that lies between Feltro in Venetia and Montefeltro in Romagna. Political hopes change more often than most, and Dante himself fixed his hopes on various leaders during the course of his life. The obscure line that names the birthplace as the nation of *il Veltro* (1:105) applies best to Can Grande:

> e sua nazion sarà tra feltro e feltro.
> [and his nation will be between Feltro and Feltro.]

The third promise is more than one of immediate rescue from a serious predicament, and more than the political salvation of Italy. It is the promise of eternal life which is implied for Dante if he ascends the various heavens of Paradise. Virgil says that he will not be able to accompany the traveler there, but that he will leave him with a more worthy spirit. Beatrice is not named, but she is obviously referred to in line 123:

> con lei ti lascerò
> [with her I will leave you]

The three promises thus concern a man suffering from a mysterious but very real mental distress; a patriot exiled from a city ill-governed and without justice; and a soul which, like every other soul, is destined for eternal life.

Behind these promises there is at work a severe principle which penetrates the entire canto. Dante will not be saved without his own self-discipline. The descent into Hell will not be a sightseeing tour. And the spectacles will not only be exterior. Dante will also have to tame the various beasts that are within him. Help is promised him from a supernatural source, but that alone will not suffice. After all, the poem is called by the poet a *commedia*, which by definition implies the struggle of free will against forces that attempt to nullify it.

Thus, at the beginning of the *Commedia*, one finds the Hebraic image of man in need of God, and the classical image of man willing to help himself and exercise self-discipline. These two themes, the unseen God and the development of selfhood, will never be lost sight of.

In the first canto we witness a dramatic action—a man reaching the brink of despair where life is suddenly cast in the form of a dark wood. The confusion of Dante's spirit is here depicted in the tangled mesh of many growths: it is the sudden realization that he has gone too far in disorder. No one form of this disorder can be distinguished any longer: the multiple disorders have grown so closely together that their origins have been obscured.

Then, as Dante begins to climb the hill, three beasts arrest his progress as if they were the habits of disorder that keep him from emerging from his deep trouble. He can see the sun, and can thus hope that a cure may yet be effected. But in the action of the canto, the beasts appear and perform their function after Dante has seen the sun. Hope again has been blotted out, and the despair, the throttling sensation produced by dense, overgrown vegetation, is more marked than ever.

More than half of the canto, beginning with line 61, concerns the meeting with Virgil. Dante's bewilderment changes to awe. It is more than a meeting with a great poet of the past, because Virgil is Dante's poet. Dante has suddenly, unexpectedly found both his way and his predecessor:

> Tu se' lo mio maestro e 'l mio autore [1:85]
> [you are my master and my author]

The tone of awe and the acknowledgment of derivation are the same as those expressed by Eve to Adam in *Paradise Lost:*

> My author and disposer, what thou bidds't
> Unargued I obey. [4:635]

Eve, in her love for Adam, and Dante in his love for Virgil, both recognize their guide and their authority.

Thus, the first sixty lines of canto I reflect the Hebraic theme of man's estrangement from God, a theme never absent from the entire *Commedia*, because it emphasizes man's dependence on the Divine. But in the last seventy-six lines, the appearance of Virgil and his words of promise represent the classical strand in the poem by emphasizing the more purely human power of man to discover his true self.

Principal Signs and Symbols

1. *Dante*: the poet who is also the Christian sinner.

2. *Virgil*: the poet who is also human wisdom, the best that man can become without belief in Christ.

3. *The wood (la selva)*: the error that hardens the heart or blinds the eye.

4. *The three beasts (le tre fiere)*: the three types of sin that

precipitate a soul into one of the three divisions of Hell (see canto II):

    (a) the leopard (*la lonza*)—self-indulgence, carnality;

    (b) the lion (*il leone*)—violence or bestiality;

    (c) the wolf (*la lupa*)—malice involving fraud.

    5. *Il Veltro* (the greyhound): the hoped-for leader the world continues to expect even today.

CANTO

2

The Three Ladies

DANTE'S DOUBTS concerning himself are so deep and serious that Virgil's speech in canto 1 cannot alleviate them. Soon after assuring Virgil of his faith, he is assailed again. And this time the doubts are fixed totally upon himself, his weakness, his sense of inferiority. "Can you see enough strength in me," he asks Virgil, "to accompany you along the hard pass?"

> guarda la mia virtù s'el' è possente [2:11]
> [consider my worth, whether it is sufficient]

His renewed fears may have something to do with the coming of night, announced in the opening line,

> Lo giorno se n'andava
> [the day was disappearing]

It is the evening of Good Friday. First, the poet invokes the help of the Muses, and then turns to Virgil. When he speaks of the great figures before him who have visited the world of immortality, his sense of inferiority deepens. Dante first mentions Aeneas, the hero celebrated by Virgil, whom Dante associates with the founding of the Empire. Second he speaks of Saint Paul, who is associated with the founding of the Church. The experiences of Aeneas and Paul with the unseen had been for the highest purpose, and Dante sees no possible comparison between them and himself. Why should he go? He is not Aeneas, he is not Paul. Dante's words are bare and dramatic:

> Io non Enëa, io non Paolo sono. [2:32]
> [I am not Aeneas, I am not Paul.]

This striking comparison, which underscores the motivation of Dante's poem, namely the experience and the salvation of a single man, at the same time clearly defines Dante's belief in the Empire and the Church. Dante interprets the prophecy of Rome's future greatness in book 6 of the *Aeneid* as the prophecy that pagan Rome will bring about Christian Rome. The name of Rome, which symbolizes the organization of justice, will exist also for the sake of the papacy to protect man's faith in God.

In his second epistle to the Corinthians (12:2–4), Saint Paul speaks of his mystical elevation to the third heaven. Now Dante, after there has been time for him to recall this and to ponder his inconsequential position and relative insignificance, begins to wonder how Virgil, a pagan, can lead a man like himself through the Christian realms of Hell and Purgatory. The questions multiply fast in his mind. Why did Virgil come to him, and did he come through his own will and his own power?

Most of the canto is given over to Virgil's reassurance. He explains carefully and methodically why and how he came to Dante. He explains—and this is the major revelation of the canto—that the help and comfort he is offering were willed in Heaven. He is the mere instrument of a divine plan. Dante's self-doubt is of such a nature that he has already unwilled what he had decided; and Virgil, as a doctor of great wisdom, knows that only clear, straightforward reasoning will restore the traveler's confidence. The arguments of his story are personal and supernatural at the same time. Dante's will is to be strengthened and completely made over.

As Virgil speaks of what was willed in Heaven, we realize we are listening to the real beginning of the *Commedia*. Understanding is all that is necessary to free Dante from his dread, and irresolution can be remedied by the steadying force of clarification. Virgil here acts as both psychologist and literary doctor. As the narrative unfolds, Dante learns that three ladies in Paradise (*tre donne benedette*, 2:124) are concerned for his welfare, and of course, ultimately, about his salvation. Virgil is their emissary.

It was the Beatrice of the *Vita nuova* who first came to Virgil where he lives "suspended," and who spoke to him directly. It is highly probable that Beatrice Portinari, whom Dante had loved, knew Virgil's poem, or at least knew the importance the *Aeneid* had for Dante. It is certainly implied that Virgil was her own choice, when she learned that someone had to be found to help the man she loved. The tercet in which she names herself to Virgil, and states that she comes from a place to which she wishes

to return, explaining that love caused her to come and speak to
him, is one of the simplest and most moving of the canto:

> I' son Beatrice che ti faccio andare;
> vegno del loco ove tornar disio;
> amor mi mosse, che mi fa parlare. [2:70–72]
> [I am Beatrice who urge you to go.
> I come from a place where I desire to return;
> love moved me that makes me speak.]

As Beatrice had been the most closely related to Dante in the
human sense, so she is the most active character in the opening
of the *Commedia* in coming to Virgil in the periphery of Hell and
soliciting his help. After explaining to Virgil that she acted out
her love for Dante, (*amor mi mosse*), she speaks two lines both
mystifying and heartening:

> Quando sarò dinanzi al segnor mio,
> di te mi loderò sovente a lui [2:73–74]
> [When I am before my Lord,
> I will often praise you to him.]

With these loving words, Beatrice promises an intervention.
What reason could she have, save that of liberating Virgil from
hell? A reader today, like a reader of the past, knows that Dante's
Catholic theology of Hell makes it impossible for a condemned
soul to leave his state of damnation.

This ending of Beatrice's speech to Virgil may well be one
example—and there are others in the *Commedia*—of Dante's
personal feelings taking precedence over the strictures of his
religious creed. Is Beatrice holding out the hope that the laws of
theology may be broken in exceptional cases? At the beginning
of this long poem, these two lines of Beatrice would seem to say
that we are reading not only a work of medieval inspiration, but
one that transcends all ages in order to represent and interpret
what is eternally universal and human. Is Dante trying to say that
the humanity of a man may be such that it will be able to temper
the law of God's love as interpreted by the Church?

Dante is not only a Christian and a man of deep feeling; he is
also a poet who in the freedom of his creation magnifies or transcends codes, laws, and customs. He makes Hell more terrifying
than it is in theology, and at certain moments, as in these lines of
Beatrice to Virgil, he makes his readers feel that God's mercy
transcends his justice; that Hell is an abstraction more than a

reality; that Hell is the experience of life; that the other world is that place where the static characteristic of sin will be changed into a state of progress from sin to repentence and thence to salvation. The artist is the man who always outstrips his conscious intention, and who in his work comes upon secrets of the universe and of the human mind he could not have discovered in a state of pure consciousness.

The three ladies of this second canto—the Virgin (Mary's name is not used in the *Inferno*), *Donna è gentil nel ciel* (2:84—there is a noble lady in Heaven); Lucia, the saint whom Dante venerated (*il tuo fedele*, 2:98—your faithful one); and Beatrice (*loda di Dio vera*, 2:103—true praise of God), so active in her help to Dante—are often looked upon by commentators as representing mercy (Mary), grace (Lucia), and wisdom (Beatrice). They might also illustrate the three phases of grace as described by Saint Thomas. The grace coming from Mary, mother of God and queen of Heaven, would be *prevenient* grace (the first impulse in a sinner to repent), as it comes to him undeservedly. Lucia is *operant* grace, which allows a sinner to desire the good and to do it. Beatrice would be *perficient* grace, which causes the repentent sinner to persist in the doing of good.

Such an interpretation would serve as a pattern of formal theology, but the real importance of the three ladies (*le tre donne*) in the poem is that their presence shows all Heaven concerned with saving a lost soul. This trio of ladies also testifies to the most significant function of woman throughout history: the mercy they show to all creatures, their loving gentleness, their compassion.

In canto 2 it is possible to say that the *Inferno* starts in Paradise, in the heart of the Virgin Mary. The *Commedia* thus starts at the place to which it will return. After his serious doubts, Dante is heartened and willingly follows Virgil into eternity. Since Virgil has named the three phases of the journey, we know in advance that Dante will overcome the terrors of Hell. The poem is indeed a comedy, that is, a form of writing which begins in fear and ends happily. And Beatrice, in her words in canto 2, guarantees this happy outcome when she tells it to Virgil in the ordinary speech of Florence.

But despite this excursus into theology, Virgil dominates the canto. In the third line from the end, Dante addresses Virgil with words that will be repeated many times throughout the poem:

tu duca tu segnore e tu maestro [2:140]
[you my leader, lord, and master]

This knowing, wise spirit will continue his role of guide through
all of the *Inferno* and most of the *Purgatorio*. There, in canto 30,
he will be replaced by Beatrice. In terms of theology, it would
not be appropriate for Virgil to lead Dante through the *Paradiso*,
but by the time he does disappear from Dante's sight, he has
grown into such a loving counselor that the poet weeps.

There is one almost terrifying line in canto 2, in Beatrice's
speech to Virgil, when she says to him:

> la vostra miseria non mi tange [2:92]
> [your wretchedness does not touch me]

She is saying that her state of grace does not allow her to feel pity
for Virgil's state of damnation, even the mild damnation of limbo.
The strictness of the theology concerning Hell is contained in
these few words.

Who is Virgil, then, and why was he chosen for a mission
which reminds him every step of the way of his own eternal
plight? From his very first words in canto 1,

> Non omo, omo già fui [1:47]
> [I a not a man, I was a man once]

he takes over full command, and often steals the scene from the
real protagonist. He is the best representative of humanity, a man
as perfect as is possible without divine grace. Virgil is thus natural
religion at its highest, a great poet who lived in accordance with a
morality of moderation, and who believed in a world-state governed by reason.

The relationship between Virgil and Dante grows warm and
rich but also ambivalent. On the whole, Dante plays the part of
disciple-pupil, weaker than his master. Yet Dante is a child of
grace, and Virgil is not. One line in the seventh canto of the
Purgatorio is perhaps the clearest clue to Viril's exclusion: *per
non aver fe*. He did have sufficient faith to warrant salvation.
Already in canto 2 the relationship is lively. The master-poet of
the Latin world has already severely reprimanded the child of
grace in reminding Dante of his cowardice:

> l'anima tua è da viltade offesa [2:45]
> [your spirit is overcome with cowardice]

Virgil is indeed the *maestro* as the two figures set out to move
through all of Hell, where they will later come upon several
figures from book 6 of the *Aeneid*.

Principal Signs and Symbols

1. Three images of help: in the order of their appearance in the poem, Beatrice, Lucia, and Mary; in the order of their help to Dante, Mary, Lucia, and Beatrice.

Mary: the mother of God, and the mediatrix between man and God.

Lucia: a virgin martyr of the third century, patron saint of those with poor sight.

Beatrice: beloved of Dante Alighieri.

2. *Virgil*: the guide. Dante at this moment is possibly outside divine grace, and answers Virgil, who is the voice of poetry and human reason. Dante thus establishes a relationship between art and religion.

CANTO

3

The Vestibule
(*Acedia* in Baudelaire and Eliot)

AFTER THE PRELUDE on earth (canto 1) where Dante, having lost
his way, is impeded by three beasts, and after the prelude in
Heaven (canto 2) where three ladies use their supernatural powers to help Dante out of his predicament, the poet, on his walk
with Virgil through the wood, abruptly finds himself at the gate
of Hell, and there reads the inscription over the "honest gate"
that tells in nine lines what Hell is, the reason for its creation and
its eternity.

The first three lines contain the strongest anaphora in the
Commedia, the repetition three times of *per me si va.*"If you go
through me," you go through, first, *la città dolente.*Hell is organized in the form of a city, but a city of pain, and therefore one
that resembles all the cities of the earth. This pain is forever, we
are told in line 1 (*etterno dolore*), and the inhabitants of the city
are lost (*la perduta gente,* 3:3). Hard, firm, specific lines, this
opening tercet, which is the real opening of the *Inferno.* The

The second *tercet,* as relentless and specific as the first, is the
description of the maker of Hell, *Il mio alto Fattore.* God himself
made Hell, because of justice. He had to. This fourth line is the
whole concept of the *Inferno:* Hell was made because of sin that
has to be punished. This God who made Hell is a triune diety.
The three names of Power, Wisdom, and Love are the names of
the Trinity, and they were all utilized in the making of Hell.
"Power" (*la divina Podestate*) is the Father, able to carry out
justice; "Wisdom" (*la somma Sapïenza*) is the Son who in his
wisdom adjusts the punishment to the sin; "Love" (*il primo*

Amore) is the Holy Spirit who in making Hell protects all the good people throughout the world and makes love on earth possible. *Giustizia is the* first world of the tercet, and *Amore* is the last. Justice is the reason for Hell, but underlying justice is love.

Before Hell was created (3:7) other eternal things were created by God, apparently the angels and the heavens. Like them, Hell is eternal, an eternal testimonial to God's justice and love. The last line of the inscription is usually interpreted as being an imperative: "leave every hope you who enter":

Lasciate ogne speranza, voi ch'intrate.

A more subtle reading would interpret *lasciate* as in the indicative mood: "You who are entering Hell have already abandoned hope." Whatever the grammatical interpretation, this ninth line raises one of the great problems of Dante's conception of Hell: Is it a realm where there is no free will? If there were free will, Hell would have a purgatorial aspect.

This may be the question in Dante's mind when he tells Virgil that the meaning of the gate inscription is obscure to him:

Maestro, il senso lor m'è duro. [3:12]

Virgil, in his answer that occupies five lines, gives the first commentary on the text of the poem. His reply is a definition of who the damned are. They are the ones who have lost the good of the intellect:

hanno perduto il ben de l'intelletto [3:18]

This is a phrase from Aristotle that was used extensively by medieval philsophers, and by Dante, in prose and verse. The phrase, which appears in book 6 of Aristotle's *Ethics* as well as in Dante's *Convivio* (2:14, 38–44), signifies the power of man's intellect to know God. In purely philosophical terms, the good of the intellect would be man's intuition of truth, and in purely religious terms, it would be man's vision of God.

The spirits in Dante's Hell, through the exercise of their free will during life have repudiated this relation of their intellect to God, and are thus eternally tormented. Do they continue in Hell to repudiate this relationship and thus exercise free will? This is something that must be examined as Dante's journey continues. Dante has told us in the gate inscription, which he invented, that love is the foundation of Hell. But should not all punishment be remedial? There is such emphasis on justice in this first *cantica* that the reader will tend to forget the theme of mediation which pervades the entire *Commedia*.

Belief in Hell remains today a tenet of Catholic faith. It has to exist if there is to be justice. But a Catholic today has the right to state: "I have no way of knowing whether any spirit is actually there, and I tend to believe that God's mercy is such that Hell is empty."

In this introductory part of the canto we witness an exchange of feelings between Dante and Virgil which will later recur. Dante is distrustful, and Virgil calls him a coward—the word *viltà* (3:15) is strong. And indeed, throughout the *Inferno* and the *Purgatorio*, Dante is a man lacking bravery. It is Virgil who is the courageous figure, the knowing guide who never forgets that the mission he is conducting is willed in Heaven and is therefore promised success. Virgil is often described, as in the beginning of canto 3, in opposition to Dante, as the teacher happy to answer questions and to impart knowledge *con lieto volto*, "with a cheerful face" (3:20)—an attitude which contrasts with Dante's bewilderment.

Just beyond the gate, in that part of Hell usually referred to as the "vestibule," Dante first hears and then sees a large group of spirits. The poet does not give a name to this first group he encounters, and he does not name any single figure in it. This absence of names, a practice contrary to Dante's habit in other cantos, gives to this passage of forty-seven lines (3:22–69) an air of darkness and mystery. Italian commentators usually refer to these sinners as the *ignavi*. The word *ignavo* denotes cowardice, sloth, indolence. Various terms have been used in English: "neutrals" is perhaps the best, but "trimmers" occurs also. A trimmer is one, who, for reasons of expediency, will change his position or modify his belief.

Dante is scornful of this sin of ambivalence, which is illustrated by both men and angels. He is shocked by the large number of sinners, and compares them to grains of sand: they are *come la rena* (3:30) when the wind blows over the sand. The image is carefully chosen to demonstrate not only the number of sinners, but also the sterility implied in the sin of not choosing. We see them rushing about without any goal, scattered, blown by every wind of fortune. No specific blame can be attached to them, but there is also no reason for any praise. The words *sanza 'nfamia e sanza lodo* (3:36), "without blame and without praise," indicate their sin, a nameless sin, indeed, and they are grouped with those angels who were neither rebellious nor faithful: *cattivo coro / de li angeli* (3:37–38). *Cattivo* means "wicked" in Dante, but has lost today its full meaning, as its French form, *chétif*, has lost the full moral meaning it had in medieval writings.

These sinners are beneath contempt, and Virgil suggests that he and Dante move quickly out of the vestibule. At that moment Dante sees a whirling banner and behind it so long a line of people that he would not have believed death had undone so many. (These words have become familiar today because of Eliot's use of them in *The Wasteland*.) Dante recognizes one figure, who is designated in a totally mysterious way as one who made "the great refusal" (*che fece per viltade il gran rifiuto*, 3:60). Might he be Pope Celestine V, who abdicated in favor of Boniface VIII? This is highly probable because of the role Boniface VIII plays in Dante's life and poem.

These "neutrals," the least guilty in Hell since they are just inside the gate and unjudged by Minos, are stung by hornets as worms suck up their blood and tears. Their plight, which is that of all the inhabitants of Hell, is their lack of hope for death:

> Questi non hanno speranza di morte [3:46]
> [these do not have hope for death]

It would be reasonable to think of death as the end of pain. The living tend to think of death as that event which ends their suffering, but the damned cannot hope for an end to their punishment.

This passage has had an impact on Baudelaire and T. S. Eliot. The movement of persons through a city in *"Les sept vieillards,"*

> Fourmillante cité, cité pleine de rêves,
> [Swarming city, city full of dreams]

is described in a supernatural light, and used in "The Burial of the Dead":

> Unreal city
> Under the brown fog of a winter dawn,
> A crowd flowed over London Bridge, so many,
> I had not thought death had undone so many.

In Dante, this sin is the selfishness of not having taken sides. The corresponding state, for Baudelaire and Eliot, is apathy and ambivalence. As it deepens in man, it becomes more serious and is named *acedia* by Dante, Baudelaire, and Eliot.

Eliot's "The Hollow Men" also seems to make an allusion to canto 3:

> Those who have crossed
>   ...to death's other Kingdom
> Remember us—if at all—not as lost
> Violent souls, but only
> As the hollow men
> The stuffed men.

The *ignavi* of Baudelaire and Eliot are not goaded by hornets and wasps, but their sin is looked upon as one of the most serious of modern man. It is the sin of the uncommitted, of the over-intellectualized who see reasons for holding every belief, but not enough reason to hold to only one side.

Through the dim light, Dante and Virgil can distinguish persons on the banks of a river. The second part of the canto begins here with the appearance of a boat with an old white-haired man in it. The river is the Acheron, the first of the rivers of Hell, and the ferryman is Charon. Many of the elements of this passage are drawn from the sixth book of the *Aeneid*, although Charon is considerably changed. There is indeed a Virgilian Charon, but Dante's is drawn more from Greek mythology. In the *Commedia* the poet transforms this mythical figure into a demon who both punishes the sinners and ferries them across the Acheron to Hell proper. It is clear now that the vestibule of the neutrals is but an introduction to the first circle.

Charon welcomes his legitimate passengers, but tells Dante, whom he recognizes as not belonging among the damned, to go another way. Virgil quiets him down with a few strong words, and the scene reverts to the naked souls blaspheming and cursing God. Their inner spirit is totally infernal, and Charon beats them with an oar as he gathers them into his boat.

This dramatic moment is cast into a six line image of autumn leaves falling from the branches to the ground. Thus these spirits, the evil seed of Adam, come together for the boat's crossing to the other shore. They fall into place in the same way that the falcon is called back to the earth by the whistle of the falconer,

> come augel per suo richiamo [3:117]
> [as the bird at its call]

The *richiamo* is the summons, the bird call. In French it is *le réclame* (as opposed to *la réclame* meaning "advertisement"), the medieval whistle, which Baudelaire uses in his sonnet *"Recueillement"*: *"tu réclamais le soir."*

In the *Aeneid* the spirits are "thick as the leaves, thick as the birds flock shoreward," but in Dante the bough sees its leaves *(il ramo / vede... le sue spoglie,* 3:113–14) and the use of the *richiamo* indicates that the bird comes down from the sky willingly to its lure. These spirits are eager *(pronti)* to cross the river. Their fear has changed to desire. It would seem that their sin calls for their punishment.

The poet does not tell us whether he crosses in Charon's boat or by some other way. The dark landscape suddenly *(la buia campagna,* 3:130) dominates the scene with an earthquake A red blaze flashes and Dante falls like a man overcome by sleep:

> e caddi come l'uom cui sonno piglia [3:136]
> [and I fell like one whom sleep seizes]

Thus the voyage into Hell has begun, and the reader can already sense that this voyage is that of self-knowledge, the knowing of all the possible deeds an individual can perform. The setting, as always in Dante, is skillfully married to the thought of the canto: the gate, the vestibule (not Hell, but the outer fringe of Hell), crowded with those who never reached any decision, the uncommitted, as we would say today, those who run after each new banner but who never grasp it in their hands; Charon, an indestructible personnage from Greek folklore; the Acheron; the passage into Hell that is eagerly consented to by the sinners; the earthquake and Dante's loss of consciousness.

The action is so continuous it is hard to realize that with the trembling of the earth and the flash of crimson fire, the transition between temporal life on earth and eternal death in Hell has taken place. Dante passes quickly through the vestibule of the neutrals. He does not describe or name any individual, and characterizes the group in very few words. The analysis and portrayal of the sin of the *ignavi* will have to be done much later by Baudelaire and Eliot.

Principal Signs and Symbols

1. *The gate (la porta):* through it one enters *la città dolente,* "the city of desolation."

2. *The vestibule:* the part that leads to Hell itself, where the

"neutrals" are forced to run aimlessly after a whirling banner. In their lifetime they followed no banner, no leader. The sin is the sin of inactivity.

3. *The good of the intellect* (*il ben dello intelletto*): on entering Hell (3:18), Virgil describes the damned as those souls who have lost the good of the intellect. This would be the *summum bonum* (the supreme good) or God. For Dante, as for Aquinas, the intellect means the reasonable soul of man.

4. *The Acheron*: this river marks the outer boundary of Hell proper. The origin will be explained in canto 14, lines 112–20. It is called "the sorrowful shore of the Acheron" (*la trista riviera d'Acheronte*, 3:78).

5. *Charon* (*Caron*): the ferryman of the dead. He is called here "a demon" (*Caron dimonio*, 3:109).

6. *Nakedness:* the spirits are described as naked in line 100 (*Quell'anime eran nude*). Except for the hypocrites in canto 23, the spirits in Hell are naked, although this is seldom mentioned by Dante.

CANTO

4

Limbo (First Circle)

THERE IS NO WAY of knowing how long Dante sleeps. According to the rigorous chronological plan of the poem, the descent through Hell occupies about twenty-four hours, but we are really outside of time during this period.

The sleep, perhaps equivalent to a spiritual death or a moment of grace, is long enough for the poet to be rested when he opens his eyes. The words *occhio riposato*, in the fourth line, remind us that "eye" (*occhio*) is the most often used noun in *The Divine Comedy*. All of Hell is dimly lit—no sunlight penetrates to any of its parts. Dante has to strain his eyes to see, and here in limbo one has a sense of Dante trying to penetrate the dark to see the noble figures he is anxious to meet, and striving also to comprehend and perhaps accept the harsh theology represented in this first division of the underworld.

The theological reasons for assigning unbaptized infants and the noble human figures who lived before Christ to Hell are so hard to follow that the mind clings to the word *sospesi* (4:45) which fills the canto. These spirits are "suspended" between the states of condemnation and salvation. Dante the theologian and Dante the man are in conflict here, and the conflict does not stimulate his greatest poetical powers. He is content to draw pictures as best he can of a dignified scene, of honorable men, using the word "honor" five times within twenty-five lines, while listening to a more than garrulous Virgil point out his own circle and his companion poets who dwell in this strangely neutral and lifeless scene.

The word *limbo* comes from *lembo* meaning "hem" or "margin." We are on the outskirts of Hell. We have not yet met Minos, who judges the damned. Here on the brink of the abyss of Hell, Dante pauses and hears the accumulated wailings of all the spirits resounding in his ears like continual thunder. He sees Virgil grow pale, *tutto smorto* (4:14), and wonders how he can follow so fearful a guide. Then when he hears the explanation, given briefly and in abstract terms (these spirits in the first circle lived before Christ and thus could not worship God in the right way) he feels overcome with sadness. He knows he will meet among the "suspended" spirits many of great worth.

Here, more than in any other section of Hell, damnation has a sense of beauty about it, a degree of greatness and goodness. Virgil is its hero. He talks about his eternal abode where there are no cries and no torture, and presents it to Dante in the aspect of a school (*la bella scola*, 4:94) or a company (*con molti compagni*, 4:121; *la sesta compagnia*, 4:148). This motif of the group is accompanied by the motif of two singular figures who stand somewhat apart from the group and represent it: Homer, the first of the poets of antiquity (4:86), and Aristotle, "the master of those who know" (*il maestro di color che sanno*, 4:131.)

Dante's sleep, broken at the beginning of the canto, may be recalled by the reader when Homer, "the sovereign poet," appears, because of the sleep of Odysseus in book 13 of the *Odyssey*, when his sailors took him back to Ithaca. The theme of sleep initiates the canto and would seem to bear some relation to the sin or lack of sin that explains limbo. These spirits are not damned, but "suspended" in exile from Heaven and from God for having failed to acknowledge and worship him. *Non adorar debitamente a Dio* is the key line of explanation (4:38), "They did not worship God as they should have." Theologically, there is vagueness and hesitation in the canto, and we can almost surmise that limbo is another break in the walls of Hell, that there is hope behind the obdurate laws.

Dante's sadness,

> Gran duol mi prese al cor [4:43]
> [great sadness took me at the heart]

urges him to ask the question: "Did anyone leave limbo?" Virgil's answer is affirmative. Christ, at his death, came to this part of Hell and released his Jewish ancestors. This is called the "harrowing of Hell" and is related in the apocryphal book, the Gospel of Nicodemus. The name of Christ is never spoken in Hell. Virgil refers to him as *un possente* (4:53), "a mighty one" who came to liberate Adam, Abel, Noah, Moses, Abraham, David, Jacob, Isaac, and many others not named specifically.

In referring to this act of Christ, Dante reapplies the doctrine of the chosen people. He thus adheres to a theological belief of the Middle Ages, but shows such admiration for the heathen of antiquity that his heart seems to oppose his mind. Is he protesting against a theological law, or is he indicating some future possible mitigation of the rigorous law? A faint motif of protest moves through *The Divine Comedy* as an undercurrent. "Protest" is perhaps too strong a word—it might be best described as the vain struggle of a finite mind to come to terms with the infinite.

Limbo was as overpowering a problem for a mind of the fourteenth century as it is for a mind of the twentieth. In light of Christian theology, what can be said concerning such eternal figures as Socrates, Plato, and Aristotle, the three among all those named who would have the most meaning for us today? Dante does the best he can to rescue such men from ignominy, by casting limbo in the shape of Elysium. His picture is a Greek elysian field where the good live after death as in classical mythology. Virgil summarizes the fate of the good heathen in the words, "without hope we live in desire":

> sanza speme vivemo in disio. [4:42]

"Living in desire" would be salvation, but "living in desire without hope" is limbo.

We are now at the scene of Dante's recognition of those Greeks and Romans, his literary masters, representing his preferences, who are joined with Virgil and whom he finds joined in Hell. The canto is more than half over before any spirit speaks to Dante and Virgil. Then in line 80, ons of the spirits—it is not clear who—greets Virgil:

> Onorate l'altissimo poeta
> [honor the great poet]

Virgil, who had left the group, is now welcomed back into it.

The first group, composed of poets, is led by Homer, appropriately enough since Homer's myth of the apocalypse is the basis of *The Divine Comedy*. Although Dante did not read Greek and probably did not read Homer even in translation, the Roman poets whom he studied had ascribed first place to Homer. "Sovereign poet" Dante calls him in line 88:

quelli è Omero poeta sovrano
[that is Homer, the sovereign poet]

The four Latin poets represent the major poets of Dante's literary culture: Virgil first; then Lucan who sang of Caesar and the Empire in his *Pharsalia;* Ovid, whose *Metamorphoses* are used by Dante; and Horace, both satirist and lyricist. They give to Dante the sixth place and thus honor him. Is this pride on the part of Dante? Possibly. But it can easily be argued that the literary world today would place Dante, not sixth in such a group, but beside Homer, as the second poet.

The poets then move toward a light which seems to come from a castle and a green meadow. There are seven walls and seven gates in this noble castle, which is surrounded by a small river. The poets come to a fresh green meadow.

The second group of spirits in the meadow is composed of Romans and Trojans, active spirits who once engaged in war. There is also one Arab. Thirteen are mentioned, eight of whom are women. There are no Greeks here.

The third group is made up of scientists and philosophers. Nearly all of these are Greek. Here the central figure is Aristotle. They have a light of their own in this dark region, and converse with one another, thus maintaining in limbo their speculative attitudes and interests. The problem of what to do with men like Socrates and Plato must have been puzzling for Dante. Saint Thomas had put them in Hell. Dante does better by putting them in a limbo of their own. These spirits have not been formally condemned.

Dante seems to feel more sympathy for the Greek and Roman second half of limbo than he had shown for the Jewish-Christian first half. The scholastic philosophers spoke of a limbo for unbaptized babies, and another limbo for the heathen fathers. Dante fuses these into one. The vestibule of the neutrals in canto 3 was his own invention, and there is a significant relationship between Dante's vestibule and his limbo. The vestibule exists for those spirits who made no choice in their lives; limbo is reserved for those spirits who were given no choice.

The picture is a symposium. Its hero is Virgil and he is very much at home. It is also a fantasy scene in which there is almost no talk, a circle of suspense. The words in line 45 pervade the canto: *eran sospesi*—they were suspended. And Dante also appears "suspended," hesitant in his description, uncertain of the meaning of this scene, which for us today is too close to allegory.

The figure of Aristotle is memorable. In his *Nicomachean Ethics*, which Dante knew in translation, the underworld has two divisions: upper and lower Hell. In upper Hell, the sins punished are those of incontinence. In Dante's Hell, the vestibule and the six upper circles are also the places where incontinence is punished. It is difficult to understand how incontinence applies to the neutrals of the vestibule and to the worthy heathen of limbo. Were they deficient in the exercise of their will? Were they faulty in willing the highest good? It is hard to reach a satisfactory answer to this basic question, and a modern reader has to rely on the fact that these noble figures have not been judged as the truly incontinent have been judged.

Principal Signs and Symbols:

1. *Limbo* (4:45) or the first circle of Hell: dwelling of the unbaptized and the virtuous pagans. Baptism is the first sacrament, and has been called the "gateway to faith," although this definition is not accurate. Faith is a gift from God. Baptism, as the first sacrament, opens the way to the other sacraments.

2. *The suspended* (*sospesi* 4:45): these spirits know no torment. They are excluded from Heaven and from the other parts of Hell. They live in desire, but without hope.

3. *The harrowing of Hell* (4:52–53): this is mentioned by Virgil and refers to Christ's descent into limbo to liberate the souls of the Jewish patriarchs.

4. *The noble castle* and *the green meadow* (*un nobile castello e il prato di fresca verdura* 4:106–11): this seems to be Dante's version of the elysian fields.

5. *Homer, the sovereign poet* (*Omero, poeta sovrano* 4:88): he carries a sword because his name is so closely associated with the Trojan War.

6. *Aristotle:* "the master of those who know" (*il maestro di color che sanno* 4:131).

CANTO

5

The Carnal Sinners (Second Circle)

THIS MOST MEMORABLE of all the cantos, the one that has been commented on more lavishly, more sentimentally, than all the others, begins with a graphic picture of Minos, judge of all Hell. We then move to the second circle proper, that of the sensualists, the lustful. They exist in an eternal tempest, blown about by the winds of a hurricane. A catalogue of names of famous lovers completes the general picture of the circle of the *lussuriosi*. The second half of the canto is given over to Francesca, who tells Dante of her love for the spirit with her. Paolo does not speak, and Dante speaks very little. It is Francesca's poem, said with such feeling that at the end Dante loses consciousness and collapses. The contrast with canto 4 is strong: after the elegiac tone of Elysium comes the tragedy of love.

Minos, who is described in the opening twenty-four lines, is the mythological figure changed into a demon by Dante. As he appears in Virgil amd Homer, Minos is the son of Zeus, the law-giver, and for that reason is the judge of the dead in Hades. In the Greek story, this king of Crete maintains his godlike attributes in his post in the underworld. But the strong gothic strain of Dante's art demonizes him. Each sinner confesses to Minos, who with his tail then girds the sinner with the number of coils that correspond to the position in Hell he is to occupy, after which he is hurled by a flash of Minos' tail to the appropriate circle. Like Charon, Minos warns Dante not to go any farther, but again Virgil states that Dante's pilgrimage is willed in Heaven.

A chief characteristic of Dante's art is his skill in creating an environment for each of the sins. The tempest of winds, *la bufera infernal* (5:31), that never rests, corresponds to the nature of carnal sin. In one single line (5:39) the poet defines what these sinners (*i peccatori carnali*) did. They subjected reason to desire:

la ragion sommettono al talento.

This key word, *talento*, has many meanings in Italian: "talent," "genius," and "pleasure" are some of the obvious meanings, although "will" or "disposition" can also be implied. These meanings lead to Dante's use of the word in line 39 as "desire" or, in the specific sense of canto 5, "concupiscence." The line is an abstract statement, but is charged with the ethical significance of the second circle. When a man is unfaithful to the direction of reason, of his rational intellect, he knows no rest. Sexual desire, as well as the sexual act, can never be satisfied, never at rest.

The wind storm both reflects the sexual sin and punishes it. The second movement of the canto (5:28–45) is given over to the general picture of the environment and the punishment. Then Dante, as will happen over and over again, after becoming curious about individual spirits in the scene, asks about them and hears some of them identified by Virgil (5:46–72). The sinners appear like birds trying to fly in a strong wind. Some are buffeted in every direction like starlings (*stornei*) unable to keep a course, and others, like cranes (*gru*) follow one another in a long line. But all wail and are tormented. The picture of helplessness dominates this introductory scene, where the punishment is lighter than in other circles because there is less will, less self-determination involved in an act of carnality. The word *lussuria* itself (lust) is in line 55.

Seven sinners, four women and three men, are named by Virgil: Semiramis, queen of Assyria, Dido, mistress of Aeneas, Cleopatra, and Helen of Troy—women from legend and history who sinned for love. Achilles, Paris, prince of Troy, and Tristan, lover of Iseult, are the three male figures.

Dante notices two spirits fluttering in the wind, and asks to speak with them. The story of Francesca and Paolo was contemporary and known directly to Dante. He speaks of this encounter as if his readers were familiar with the details of the famous and tragic tale of the murdered lovers. Two feudal families, involved in a long dispute, tried to end the quarrel by a marriage. Francesca was the daughter of the Polentas of Ravenna, and Paolo was the son of the Malatestas of Rimini. But Francesca was married off to Paolo's brother, Gianciotto. This name is a fusion of Giovanni and Ciotto. "Ciotto" is the same word as *zoppo*, "lame." During the ten years of this marriage, love grew between Francesca and Paolo, the handsome brother, who also was married and father of two children. The love affair was thus doubly adulterous. Gianciotto found his wife and brother together and stabbed them to death. Dante assumes his readers know the facts of the incident and concentrates on what we might call a psychological interpretation of the story. The poet uses only Francesca in order to give a sense of both the power of her love, which continues in Hell, and of its tragedy.

As Francesca relates her story to Dante, during the brief time that the wind dies down and is silent, the facts are revealed, but are softened by Francesca's character, and changed into the universal story of a love that destroyed two human beings. Francesca relates four stages of the experience: first the weakness of love, the gradual yielding to a forbidden sentiment; then full passion, the overwhelming desire for love with the knowledge that it is wrong (this second stage is implicit in Francesca's story); third, the act of adultery, or the realization of passion, which again is modestly implicit in the recital; fourth, the betrayal-murder, which comes with such abruptness that it plunges the lovers into the eternal whirlwind where Dante finds them.

The scene in Hell, along with Francesca's story, make these seventy lines into the leading document in world literature on passionate love. It is love that is simultaneously rapture and torment, both joy and cruelty, both heaven and hell. Love, when it reaches its sexual fulfillment, demands that the lovers be together. Dante, in his power as a poet, has imagined the two lovers bound together endlessly, whirling in the winds of the second circle of his Hell. But the lovers' very closeness is a constant reproach that one makes to the other for committing the sin that has separated them from eternal happiness. Paolo, who is silent in the canto until he begins to weep (*l'altto piangëa*, 5:140), "the other one was weeping") is inseparable from Francesca, but he is also her punishment and her sin. Unless he is seen this way, neither the canto nor Dante's conception of the *Inferno* mean a thing.

Dante asks the two spirits to come and speak with him: *venite a noi parlar* (5:81), and they come like doves borne through the air. Francesca speaks, beginning in line 88, with extraordinary frankness and pathos. But we can never forget that it is also the poet speaking as he reimagines the story, dealing with love as he had already expressed it in earlier works. In her opening words, Francesca, greeting this man from the earth, says that she would pray for him if the king of the universe were her friend. This one line,

se fosse amico il re de l'universo, [5:91]

seems the most heavily charged with pathos. It stands at the beginning, and the rigors of its doctrine can never be forgotten by the reader. Francesca cannot pray because she is in Hell.

The sketch of her life (she was born in Ravenna) is condensed into her love. *Amor*, used as anaphora at the beginning of three successive terzinas, is her life story. She says that love first seized Paolo. But he was taken from her, and the manner of his death still offends her. This *modo* may refer to the abruptness of the murder which gave Francesca no time for repentance, or it may be the brutal violence of the slaying which offended her sensibility. The second terzina tells of love as it affected Francesca, giving her such pleasure that it does not leave her even here in Hell. The third mention of *amor* is as the force that led both Paolo and Francesca to death:

Amore condusse noi ad una morte. [5:106]
[Love led us to one death.]

Dante lowers his head at these words, and Virgil has to interrupt this meditation to ask Dante to express his thoughts. The poet is wondering about what led up to the sin, and he addresses Francesca by name for the first time, asking her questions that any doctor might ask: How and under what circumstances did the experience of love allow you to know uncertain desires (*i dubbiosi disiri*, 5:120)? Dante knows that the formal sin was adultery, but he is curious to know how it came about. Francesca then tells him in the following eighteen lines the tragic story which has justifiably won world fame.

The opening tercet is a preface, a general account that reminds us of the present setting from which we will hear the story. "The greatest suffering," Francesca says, "is the memory of happiness in a state of wretchedness." And Virgil, too, knows this. The line

Nessun maggior dolor [5:121]
[no greater pain]

comes verbatim from Boethius' *The Consolation of Philosophy* (book 2), and it is used by Dante as a philosopher might use it: at the beginning of a narrative that treats of ecstasy and its consequences. The reading of a book led to the sin. It was the story of Lancelot's love for Queen Guinevere and their betrayal of King Arthur in their act of adultery. So, we are to understand that Francesca and Paolo met many times, ostensibly to read together, but subconsciously to provide the occasion for lovemaking. The meetings, the readings about love, the parleying with love, the deceit, initiated gradually but deceit nonetheless—this is the mode that characterizes Francesca and separates her from Beatrice. *I dubbiosi disiri* might be translated by "dangerous desires."

The reading of the story (*quella lettura*) brought them to the moment of self-yielding, and then in words that are tender but totally explicit, Dante describes the kiss that marks the transition from the couple's vicarious enjoyment of Guinevere's smile (*il riso*) to Francesca's mouth (*la bocca*). It is the shift from a book about life to life itself; the kiss that sealed their fate and joined them forever. There was no need to read farther. In one line is contained unsaid the consummation of the love of Francesca and Paolo:

> quel giorno più non vi leggemmo avante. [5:138]
> [that day we read in it no farther.]

Galeotto was the book, says Dante, but in the story Gallehaut was the go-between, Lancelot's friend: the act of reading function as Gallehault's role in the story.

The last four lines of the canto move quickly. The two lovers have revived and relived their love, while Dante, overcome with compassion, sinks down as if suddenly dead:

> E caddi come corpo morto cade. [5:142]
> [And I fell as a dead body falls.]

The contrast is striking as the living man in the scene loses his senses just before the two lovers are whirled away from him in the next gust of wind.

Cantos 3, 4, and 5 form an introductory unit to Hell that concerns choice and free will. In the vestibule of canto 3, the *ignavi* are shown as spirits who had shied away from making any choice. Limbo in canto 4 holds those who had never been given a choice: unbaptized babies, worthy pagans, and worthy Hebrews. The *lussuriosi* of canto 5 did make a choice, and Dante's art in the Francesca story makes that choice plausible, recognizable, and deeply human.

This is one of two sins in Dante's poem that is shared. (see canto 26). Francesca and Paolo chose to be together in life and so they are together in eternity, but the poet turns this bond into their punishment. The gracious way in which Francesca speaks to Dante, and consents to tell him her story, reveals her character. She has kindness and nobility of spirit; she thinks of the pleasure of the other; she will not say no. It is the woman's story, not the man's—it would be improbable for Paolo to speak in this fashion. In the unfolding of passionate love, the woman is the passion itself, the one exalted by passion, and the man is the instrument of passion, the one who initiates it and brings it about, but who participates in it less. He quickly becomes the spectator of the emotion he has helped to create, albeit a loving spectator. That is precisely Paolo's role in canto 5. His stature as a man would be diminished if he were used to illustrate the passion that belongs more to Francesca.

The seventh section of Joyce's *Ulysses* is the windy chapter, relating to the story in Homer of Aeolus, keeper of the winds. Aeolus had six daughters and six sons. These girls became the wives of their brothers. Thus the noisy wind of Aeolus is associated with illicit love. Stephen Dedalus calls lust his dearest sin. He quotes four phrases from canto 5 as he thinks of the rhymes of a poem he has written on the beach. This thought leads him to recite the three rhymes of lines 92, 94, and 96:

> la tua pace
> che parlar vi piace
> mentre che 'l vento, come fa ci tace.

He hears the rhymes as he sees three young women approaching him in the three colors of green, rose, and russet. They seem to be entwined, as the rhymes are, in the mauve-purple dark of the beach: *per l'aere perso* (5:89). It is the dark, ominous atmosphere of canto 5 at the moment when the wind quiets down during the moment of communication between Francesca and Dante.

John Keats, in his sonnet "A Dream," imagines himself as Paolo:

> But to that second circle of sad hell,
> Where 'mid the gust, the whirlwind...
> ...Pale were the sweet lips I saw,
> Pale were the lips I kiss'd, and fair the form
> I floated with, about that melancholy storm.

Francesca, daughter of Guido da Polenta, who probably gave protection and hospitality to Dante during his exile, is the first spirit who speaks to Dante in Hell. Her episode is too often used to illustrate Dante's power of empathy and his warm tenderness. But the real importance of the passage is the skill with which the poet describes the soul's first opening out to sin, the consent to sin which the world is ready to excuse because of its allegiance to love.

Principal Signs and Symbols

1. *The tail of Minos* (*la coda*): measures the gravity of the sin. Minos, a god of antiquity, is here medievalized.

2. *Lust* (*talento*): the least punished sin in Hell.

3. *The infernal storm* (*la bufera infernal*): the wind (*il vento*) is the punishment that suggests lust.

4. *Galeotto was the book* (*Galeotto fu il libro*): Gallehault was the intermediary between Lancelot and Guinevere, as the book was the intermediary between Paolo and Francesca.

CANTO

6

The Gluttons: Ciacco (Third Circle)

GLUTTONY FOLLOWS LUST in Dante's scheme of sins, and thus is considered more serious, more punishable. Eating and sexual appetite are indeed closely related because one can easily replace the other. It is unusual, however, for the two appetites to function simultaneously: overeating is often the sign of sexual privation or at least of sexual dissatisfaction.

Canto 6 is closely related to canto 5 because of this relationship between gluttony and carnality, and at the same time distinct from it because we move from a sin that is mutually enjoyed to a sin that is solitary, one indulged for its own sake. The shift from carnality to gluttony is explicit and dramatic, and through the setting and the figure of Ciacco, Dante makes us feel the heavier toll it takes on the soul. *La gola* is Italian for "throat." *La golosità* is gluttony, and *i golosi* are the gluttons.

After the winds of canto 5, we enter the more biblical atmosphere of the plague of rain, *(la pioggia)*, sleet, and snow in this third circle. After the noise of the storm, with its howling and force, we come to a repulsive place of filth. This is the briefest of the cantos, and describes, after the physical elements, the demon at the entrance and one of the figures inside, adding a note on eschatology at the end.

Line 13 introduces the demon guard of the third circle, Cerberus, a three-throated doglike figure:

> Cerbero, fiera crudele e diversa
> [Cerberus, a monster fierce and strange]

In the *Aeneid* (book 6) and in Greek mythology, Cerberus also appears with three throats and three heads. He guards the entrance to Hades not out of gluttony but out of the terror of death. In Dante he has red eyes, a black beard, clawed hands, and he barks over the spirits immersed in the filth. The incessant rain makes them bark like dogs as they turn from side to side, each one making a shelter for the other.

Virgil treats Cerberus not as a demon, but as a figure of terror, and Dante portrays him as a figure of gluttony. His human elements—a beard and hands—indicate that he has been metamorphosed into a demon from a human form. He illustrates gluttony by swallowing earth, and punishes the sinners by clawing them. Cerberus is thus both the sin and its punishment. The adjective *diversa*, used to describe Cerberus, has many meanings. Here it would seem to be "strange" or even "disgusting." The word *vermo* (worm) allies Cerberus with the serpent or the dragon: *Cerbero, il gran vermo* (6:22). When Virgil throws fistfulls of earth into the ravenous gullets of the creature, he repeats what the Sibyl does in the *Aeneid* with honey cakes, which she uses to quiet the beast.

One of the shades sits up and speaks to Dante, who does not recognize him. Gluttony has disfigured him and the mud in which he lives has befouled him. The spirit wants to be recognized:

> riconoscimi, se sai [6:41]
> [recognize me if you can]

This is the first Florentine Dante meets in Hell. In introducing himself, he announces this fact: "The citizens of your city called me Ciacco because of the grievous fault of gluttony":

> Voi cittadini mi chiamaste Ciacco:
> per la dannosa colpa de la gola [6:52–53]

Ciacco, possibly a corruption of Giacomo, means "hog" in Florentine dialect. Dante, who feels deep sympathy for Ciacco on seeing his plight, was twenty-one when Ciacco died. The man was well known in Florence for his wit, his story-telling skill, and for his foul language; he was often invited to dinner to provide amusement for the guests. Villani, in his *Chronicles*, speaks of this kind of man—*uomini di corte*, men of the court or men invited to banquets, newsmongers—whose speech could be both amusing and malicious. All that is known about the real Ciacco is here in canto 6 and in one of Boccaccio's *Decameron* stories (IX, 8).

Dante recognizes Ciacco and feels pity for him, pity strong enough to cause him to weep. But his feelings are not as overpowering as they were for Francesca, and we will notice as the journey continues that Dante's pity for the souls in Hell diminishes. Without transition, Dante initiates questions about Florence. In this conversation the reader learns that the spirits can foresee the future. This is the first of many references to Boniface VIII, the reigning pope in 1300.

Ciacco's power of seeing into the future reveals to Dante the greater strife that was to come to Florence in the bloody struggle between the two political parties: the Whites (*i Bianchi*), Dante's own party, and the Blacks (*i Neri*). Dante had already lived through this feud and been exiled because of it in 1302. But his journey through Hell takes place in 1300, and he assigns to Ciacco the task of foretelling the future events. Dante's questions are brief and general at first: "Are there any just men in Florence? What are the reasons for such strife?"

The word *giusto*, which Dante uses in his question (*s'alcun v'è giusto*, 6:62), is used again by Ciacco in his mysterious answer: "There are two just men" (*Giusti son due*, 6:73). The sound of the sentence is biblical ("Peradventure there be fifty righteous within the city," Genesis 18:24). No provable identification has been demonstrated, although the most pleasing is the theory that the two just men were Dante himself and his friend Guido Cavalcanti. Ciacco's answer to the second question addresses itself to moral concerns rather than political: "Pride, envy and avarice are the sparks that have set the hearts on fire" (*superbia, invidia e avarizia*, 6:74). Ciacco denounces Florence because of the moral traits of its citizens, thereby demonstrating his own high moral character. Like other spirits whom he mentions to Dante, Ciacco is consigned to Hell because of a personal vice. The law gradually becomes clear: one private vice is enough to condemn a man who in every other respect was a law-abiding and conscientious citizen, a man good in the sight of God and his neighbors.

Dante pursues his questions with great specificity. He lists five names of notable Florentine citizens and asks if they are in Heaven or Hell. Ciacco's answer is brief: all five inhabit lower parts of Hell. The glutton then requests of Dante something that will be asked often during the rest of the journey. "When you are in the sweet world,"

Ma quando tu sarai nel dolce mondo, [6:88]

"speak of me to the living." He wants to be remembered on earth. In his briefly phrased request, in almost the same sentence, Ciacco appears wise and omniscient, a prophet even, and movingly human, an object of pity.

Ciacco then quickly disappears from sight, and Virgil comes to the front in just a few lines which he exchanges with Dante on a problem of eschatology. It is an important passage (6:94–115) for an understanding of the condition of the souls in Hell and of what will happen to them after the second judgment, that made by Christ himsèlf. Virgil begins the discussion by reminding Dante that at the second coming of Christ, each soul will return to its grave and put on its body. Dante then asks if the soul will suffer more in its recovered body; Virgil replies in the affirmative. The more perfect the soul and the body become, the greater the pain, the greater the capacity to suffer.

Ritorna a tua scïenza [v. 106]
[return to your learning]

Virgil says to Dante. This is obviously a reference to Saint Thomas Aquinas and to the detailed reconciliation the philosopher made in the thirteenth century between Aristotle and the Bible.

If Minos is the first judge the soul meets in Hell, Christ will be the second, and his judgment will confirm the first. In verse 96, Christ is referred to with the words la nimica podesta, "the enemy judge." Thus Virgil replies to Dante in words of Saint Thomas, and behind him, Saint Augustine. There is no hope for these souls, only deeper damnation. The disquisition on theology is cut short when in the last line the fourth circle is announced.

The sixth canto is one of striking contrasts and wonderment for the traveler. Behind the figure of Ciacco, the story-teller at banquets, the man who bought his dinners with his licentious speech, we sense the ongoing punishment of the gluttonous and their misery in the slime. The dog-demon Cerberus, at the beginning, has been momentarily quieted. When Dante asks about his city, we learn simultaneously of the evil that awaits Florence and of the high moral traits of Ciacco, who speaks with his gift of seeing into the future. And then, as a kind of postscriptum, Virgil speaks of the aggravation in the penalty of lost souls after the day of judgment. The canto contains the first conversation about Florence, and hints at Dante's agony when he learns about the fate of some of the good citizens of his city (6:79: *i degni,* "the worthy ones"), men who had once set their minds on doing good in the political sphere (6:81).

In this world of the gluttons we are far from the mystical meaning of eating with which the Bible begins and ends. Adam's and Eve's sins are related to the act of eating, and at the end of Holy Scripture, Christ appears as the Lamb, the body of God, to be eaten. The book begins with a warning not to eat what is forbidden by God, and ends with an invitation to eat the very body of God.

Principal Signs and Symbols

1. *Cold and heavy rain (piova fredda e greve,* 6:7–8): the physical punishment for spiritual wickedness, degrading self-indulgence.

2. *Gluttons:* third circle sinners who represent suffering for the lowest kind of sensual gratification.

3. *Worm:* the Italian *vermo* is one of many words for "monster."

4. *Cerberus (Cerbero):* the three-headed dog in Homer and Virgil, and here in Dante the representation of voracious appetite.

5. *Vanità che par persona* (6:36): "emptiness which seems a body." The spirits in Hell have only the appearance of their bodily forms. They are airy shapes, although they can be tortured.

6. *Ciacco:* the shade of a citizen of Florence. The nickname "Ciacco" means "pig."

7. *Florence:* called here in line 49, *la tua città,* "your native city," and then, in line 61, *la città partita,* "the divided city."

8. *The wood party (la parte selvaggia,* 6:65): the "Whites," some of whose leaders had come from the country around Florence. They opposed the more aristocratic "Blacks." The man *che testé piaggia* (who keeps tacking, who sits on the fence, 6:69) is

Boniface VIII who finally favored the Blacks by promoting the decree that banished the Whites in January 1302.

9. *Day of judgment*: referred to in 6:94. See Matthew 25. The *nimica podesta* is Christ, "enemy of the wicked" (6:96).

10. *"Return to your learning"* (*ritorna a tua scïenza*, 6:106): this would be the philosophy of Aristotle as adopted by Aquinas.

11. *Plutus* (*Pluto*, 6:115): "Here we found Plutus the great enemy." Pluto, the god of the lower regions, was often confused with Plutus, the god of riches in the medieval tradition.

HELL Canto 7

CANTO

7

The Avaricious and Prodigal (Fourth Circle)
The Wrathful and Sullen (Fifth Circle)

THE FOURTH CIRCLE is introduced by a violent, unintelligible cry from its demon-guard, Plutus, god of wealth in Greek mythology. We are in the next-to-last circle of that part of Hell where the sins of incontinence are punished, and already the way seems long and diverse since Dante encountered the three beasts (*le tre fiere*) of canto 1, heard of the three ladies (*le tre donne*) of canto 2, moved through the vestibule of the will-less (*gl'ignavi*) in canto 3 where the boatman Charon appeared, and met the suspended ones (*i sospesi*) in limbo, the first circle, of canto 4. The long-tailed demon Minos introduced all of Hell as well as the second circle of the carnal sinners (canto 5), where Dante heard the sad story of Francesca. Immediately behind us, in canto 6, lies the third circle of eternal rain, where the demon Cerberus rules over the gluttons and where the Florentine Ciacco had spoken to Dante of their beloved city.

There had been no mutuality amid the cold of the gluttons. Obsessed with self-satisfaction, the glutton is blind to others. Dante, in fact, uses the word for "blind," *cieco*, when he calls the gluttons "other blindmen," (*altri ciech*, 6:93). After passing Plutus, who appears in the form of a wolf (*lupo*) with swollen cheeks as if his mouth and throat were a reservoir of wealth, we find that the fourth circle is the place where the avaricious and the prodigal are punished, and punish one another. It is a fantasy scene which pictures a joust (*giostra*) wherein two opponents rush toward each other, each bent on demolishing the other. The greed of hoarding is thus opposed to the greed of squandering.

This is a community of opposites and of oppositions. In another
scene one party (or one gang) rolls great stones against the other.
It is an action of pure futility, motivated by pure hatred.

The image of a deadlock is uppermost in the scene. One side
yells *"Perché tieni?"* (7:30), "why do you hold (like misers)?"
And the other yells *"Perché burli?"* (7:30), "why do you throw
away (like spendthrifts)?", and we feel the impasse in which an
economy of parsimony is offset by an economy of waste. The
scene of community is dominated by a perverted communal
spirit: all are against all in this clash of greeds. This image of
society is one of extreme anarchy, and the question arises in the
mind of the reader: How has society reached this point? How has
society reached so quickly this state of disintegration?

Dante has wisely placed in this same canto the introduction to
the fifth circle, the marshy river Styx, which contains the wrathful. On the surface of the Styx a savage discontent is visible as the
souls snarl and rend themselves. It is the picture of active wrath.
At the bottom of the marsh lie the more passive, more sullen
figures of wrath, who gurgle a hymn of hatred.

This fifth circle is indeed the climax to all the circles of incontinence, for here passion and greed have become impotent
frustration. This extreme point of anger in its two aspects of
snarling and sullen anger, began invisibly in the second circle,
with the tender indulgence expressed by Francesca. Dante in-
tends us to realize that it is not unrelated to the joyless morality of
limbo, in the first circle, to the indecisiveness of the souls in the
vestibule of Hell, and to the soul of the man Dante in the *selva
oscura* of canto 1 where he meets the first beast, the gaily spotted
leopard. Within the structure of his poem on Hell, the detailed
description of that encounter with the leopard explains all the
sins of incontinence, beginning especially with the unwise yet
loving indulgence of Francesca and ending with the inarticulate,
frustrated wrath of the unnamed souls lying at the bottom of the
Stygian marsh.

The end of the passage on the leopard in canto 1 gives a possible clue as to the extent of these sins of incontinence and to the
insidious deepening of significance as we go from the first to the
fifth circles. The agile beast (*la lonza leggiera*) gave to Dante a
sense of hope at the very beginning of his climb, in verse 41 (*a
bene sperar*). The leopard appeared so attractive that it hardly
seemed to be a hindrance to Dante. Similarly, the sins of the leopard are those that at first appear to us inoffensive, sins easily over-

come. The opening sections of Dante's poem are indeed suffused with hopefulness. Hell is perhaps not as terrifying as has been claimed. The souls in the vestibule had been tolerant in life. How hard it is to distinguish excessive or sinful tolerance from genuine tolerance! The pagans in limbo were good men, gifted in thought and deed. In the second circle, love is a part of carnality, and we all know how important love is in the world. As we watch the *golosi* in the third circle, we may wonder if it is easy to draw a line between the *gourmands* and the *gourmets*. And now in the fourth circle we remember that thrift and generosity are words that might be applied to hoarding and careless spending. The series ends with the fifth circle, where the wrathful, visible in the Styx, and the sullen, consumed by hatred, are invisible in the bottom of the marsh. These are the last of the sins that had appeared in their earliest manifestations as not too serious, and even attractive, to the sinners.

This is a canto rich in its complexity, and one so charged with poetic detail that the reader forgets how much space is being covered in Dante's journey. Plutus appears in the figure of a cursed wolf (*maladetto lupo*, 7:8) whose unintelligible sounds even Virgil does not attempt to translate. Avarice, the sin of the clergy, is apparent in Plutus' inflated face (*enfiata labbia*, 7:7). His swollen cheeks contain whatever is being hoarded. This bestial figure, after one stern reprimand from Virgil, collapses as, when the mast breaks, the sails fall to the deck of a ship.

According to the proverb, extremes meet in the contra-dance, or round-dance (*la ridda*) where the avaricious and spendthrifts clash together. The misers have shorn locks (*crin mozzi*, 7:57). Dante is moved to pity by the scene before him and feels that he should recognize some of the figures, but Virgil reminds him that these souls were so undiscerning in life that their faces are indiscernible in Hell. No one is identified in this circle. All the gold they hoarded or misspent in life will not allow them any rest in their endless butting against one another.

The name of Fortuna is first spoken by Virgil (7:62) as he comments on the principal scene of the canto, and almost immediately Dante picks up the word and asks pointedly and simply who this Fortuna is (7:68): Does she control the world? The tone of the canto changes then from the grotesque to a clear disquisition on the meaning of Fortuna, no longer a pagan goddess, but a creature of God, one of the blessed (*ella s'è beata*, 7:94) who is responsible for dispensing wealth. The brief

passage of thirty-five lines is almost a foreshadowing of the
Paradiso. Christians traditionally prefer to use the term "Providence" rather than "Fortune" in designating God's power over
worldly possessions. The biblical phrase from Job is the most
often quoted in this regard: "The Lord gave, and the Lord hath
taken away, blessed be the name of the Lord." In other words,
the wisdom of the Lord, his inscrutable purpose, does not allow
earthly wealth or property to stay too long with any one person,
family, or nation.

Boethius' *The Consolation of Philosophy* is a text echoed in this
passage on the mutability of man's fortune. Boethius was translated by Chaucer, and his own translation-commentary of Aristotle was widely used by the scholastic philosophers. Dante in-
corporates in his description the two leading attributes of Fortuna: the swiftness with which she acts (the word *veloce* is in line
89) and her unpredictability (or inscrutability) as expressed by
the traditional image of "the wheel of fortune"; as Dante says,
"in the sphere she turns" (*volve sua spera*, 7:96). The figure of
Fortune is the quiet, serene counterpart to the howling Plutus
and to the blind madness of giving and taking, visible in the
prodighi and the *avari*. Dante closely follows the interpretation
of Boethius, but he is bold in assigning to Fortune the rank of an
angelic intelligence, an "angel of earth," as she is sometimes
called.

Moving past a spring and a trench and following murky water,
Dante and Virgil come to a marsh. It is the Styx, one of the
classical rivers of Hell, and it constitutes for Dante's purpose the
fifth circle. In the bog naked spirits fight and tear one another
with their teeth. These souls are those who were overcome by
anger in life. Others, according to Virgil, are invisible in the
black mud below. In them anger had turned to sullenness. Dante
hears them speak: *Tristi fummo,* "we were sullen, and bore
within ourselves a sluggish smoke." The word for sluggish is
accidioso, the key to this sin of spiritual sloth, and which will be
developed further in the *Purgatorio*. The two groups of the fifth
circle are not in opposition and do not punish each other, as the
two groups of the fourth circle did, and there is no monster
guarding the entrance.

Whereas Aristotle and Aquinas divide the wrathful into three
classes—*acuti* (quick-tempered), *amari* (sullen), *difficiles*
(vindictive)—Dante has only two categories: active and passive
wrath. In the first we witness a scene almost like a street fight,

with figures gouging and biting one another. In the second are the brooders, submerged in the mud. Because of the word *accidïoso* in line 123, some commentators believe these sinners to be slothful. But the emphasis is on *tristi*, meaning "sad" or "sullen" (7:121–23).

In the fourth circle sin begins to strive against itself in the strife between miserliness and extravagance. In the Stygian bog, sheer anger (*ira*) is demonstrated as it turns outward, almost in the form of anarchy, and as it turns inward in those souls beneath the surface. The canto as a whole marks the end of the first division of Hell. The ending of this long itinerary of incontinence is the Styx, a word meaning "hateful," where the feeling of resentment in man grows into active hatred and passive sullenness.

Principal Signs and Symbols

1. *The joust* (*la giostra*, 7:35): the image of mutual antagonism, the futility of war, classes, gangs. Here the hoarders and spendthrifts are opposed and joined in a scene of futility. *Riddi* in line 24 is from the verb *riddare*, based on the noun *la ridda*, a round dance.

2. *The Styx:* the second river of Hell appears as a marsh (*una palude*, 7:106) containing the wrathful on the surface, and the sullen underneath in the mud. The word "Styx" means "hateful" and is sometimes interpreted as meaning "sadness.'" It is the fifth circle and also the boundary between upper and lower Hell.

3. *Fortuna:* the pagan goddess is christianized by Dante and made a servant of God as she carries out the divine purpose on earth. The image of a "wheel" is in the word *vicenda* (7:90) meaning a "turn" or a "change." The turning of the wheel brings about disaster or prosperity. In his use of the figure of Fortune Dante does not mean to deny free will.

CANTO

8

Wrath and the Gates of Dis

IN CANTO 8 one of the wrathful appears before Dante and is recognized by him, but prior to that episode which, although brief, dominates the canto, a small boat with one oarsman moves swiftly through the air and the water of the Styx. It is Phlegyas, who in Greek mythology had set fire to Apollo's temple at Delphi and was condemned to Hades. Before Virgil speaks his name, the boatman gloats that he has caught another guilty soul.

The opening of this canto,

> Io dico, seguitando, ch'assai prima
> [I say, continuing, that long before]

is responsible for a legend that has no documentary support. Many early commentators believed that Dante composed the first seven cantos before he went into exile, and then resumed work after the interruption. The theory is based on the word *seguitando* in the first line.

Two lights appear at the top of a high watchtower, and another light signal farther off answers back to this outpost of the city of Dis, the second section of Dante's Hell. The movement of the entire canto is fast, melodramatic, and mysterious. Dante is at a very high point of excitement and wonder. Moreover, he is to play an important part in the action of the canto. For the first time Dante is taken to be one of the sinners arriving in order to allocated. Phlegyas is delighted over this, but is immediately set right by Virgil who says to him: "You cry in vain" (*tu gridi a vòto*, 8:19). The boatman, as intemperate as those he guards, behaves as if he has been cheated. Phlegyas reminds us of Charon, although he is human in his appearance.

Between lines 31 and 63 occurs an episode that has been variously interpreted. Virgil enters the boat first, followed by Dante, who realizes that his body has weight and causes the boat to appear laden (Virgil's form is weightless). When the boat moves off, it cuts deeper into the waters of the Styx than it normally would. As they cross the stagnant channel, the action of the scene begins immediately with the appearance of a figure covered with mud. The spirit's opening words indicate that he knows Dante is still alive:

Chi se' tu che vieni anzi ora? [8:33]
[Who are you who come before your time?]

Dante replies that he is merely passing through, and asks the spirit who he is. Because of the mud, Dante does not recognize him at first. The evasive answer of the spirit is pitiful and almost resembles repentence:

Vedi che son un che piango. [8:36]
[You see I am one who weeps.]

The sadness of this spirit is offset, and dramatically so, by Dante's reply in which he says he now recognizes the spirit despite the filth covering his body. "Accursed spirit," Dante calls to him, "remain in your weeping and wretchedness" (8:37–38). When the figure stretches its two hands out to the boat, Virgil thrusts him off with words as strong as Dante's: "Go off with the other dogs" (8:42). Then comes the most startling moment, when Virgil, having cast off the spirit, embraces Dante, kisses his cheek, and says to him words that are traditionally addressed to the Virgin Mary: "Blessed is the womb that bore you" (8:45). In this way Virgil rejoices over Dante's strong sense of indignation (Alma sdegnosa, 8:44). After giving this biblical salutation, Virgil emphasizes the arrogance of a spirit who is not remembered on the earth as having done any good and who therefore demonstrates greater fury in Hell. There are kings, he says, now living in the world who will be one day, like this spirit, swine in the mire (8:49–51).

Eugène Delacroix, in one of his larger paintings, has caught the violence with which the spirit tries to stop the boat carrying Dante and Virgil. Dante's anger, ironically and mysteriously, grows beyond that of the sinner. The poet wants to see the spirit plunged deeper into the Styx. Virgil approves of the wish and promises that before the shore comes in sight, he will have satisfaction. Not until we reach this point, the end of the passage, do we hear the name of the sinner, Filippo Argenti, yelled by the other sinners who set upon him, an action not entirely necessary since Filippo begins to gnaw himself in an act of self-torture.

If there is no break in the composition of the poem between cantos 7 and 8, there is certainly a change in Dante's attitude. The canto is memorable not so much for the wrath of Filippo Argenti as for Dante's wrath, and Virgil's, too. Of the three characters (this is the first scene which has three participants), Filippo himself is the most humble in his second deeply pathetic speech: "see, I am one who weeps." A Florentine, he belonged to the political party opposed to Dante's. He was a *Nero*, one of the Blacks, a man of wealth who acquired the nickname Argenti because he had his horse shod with silver. He was a muscular man, of large stature, an athlete, but known especially for his violent temper. Here in the mud of Hell, he continues to act out his temper. Delacroix has him sink his teeth into the boat as an expression of anger.

Filippo Argenti's first question to Dante may be interpreted as an insult: "Who are you coming here before your time?" This may imply that Dante is so wicked that he is in the swamp before his death. Filippo conceals his identity when he answers Dante's question with the words: "Isn't it enough to see I am a spirit suffering?" The extravagance of Filippo Argenti is made more of in Boccaccio's *Decameron* (9:8), where he is presented as an arrogant nobleman of the Adimari family who hates all the citizens of Florence. According to records, he was not a criminal, but an imperious horseman, here dismounted forever in the mud of Dante's Hell.

Until this irruption of Filippo Argenti, Dante had shown two strong emotions: pity and fear. The rage he feels in canto 8 is his third emotion, and it is possible that he has been contaminated by the presence of the wrathful. All four speakers in the canto, Phlegyas, Virgil, Dante, and Filippo Argenti, exhibit anger. Classics scholars remind us that the Greek poets castigated anger and urged a spirit of pardon and moderation. Even if the gods expressed anger, men should not. On the whole, the Latin writers maintained this attitude. In his treatise *De ira*, Seneca states that there is no justification for anger. And yet God's anger is expressed in almost every book of the Old Testament. Saint

Thomas Aquinas avoids speaking of divine anger, and emphasizes the doctrine that God, in willing justice, wills punishment at the same time. The episode of Christ's attack on the moneylenders in the temple is certainly a flare-up of anger, but Christ's teaching and his example underscore leniency and understanding rather than anger.

We will see that the Filippo Argenti passage is not the only example of Dante's wrath. It is merely the first and almost unexpected instance of anger in the poem's protagonist, and it continues in varying degrees of exhilaration and even delight. This psychological change in Dante indicates a lessening of his fear of Hell, although in the final episode of the canto his emotions of fear take over again as he sees the devils at the entrance to the city of Dis.

It is an elaborate approach to Dis, Satan's stronghold, this second part of the *Inferno*, that carries over into canto 9. Both the space allotted to this section and the opposition to Dante, the traveler who is not yet dead, indicate the importance of shift from the sins of incontinence to the sins of violence.

> La città c' ha nome Dite [8:68]
> [the city that has the name Dis]

is the whole of lower Hell. It appears with ramparts and is moated by the Styx. The iron walls of the city are the image of obstinacy, the willful determination to perpetrate violence and fraud, which are the two categories of sins that are punished in Dis.

From this point on, there is no trace of self-deception in the sinners of Hell, no trace of the easily moving leopard. Evil will be as clear as the walls made red by the fire that burns within them. The episode with Filippo Argenti is perhaps best explained as Dante's introduction to an evil that is fully conscious of itself. On realizing its danger and its degradation, he turns on it with strong indignation. Virgil, when he sees this in Dante, uses words associated with the conception of Christ when Mary felt the stirring of the child within her. The new division in Hell is clearly marked by Dante's new attitude. Until this point nature in the form of wind, rain, and mud formed the environment. But we have now passed through the suburbs and face the city itself with its tower, walls, and battlement. It is the city, organized and powerful as sin itself.

The entire canto is full of movement, both in its panorama and in its drama. Everything—speeches, action, characters—is vivid, intense, rapid. When in line 82 Dante sees more than a thousand spirits on the gate, presumably those angels that fell with Satan, a new fear strikes him, because they deny him entrance. He still belongs to the living and therefore has no place in Hell. Virgil then takes over the final action and indicates that he will speak to the devil guardians. They say that he should come alone, and let the other figure return. Dante's discouragement and fear are such that he suggests he and Virgil retrace their steps.

In line 97, Dante refers to the seven times that Virgil had already restored him. The number seven is indeed accurate is one remembers the role of Virgil with the wolf, Charon, Minos, Cerberus, Plutus, Phlegyas, and Filippo Argenti. As soon as Virgil speaks words of comfort, and promises not to leave Dante, the action starts up again. As Virgil approaches the gate, it is closed in his face. With the resistance of the devils, who once opposed Christ's descent to Hell at the main gate bearing the inscription, Virgil's anger flares up again. The end of the canto is not the end of the episode. We realize the action will continue as Virgil points out an approaching figure who will solve the problem.

Principal Signs and Symbols

1. *Phlegyas (Flegias):* a king in mythology who in his rage set fire to Apollo's temple, and here in canto 8 is ferryman on the Styx for sinners who pass from the fifth circle to Dis.

2. *Filippo Argenti:* a Florentine of the Adimari family, known for the violence of his temper.

3. *City of Dis:* the whole of lower Hell. Its ramparts and the Styx form a circle around the pit. Virgil uses the name "Dis," the classical name for the king of Hell (Dis or Pluto). Dante, as a Christian, will call this king Lucifer, Satan, or Beelzebub.

4. "More than a thousand rained from Heaven" (8:2–13): These are the angels that fell with Lucifer, according to the Christian tradition. In lines 124–25 the rebellious angels (now demons) tried to deny Christ's entry into Hell by barring the "less secret" gate (the gate of canto 3).

5. The "one by whom the city shall be opened to us" (*tal, che per lui ne fia la terra aperta,* 8:130) is the angel of the next canto.

CANTO

9

The Furies and the Angel

FROM THE MIDDLE of canto 8 where the city of Dis is named with its citizens and its garrisons (8:68–69), to the last quarter of canto 9, we see a veritable melodrama unfold in the struggle of Virgil and Dante to enter Satan's city. If we use the term "drama," it is convenient to see the action as divided into four movements or acts (the first two have already taken place in canto 8).

1. The fallen angels over the gate admit Virgil but not Dante. Dante is so disheartened that he is willing to go back (8:82–102).

2. Virgil parleys with the angels (or devils) and is repudiated. The door is closed in his face (8:103–30). This end of the second movement is colored by Virgil's anger, a strong feeling comparable to that expressed earlier in the canto by both Dante and Virgil over Filippo Argenti.

3. The third act takes place in the first third of the new canto (9:1–60) and is more complex and violent than the preceding sections. It begins, however, with a passage of introversion, of inner struggle for both Virgil and Dante. Thus far at the entrance to Dis, Virgil has failed in his efforts, but he has not in the least lost faith—he is simply puzzled that help is so long in coming. Dante, on the other hand, who closely watches Virgil's face, doubts both himself and his guide. He is polite is asking his question in the third person. "Has anyone ever come down this far from the first circle?"

discende mai alcun del primo grado? [9:17]

The first circle is limbo, home of Virgil, and Virgil knows that Dante is really asking: "Have you ever come down this far?"

Virgil's answer is affirmative as he reassures Dante: "Yes, I was here before, when Erichtho conjured me up." This allusion to the Greek sorceress may be an invention of Dante or it may be part of a medieval legend in which Virgil was regarded as a magician. At this point the devils over the gate turn from an attitude of defense to one of assault. The three Furies appear on the top of the wall and call on Medusa to turn Dante to stone. To protect him, Virgil covers Dante's eyes with his hands. The three Furies are female forms from classical mythology. They appear in Virgil's poem as the Erinnyes or Eumenides, punishers of crimes against kindred. In Aeschylus they pursue Orestes, who murdered his mother. They are more demonic in Dante than in Virgil or Aeschylus. The climax to this third part of the drama is the call to Medusa:

> Venga Medusa: sì 'l farem di smalto [9:52]
> [let Medusa come, that we may change him into stone]

Dante goes to great pains to present this entrance into Dis as a difficult adventure. It occupies the normal length of an entire canto: half of 8 and half of 9. In a geographical sense, the passage marks a shift from a country landscape to that of a city. In terms of morality, it marks the passage from incontinence to malice. In a psychological sense, it is the change from a passive will on the part of the sinners to an active will. And finally it would seem to indicate a change from an individual sin, affecting one person, to an organized sin deliberately willed and affecting more than one. The scene of wrath with the three Furies calling upon Medusa, who never appears, is quite appropriate to the city of Dis and its far more intricate organization.

Medusa, invoked but not seen, is not referred to by Virgil in book 6 of the *Aeneid*. But Odysseus, in book 9 of the *Odyssey*, is frightened that Persephone, queen of the underworld, will send one of the three Gorgons, who is Medusa. There is thus a faint connection here between Dante and Homer. Dante may have read Homer in translation, or more probably in translated fragments.

Between acts 3 and 4 there is a mysterious *tercet* (9:61–63), in which Dante speaks directly to his readers and urges them to "consider the doctrine that is concealed under the veil of these strange verses":

> O voi ch'avete li 'ntelletti sani,
>   mirate, la dottrina, che s'asconde
>   sotto 'l velame de li versi strani.

The poet never says what the doctrine is, but the lines are so close to the names of Medusa and the Gorgons that it may concern the rebel angels or any rebellion against God which hardens the heart. Whatever the exact "doctrine" is that Dante had in mind, the three lines provide an introduction to the fourth movement of the drama, which concerns divine help. In fact, this acute need for divine help at such critical moments may be the doctrine itself. Thus the "teaching" behind the verses may apply to what precedes them (the terrifying picture of rebellion) or to what follows them (the coming of the angel).

Act 4 is the happy dénouement, the appearance of the heavenly messenger (*da ciel messo,* 9:85), a strong figure walking on the Styx, as a fearful sound causes both banks to tremble. The fallen angels disperse, as fast as the appearance of a snake would cause frogs to scatter, and coming to the gate, the angel opens it with a touch of his wand. He chides the rebel angels for their stupidity in opposing Heaven, and then moves swiftly off without a word to the travelers. This move from the Furies to the will of God fills Dante and Virgil with confidence. They feel "secure after the angel's words":

> sicuri appresso le parole sante. [9:105]

The *Paradiso* is the foundation of the *Inferno*. This truth has just been illustrated, although the etymology of the word *paradiso* as *para* (against) *Dis*, the city of Dis, is not considered authentic.

The three major myths of races or civilizations on which *The Divine Comedy* is founded are present in this drama of Dante's entrance into Dis. From the Hebraic myth come the fallen angels and their opposition to God at the beginning of history. From Greece come the three Furies and their wrath against the divine order. From Christian myth comes the angel sent by God to carry out his will, an action reminiscent of the harrowing of Hell by Christ. The first part of the action demonstrated Dante's impotence and his immediate sense of helplessness. The second part demonstrated Virgil's inadequacy. Alone he was unable to enter Dis. Part three was the effort of Hell to terrify and threaten the travelers, especially Dante, when the Furies called upon Medusa. Part four was the answer of Heaven, an act of Providence in the form of a scornful angel.

The angel has forced Hell to open itself up to Dante and reveal to him the fullness of its terrors and ugliness. This strange rescue awakens in Dante a deeper consciousness of sin. In opposing the intruder, Hell marshaled theatrical devices worthy of a horror film of the twentieth century, and in opposing these devices, Heaven, in the form of a single unadorned figure, had only to touch with a wand the door of lower Hell in order to be totally effective.

After his momentary faint-heartedness, followed by his amazement at the angel's success, Dante now is all curiosity. Anxiety is followed by wonder as he enters the city of Dis and the sixth circle which lie just within the walls. It is in the form of a plain (*grande compagna*, 9:110) made uneven by graves. Flames spread among the tombs making them exceedingly hot. The lids are open, and the suffering of the spirits within the tombs is audible. When Dante asks who these people are, Virgil answers: "They are the archheretics with their followers of every sect":

> Qui son li eresïarche
> con lor seguaci, d'ogne setta [9:127–28]

The circle of the heretics in their flaming tombs illustrates this new part of Hell where the sinner's will is more obdurate. Previously, in the five circles of incontinence, the sinners had broken a moral law with full knowledge they were doing so, but were unable to resist, unable to struggle against the temptation, impulse, or habit. From this point on, beginning with this graveyard scene, the sinners have looked upon the face of Medusa and their will has hardened.

Heresy is traditionally oppostion to one or more of the dogmas of the Church. In the usual sense, the heretic accepts the Church but defies it and refuses to accept some part of the doctrine. And he tends to justify the disagreement. He is fully aware of the implications of his actions. The archheretics of the sixth circle represent something far more serious, and the terrifying symbolism of sepulchres on fire illustrates this gravity. Here the heretic is the denier of God, and heresy is therefore the denial of divine order.

The fallen angels are an appropriate introduction to the sixth circle. They have rebelled against God, although they cannot, in fact, deny him. They illustrate the will moving deliberately and actively against God. The background to this is the anger of the three Furies and the threat of Medusa. But all threats are swiftly, almost silently, effaced by the angel. A rescue has been brought about, but it is a strange rescue into a deeper gloom than we have previously seen. Dis will represent for Dante a more vivid understanding of sin in its willfulness and in its complexity. The tercet of advice, *mirate la dottrina*, is the necessary pause which turns Dante fears into wonder and curiosity. He is now prepared for the second phase of his adventure.

The sixth circle is awesome to him as he realizes that the arch-heretics, those who deny God's order, are lying in their tombs and the tombs are in flames. Disbelief in the reality of God is the first result of obduracy, and is symptomatic in those who have looked upon the face of Medusa. The scene is a cemetery, and it reminds the poet of the graveyard outside of Arles, in Provence, Aliscamps, or *campi Elysii*, where heroes of the crusades wished to be buried in company with the earlier heroes of the *chansons de geste*.

"Cowardice" is the full meaning of the word *viltà* in the opening line of the canto. Dante's pallor seems to be that of a coward. From this point to the end of the canto when the poet shows desire to see the inside of the fortress of Dis,

> e io, ch'avea di riguardar disio [9:107]
> [and I who had the desire to see]

he experiences a series of intense emotions: great fear, doubt concerning Virgil's power, terror at the sight of the Furies, wonder over the sight of the angel, and finally a full, open-eyed attentiveness fixed on the fiery tombs whose covers are raised up, which prompt his immediate question: "Who are these people we hear and do not see?"

The entire canto is an admirable prelude to the first encounter—one of the most notable encounters in the *Inferno*—just within the sixth circle and therefore just within Dis. The background for the entrance and the meeting with Farinata is Roman, Virgilian, mythological, and includes Erichtho, the necromancer from Thessalonica, for whom Virgil once descended to lowest Hell (this was doubtless Dante's invention): the three Furies, Tisiphone, Megaera, and Alecto, avengers of crime in classical mythology, and here possibly the infernal complements of the ladies of canto 2, the reference to Hecate (or Persephone) as "queen of everlasting lamentation" (*regina dell'etterno pianto*, 9:44); Medusa, whom Virgil believed able to turn Dante to stone; and Theseus, who had once descended to Hades to kidnap Persephone for his friend Pirithous.

The other half of the canto is Christian, with the sudden appearance of the angel. His coming is comparable to one of the traditionally recognized three advents of Christ (his descent to Hell, his daily descent into a person's heart, and his descent at the Last Judgment). As Christ once opened the gate of Hell, here in canto 9 an angel opens the gate of Dis. Mythology and Christian theology are both here.

The sixth circle is outside the three main regions of incontinence, violence, and fraud. Its sin is based on intellectual pride and is carefully placed after incontinence (weakness of the flesh) and before violence (premeditated sins). Since intellectual pride is not the source of a sinful act, it thus deserves its special position.

Principal of Signs and Symbols

1. *Three Furies* (*tre furïe*, 9:38): Tisiphone, Megaera, and Alecto were the avenging goddesses in Greek mythology. They may represent here the antithetical figures of Mary, Lucia, and Beatrice in canto 2. In mythology they are "handmaids" to Hecate (or Persephone), wife of Pluto, god of the underworld.

2. *Medusa:* one of the three Gorgons. Her hair had been changed into serpents so that whoever looked at her was turned to stone. She was at length killed by Perseus.

3. *The heavenly messenger (da ciel messo):* his coming at this point is similar to Christ's descending into Hell to free the chosen people.

4. *The archheretics* represent here a sin based on intellectual pride.

5. *Aliscamps*, near Arles, was famous for the tombs of Christians slain in war against the infidels. At the battle of Aliscamps William of Orange was defeated by the Saracens.

CANTO

10

The Heretics: Farinata (Sixth Circle)

THE SIN PUNISHED in the sixth circle is clearly stated in line 15 of canto 10. The archheretics are those who in life believed the soul dies with the body:

> che l'anima col corpo morta fanno
> [who make the soul die with the body]

These spirits are the deniers of immortality, and therefore of Christianity, and, in a more restricted sense, the deniers of the very basis of Dante's *Commedia*.

Canto 10 is unique for its skillful combination of thought and dramatic intensity. Although it is of average length, it seems to be a brief canto, and this brevity is mentioned twice by the poet. It is also one of the most movingly human cantos because of the two meetings with Farinata and with Guido Cavalcanti's father. The Greek philosopher whose name appears in line 14 and who personifies this particular sin is Epicurus.

Today one associates sensual indulgence with "Epicurus and his followers" *(con Epicuo tutti suoi seguaci)*, but for Dante—and this is evident in the writings of Epicurus—they denied the immortality of the soul, and thereby built their own sepulchres of fire in which the soul continues to live and suffer. The lids of the tombs are opened now, but they will be sealed up at the Last Judgment. The lesson is terrifying: the bodies of these sinners will be sealed up for eternity, as their minds had been enclosed during their lifetime within their heretical opinions. Disregarding the fiery tombs, this is the Hebrew prophetic vision in the valley of Jehoshaphat (Joel 3:2).

73

The first spirit to speak to Dante immediately draws our attention to his temperament and his political career, whereas his sin, because of which he is in his fiery tomb, is not alluded to. We see Farinata degli Uberti as a living man, as a heroic political figure, and not as one of the damned. Dante's mind is at all times filled with images of men and events especially associated with the political struggles that beset the city of Florence. This Farinata, who died in 1264, the year before Dante was born, had in 1260 won for the Ghibelline party the battle of Montaperti. A decisive defeat for the Guelfs, the victory was won in a hillside village near Siena, and it left, according to a chronicle of the day, a field red with blood. The victorious Ghibellines wanted to destroy Florence, but Farinata opposed this, and thereby saved Florence. Epic in his stature and activity on earth, this Florentine warrior, so warmly devoted to his career and his city (*quella nobil patria natio*, 10:26), shows in his face and bearing a total contempt for Hell.

Dante, by his accent or by the phrases he uses in speaking to Virgil, is recognized by Farinata as being a Tuscan:

> O Tosco che ...
> vai così parlando onesto, [10:22–23]

"You who speak so decorously, will you pause a moment in this place?" And then, more specifically: "Your speech shows you to be a native of Florence":

> La tua loquela ti fa manifesto [10:25]

Loquela is "speech" and instinctively the reader will think of the words of the crowd to Peter: "thy speech betrayeth thee" (Matthew 26:73). Peter's words betray his Lord, but Dante's words revealed his province to a man who had once defended it.

Dante puts all that he knew of this man into the brief portrait of canto 10: his strength, his grandeur, his defiance of the place in which he suffers. The fire, out of which Farinata rises up, is the punishment which he transcends in his proud attitude. This fire of the sixth circle is the last of the four elements of antiquity. Air is prominent in the second circle where the winds of lust sweep Francesca and Paolo; water dominates in the third circle in the rain that endlessly beats down on Ciacco the glutton; and the earth is the mud in which the wrathful live in the fifth circle; and now fire appears as the enduring element of the archheretics. The upper half of Farinata's body is above the flames when he rises up to greet Dante. He transcends his physical torment in order to converse with his countrymen, and Dante, the poet-countryman, transcends whatever animosity he might have felt toward this adversary in politics and war. Reverence and admiration for Farinata color all Dante's words in the passage.

Struck by the Tuscan speech of the traveler, Farinata utters with his opening words an entreaty to have Dante stay and speak with him: *piacciati*—may it please you. And then, with the mention of his "noble country," he expresses a thought not in complete harmony with his pride: "the country that perhaps I vexed too much":

> a la qual forse fui troppo molesto. [10:27]

There would seem to be the beginning of a sense of remorse in the use of the word *molesto*. And this, coupled with the word *forse*, "perhaps," is almost an impulse of tenderness. Leopardi, the nineteenth-century Italian poet, nineteenth-century Italian poet, was very moved by the use of *forse* in the Farinata line, and stressed its poetical pathos.

Dante's eyes are "fixed" *(fitti)* on Farinata and he is so overwhelmed that Virgil has to push him toward the spirit to thus initiate the conversation. Once the Ghibelline warrior has Dante's attention, he begins with an almost impudent question:

> Chi fuor li maggior tui? [10:42]
> [Who were your ancestors?]

Behind the question, Farinata is asking: "Are you my friend or my enemy?" The Ghibelline-Guelf struggle for power is still uppermost in his mind. Dante reveals his name and therefore his background, and immediately Farinata alludes to his major victories over the Guelfs. These were the two battles won 1248 and 1260.

Dante barely has the time to remind Farinata that the Guelfs returned to power after each of those battles, when a figure rises up beside Farinata and looks about him as if to ask whether Dante is accompanied. Weeping, the shade asks the poet:

> mio figlio ov'è? e perché non è teco? [10:60]
> [Where is my son and why is he not with you?]

It is Cavalcante Cavalcanti, father of Guido, Dante's best friend: the closeness of relationship between the two young poets would justify the father's hope that his son would be there.

We first see Cavalcante on his knees (*in ginocchie*, 10:54), as if impelled by the desire to see his son, and then on his feet (*drizzato*, 10:67), when Dante, unintentionally, refers to Guido in the past tense as one "who had scorned Virgil" (*ebbe*, the past definite of *avere*, is misunderstood by the father, who now believes his son is dead); finally he falls back supine in his tomb (*supin ricadde*, 10:72). Overcome with grief, the elder Cavancanti disappears from sight.

This brief painful drama is ignored by Farinata. It interrupts his conversation with Dante and offsets the political theme with its recollection of the deep friendship between Dante and Guido Cavalcanti that was to be broken by events and differences of character. Guido, one of the foremost poets of the day, to whom Dante had dedicated *La vita nuova*, was alive in the spring of 1300, the date of Dante's journey through Hell, but he was dead when Dante wrote his poem. Guido had been exiled from Florence, and then recalled, but died a few days later from malaria, in August 1300.

Unmoved by this pathetic incident, Farinata resumes his speech by commenting on Dante's words that the Ghibellines did not know the art of returning to battle. Farinata agrees and says this fact torments him more than his present suffering in his tomb. Then, because the damned have the power of seeing into the future, he predicts Dante's banishment from Florence within fifty months. Farinata thus explains to Dante the prophetic vision of the inhabitants of Hell. However, the future will be closed to them after the Last Judgment, when time will merge with eternity.

The last lines of the conversation are spoken by Farinata, thus Dante pays a homage of reverence and admiration to his political adversary:

> Qui con più di mille giaccio:
> qua dentro è 'l secondo Federico [10:118–19]
> [With more than a thousand I lie here;
> there within is the second Frederick]

Posthumously, in 1283, Farinata, along with his wife, was condemned as a heretic. The historian Villani speaks of Farinata, Cavalcante Cavalcanti and Frederick II, king of Sicily, as Epicurean heretics, men who did not believe in any future life.

This is the first reference in the *Inferno* to Frederick II, a patron of the arts, himself a poet, and one largely responsible for the revival of letters on the thirteenth century known as the Sicilian School of poetry. With every renaissance in Europe, with every revival of learning, whether in the twelfth century or the sixteenth or the early nineteenth, there have been signs of speculative thinking involving a denial of religious belief and especially belief in the supernatural. The legend behind Goethe's *Faust* is that mysterious contract between a man of learning and the devil. The illumination of man's mind seems to bring with it the reflection of demonic fire. Farinata's reference to that moment when the gates of the future will be closed (10:108) is appropriately described as the moment when man's intellect will be void:

> tutto è vano
> nostro intelletto [10:103–4]

The *Commedia* represents a summation and a culmination of the twelfth/thirteenth-century renaissance in Europe. The rehearsal of all the forms of man's knowledge is in the work as well as the various degrees of man's life in God. But the burning tombs of the archheretics are there in canto 10 to testify to the vanity of knowledge and the emptiness of man's life without God. Farinata reminds us that when time ceases, there will be nothing to know. The rise and fall of kings (Frederick II), the rise and fall of the Ghibelline party (Farinata, Cavalcante Cavalcanti) serve to remind us of the futility of man's political power and of the inevitable changes in men's fortunes that befall humanity from generation to generation.

Political power (Farinata) and artistic ambition (Guido Cavalcanti) are both alluded to in the canto, and they are both exemplified in Frederick II; but here as already in canto 5 with Francesca, and to some degree with the neutrals and the gluttons (Ciacco), the life of the poem rises out of the characters embodying the sin and their pathos. As Dante records these encounters and describes the situations, the elaborate arrangement and punishment of the sins, he himself is drawn into the life of the lost ones (*la perduta gente*). The closeness of this relationship varies in each instance. Dante feels intense pity for Francesca's plight, and he feels great admiration for Farinata. With every episode and character, one theme is constant, one theme continues and deepens as the voyage leads Dante into deeper circles of Hell and into a deeper understanding of sin: it is the ever-growing, the multiple-faceted relationship between

Dante and Virgil. The entire *Inferno* and most of the *Purgatorio* could be interpreted as a poem of friendship, as the revelation of all that life and death holds when that revelation is made by an older wiser man to a more fervent, more ambitious younger man.

At the end of canto 10, when Farinata tells Dante that he lies in his circle with more than a thousand others, and then disappears from sight into his tomb, Dante wonders about the prophecy he has just heard concerning his own exile. He turns back to Virgil, whom he calls in the last lines of the canto *l'antico poeta* and *quel saggio* ("the ancient poet" and "that sage"). Virgil tells him that eventually in this voyage Beatrice will reveal to him the way of his life *(di tua vita il viaggio)*. These words are a prophecy in themselves, and they mark the gentleness, the persuasiveness of consoling friendship.

Principal Signs and Symbols

1. *The tombs of the heretics:* these burning iron tombs designate the obduracy of the intellectual.

2. *Epicurus:* the philosopher for whom the highest good is on earth, whereas the Catholic Church teaches that the highest happiness is in the life after death. Epicurus denied the immortality of the soul.

3. *Farinata degli Uberti:* Florentine leader of the Ghibellines. Dante had asked Ciacco about Farinata in canto 6, line 78.

4. *Cavalcante dei Cavalcanti:* member of a well-known Guelf family. His son Guido was a poet and friend of Dante and son-in-law to Farinata.

5. *The queen who reigns here* (10:79–81): Hecate or Proserpina, the moon goddess. Before fifty months have passed (April 1300 to summer 1304), Dante will know how difficult the art of return from exile is.

6. *Emperor Frederick II* (1194–1250): here among the heretics because he was looked upon as an Epircurean.

7. *Cardinal Ottaviano degli Ubaldini* (1210–73): *il Cardinale* of line 120, a Ghibelline who rejoiced over Montaperti. Dante condemns him as a heretic perhaps because of his doubting the immortality of the soul.

CANTO

11

The Plan of Hell

DANTE CHOOSES this point in his poem, at the conclusion of the brilliant meeting with Farinata and Guido Cavalcanti's father, to give an interlude, an exposition of the system of punishments in his *Inferno*. The gravity of the tone of the sixth circle is enhanced by Dante's use of *voi*, the polite pronoun, in speaking to Farinata and Cavalcante Cavalcanti, the pronoun he will use on only one other meeting, that with Brunetto Latini, in canto 15. With all the other shades he uses *tu*, the familiar form of address.

Thus canto 11 is a necessary pause before the real descent into the city of Dis begins, and it serves many purposes. For the action of the poem, it reveals the knowledge of Virgil, who expounds a system of classification based on scholastic philosophy, that of Saint Thomas Aquinas, who leaned heavily on Aristotle and Cicero for matters related to ethics. And consequently it reveals at the same time a fuller insight on the part of Dante concerning the region of the dead he is crossing, thus enabling us to see more clearly the structure of the work, the highly rational ordering of sins.

Dante's mind is full of memories of the battle career of Farinata, of his proud strong nature still manifest in Hell. In a way, the great Ghibelline illustrates the hardness of the Medusa head with which Dante himself had just been threatened when he and Virgil had tried to enter the gate of Dis. The change that deeper Hell will bring is prepared in this opening image of the archheretic. The sixth circle separates the upper Hell of the incontinent from the lower Hell formed by the three circles of violence, fraud, and treachery. The sins of violence, in the seventh circle, have a deeper place in Hell than those of incontinence because they accentuate the bestial side of man's nature. They are the sins of the lion *(leone)*, the second beast encountered by Dante in canto 1. The sins of fraud or malice of the eighth circle, the most complex of all the circles, are those of the she-wolf *(la lupa)*, the third beast of canto 1.

The image of the city is everywhere in these last three circles. Violence is swift, a flaring up of the human spirit for the purpose of destruction. Fraud is a longer, slower process of deceit, a deliberate undermining of someone else's will. The treachery or betrayal of the ninth circle is treated as the most serious of all sins because in that act all human values between individuals are destroyed. Thus canto 11 provides us with a plan of the devil's city. Virgil and Dante have just seen a few of the first inhabitants, those of the sixth circle, but heresy in the Dantean sense seems to be more related to incontinence than to violence. It stands midway between the first half of Hell and the second half.

Variously called the "scholastic canto" or the "Aristotelean canto," it is a review of the criminal or moral code of behavior. It contains no picture or character that stimulates the reader's imagination, no Charon, no Furies, no Ciacco, but it presents a scheme that holds the reader's mind, and it names in line 80 the philosophical treatise that is the principal source of the moral framework of Dante's *Inferno*. Virgil, the principal speaker and teacher of the canto, calls the book *la tua Etica*, "your Ethics," which is the *Nicomachean Ethics* of Aristotle, listing

le tre disposizion che 'l ciel non vole [11:81]
[the three dispositions that Heaven does not allow]

Virgil then names them in the following two verses: incontinence, malice and bestiality:

incontenenza, malizia e la matta
bestialitade [11:82–83]

These three categories are in Aristotle and are usually translated by the terms "vice, incontinence, and bestiality (*Nichomachean Ethics* 7:1). The most likely translation of "bestiality" in Dante would be the violence of the seventh circle. Incontinence, then, would be contained in the first through sixth circles, and fraud and malice would be found in the eighth and ninth circles.

Aristotle's ethical system in anthropocentric, but when Dante
says that the three dispositions are not allowed by Heaven, he
moves into the realm of Christian doctrine.

In the unfolding of the canto, these general definitions are
prompted by a leading question asked by Dante in lines 73
and 74:

> perchè non dentro da la città roggia
>   sono ei puniti?
> [Why are not the sins of incontinence punished in the red
> city?]

The question is full and explicit because in it Dante refers to the
four leading circles of incontinence: the marsh of the wrathful *(la
palude)* in the fifth circle, the windy second circle of the lustful
(il vento), the rainy third circle of gluttony *(la pioggia)*, and the
sharp tongues of the hoarders and spenders in the fourth circle.
Virgil explains that God feels less anger toward those outside
the city of Dis, a divine distinction which, of course, is not in
Aristotle.

Much earlier in the canto, when Virgil advises a brief pause so
that the travelers may become accustomed to the strong stench
rising up from the abyss, he points out that there are three similar
circles *(tre cerchietti,* 11:17) in gradation that lie ahead and that
are the continuation of the wider circles they have already
passed through. Then the word "malice" *(malizia)* is isolated in
the text as the word most applicable to the sins of the seventh,
eighth, and ninth circles. "The end of all malice," Virgil says, "is
injury" (11:22–23). And immediately he names the two main
kinds of malice: "force" *(forza)* and "fraud" *(frode,* 11:24). These
are the two terms used by Cicero in *De officiis* I, 13. *Forza* would
mean "violence," although today it usually means "strength" or
"power"; "fraud would apply to the eighth circle. Whereas violence characterizes animals as well as men, fraud is peculiar to
man and is therefore more displeasing to God and is placed
lower in Hell. Since a person may perpetrate violence against
God, against himself, or against his neighbor, it is punished in
three distinct "rounds" *(gironi)* in the seventh circle.

Dante's system of sins is really twofold: the sins of incontinence, punished in upper Hell or the region outside of Dis,
and the sins of malice, punished in lower Hell or Dis. Dante
then divides malice into violence and fraud. In omitting any

reference to the *ignavi* or neutrals in the vestibule, to the unbaptized in the first circle or limbo, and to the archheretics
of the sixth circle, Dante implies that those sinners are not guilty
of incontinence or malice. They merely held wrong beliefs; they
were not guilty of sinful acts.

Dante, like the scholastic philosophers just prior to his time,
drew upon Aristotle's system of ethics. Aristotle had before him
the example of the Greek myths, stories incorporating ethical
problems which spoke to the people in the guise of narratives
through actions and characters and symbols. The lucid philosophical language of Aristotle is vastly different from that of
myth, and in his *Commedia* Dante retranslated the language of
Aristotle and Aquinas back into stories, the circles of his *Inferno*
where characters and situations, punishments and dramas illustrate abstract laws governing human behavior. In his *Poetics*
Aristotle claims that the richest source of myths is Homer. Dante
the Christian poet adds to the myths of Homer's epics the myths
of the Bible. In such a canto as 11, which is an exception in that it
is strategically placed just before the descent into Dis begins, he
defines the ethical terms of his poem's conception as a philosopher might.

Thus the background of the *Inferno* is a combination of the
mythical and the ethical. The myths in the narrative poems of
Homer, reworked in Virgil's *Aeneid*, and the myths in sacred
scripture, merge with the pagan rules of morality in Aristotle and
Cicero and the scholastic version of those rules in Aquinas. The
concept of Hell undergoes a considerable change as it moves from
the Hellenistic age to the Christian age. Whereas Aristotle condemns a man for an immoral act, Dante damns and punishes him
eternally only if there is no repentance. By violating the divine
order of God, the sinners themselves create their own Hell.

Immorality for the Greek mind is unwise. It is considered an
offense against prudence. For the Roman mind, it is looked upon
as illegal, an offense against the law. Dante looks upon it as sinful
or infernal, an offense against the law of God.

The end of the canto (11:91–115) is abrupt. Dante expresses his
gratitude to Virgil, whom he calls the "sun" healing all troubled
visions, and then asks a final question about the sin of usury.
In what way, he asks, does usury offend God? This time Virgil
alludes by name to the *Physics* of Aristotle, and probably to the
remark in that work that "art imitates nature" (2:2). Nature would

then be the connecting link between God and man's art. The function of man in his daily life is to labor, to toil. "In the sweat of thy brow shalt thou eat bread," (Genesis 1:28) we read at the beginning of the Bible. Usury is interest on money, and this is contrary to God's plan for the activity of man during his life on earth. The usurer is an exploiter of man's labor. It should be remembered here that usury in Dante's day was so excessive that it was close to being a form of plunder. For Dante it was the sin of an individual. Today it would be under a monopoly, when industries seize control over public conveniences, that returns from investments of capital could be called usurious.

The first round (girone) of the violent is for the sin of blasphemy, that is, violence done to God. The second is for violence perpetrated on other men. The third, referred to in lines 49 and 50, bears the mark of Sodom and Cahors. The sodomites violate nature, and the inhabitants of Cahors violate the art of God's world (the city of Cahors in southern France was famous for usury in the Middle Ages). It would appear that the word *Caorsino* in Italian was synonymous with usurer.

The relationship between Virgil and Dante throughout canto 11 is that of teacher and student. An eagerness to learn is a strong motive in the questions Dante asks as he and Virgil pause before moving on. Neither student nor teacher wishes to waste time. Previously in his journey Dante has learned by what he has seen, by examples. In this circle he learns by listening to doctrine. At the end of the lesson, in his use of the word "sun" (11:91), he pays supreme homage to Virgil, the illuminating master. In canto 1, at the time of his meeting with Virgil, Dante had called him the honor and light of other poets:

O de li altri poeti onore e lume. [1:82]

Principal Signs and Symbols

Divisions of sin (wrong behavior):
 (a) Aristotle: incontinence, bestiality, malice (or vice);
 (b) Cicero: violence, fraud;
 (c) Dante: incontinence, violence (or bestiality), fraud (or malice).
 The nine circles:

1. limbo (unbelief)

2.

3. } incontinence (leopard)

4.

5.

6. heresy

7. violence (lion)

8. } fraud (she-wolf)

9.

The vestibule (canto 3): the "neutrals" constitute a tenth division.

CANTO

12

Violence: The River of Blood (Seventh Circle)

DANTE IS SILENT throughout canto 12, despite its being a canto full of pictures and violent action. We see first an infernal landscape of broken stone, a slope caused by a landslide which occurred when Christ descended into Hell. From two scenes in particular, Dante easily learns that he is in the first *girone* of the seventh circle, the *girone* of the minotaur and the centaurs, where sins of violence are punished.

Since the minotaur and centaur combine the natures of man and animal, we are led to believe that the sins of violence are akin to the sins of bestiality. Extreme violence is depicted in the minotaur, but a sense of dignity characterizes the centaurs, who carry out their functions quietly and efficiently. In their part of the canto, the violence is in the figures submerged in the river of blood: in those sinners who did violence to their neighbor, *al prossimo*, as designated in canto 11, line 31. A violent man—a murderer, for example, or a tyrant, or a highwayman—assails the free will of a fellow man. These are among the cases briefly alluded to after Virgil and Dante meet three representative centaurs.

After infernalizing nature in this mountain scenery, Dante points out "the infamy of Crete" (*l'infamïa di Creti*, 12:12), spread out on the top of the broken cleft of rock. In just a few lines, seventeen in all, the Minotaur of classical mythology is represented as the guardian monster of the entire seventh circle, to which six cantos, 12 to 17, are devoted. Save for a brief reference in the *Purgatorio* (26:87), this would seem to be Dante's only reference to the labyrinth of Crete, designed and built by Daedalus to house the monster, the product of the union of Pasiphaë, wife of King Minos of Crete, and a white bull.

The Minotaur demanded a yearly blood sacrifice of Athenian youths. Theseus, called by Dante the duke of Athens (*il duca d'Atene*, 12:17), slew the Minotaur and was aided by Ariadne, half-sister of the Minotaur, in escaping from the labyrinth. There is a reference to this sister (*tua sorella*, 12:20), spoken as Virgil wards off the monster. Virgil's words produce a vivid demonstration of violence, causing the Minotaur to plunge back and forth and bite itself. The grotesque quality of the scene is a clear picture of evil undoing itself. This, one of the most distant myths of mankind, is a leading example, even in our modern terminology, of the sin of bestiality. The principal elements of the myth are given by Dante, fragmentarily, and build up to the specific name of the monster in line 25:

> vid'io lo Minotauro
> [I saw the Minotaur]

After escaping the danger of the Minotaur with its thrashing about, Dante fixes his attention again on the rocky descent. Virgil says that the rocks had not fallen when he first descended into Hell, and implies that the earthquake at the moment of Christ's death and descent into Hell to release his worthy ancestors (see canto 4) account for the chaotic condition of the way. The reference in this passage is to Empedocles, the Greek philosopher who accounted for the alternation of destructive and constructive forces in the universe by the alternation of love and hate between man and the gods. *Colui*, in line 38, "He who took from Dis the great prey," is, of course, Christ in the harrowing of Hell. At the end of this explanation, Virgil urges Dante to look at the river of blood (*la riviera del sangue*, 12:47) in which the violent sinners are immersed. Not until canto 14 will the river be named as the Phlegethon.

We are now at the central passage of the canto (12:46–99). It is the scene on the bank of the Phlegethon, along which centaurs run, one following the other (*in traccia*, 12:55). Boiling blood is a permanent symbol of violence in the memory of man. We still hear "my blood boils," which is an effort to express the human sentiment that can easily lead to violence. The origins of the river, the third of the infernal regions, will be soon explained in canto 14, where we will be told that it is made by men, formed by the blood shed on earth through acts of violence, and that it flows down into Hell from the body of the Old Man of Time. Dante now realizes that this ditch, containing the river of blood, is the first of the three *gironi* ("rounds" or "rings" constituting the seventh circle).

Centaurs armed with arrows are the guardians of this *girone*, and they, like the Minotaur, come from Greek mythology. Since they are half man and half horse, they are of a higher order than the Minotaur (half man and half bull.) Their function is quite clearly to punish. By the thousand they go around the ditch and pierce with their arrows whatever spirit rises out of the blood farther than the gravity of its sin permits. Dante and Virgil undergo a slight struggle with the centaurs, but they are passed in the usual way by an appeal to Dante's divine mission.

Three are mentioned by name. Chiron (12:65), the chief centaur, was reputedly the teacher of Achilles, Hercules, and others. He appears reflective and dignified as he parts his beard with the notch of an arrow. Nessus (12:67–69) is the first to speak to Dante and Virgil, and later he will carry them on his back across the river. In attempting to rape the wife of Hercules, he was killed by Hercules, but before dying, he gave Deianira, the wife, a robe soaked in his blood. This robe caused Hercules' death when he put it on. The last of the three is Pholus (12:72), about whom little is known, save the story of his drunkenness at the wedding of Pirithous and Hippodamia, when he attempted to rape the bride.

The violent man pointed out to Dante in this canto are principally tyrants, murderers, and robbers. They once acted like violent centaurs on earth and are now punished by the centaurs in Hell. As is customary in the *Commedia*, there are both ancient and modern examples. From Dante's own time, a Ghibelline tyrant is named, Azollino (v. 110), son-in-law of Emperor Frederick II, as is a fierce Guelf tyrant, Obizzo (12:111). The last example, in line 120 is of a heart dripping blood into the Thames. To avenge the death of his father, Simon de Montfort, at the hands of Edward I, king of England, Guy de Montfort stabbed to death Edward's cousin, Prince Henry, at Massin Viterbo. According to the chronicler Villani, Henry's heart was placed in a cup at the head of London Bridge where it dripped blood into the river below.

With canto 12 another day has dawned. It is now three hours after midnight. The hybrid centaurs provide a marked contrast to the cynical Minos, the loathsome Cerberus, and the grotesque Minotaur. In their attitudes, movements, and gestures, the centaurs appear almost as striking and beautiful as if they belonged to a Greek frieze. There is a strange mood of calm in the scene, as if all signs of violent behavior and speech had been silenced. Of the deeds perpetrated on earth, only the trace of blood remains in Hell. Dante's attention is more drawn to the phenomenon of the man-horse. Benedetto Croce has written movingly about this canto and called the scene a military encampment at the river of blood. Dante and Virgil are first questioned and threatened by officers of the guard, and then permitted to cross the river. Signs of discipline and severity are everywhere in the scene.

Chiron, captain of the guard, appears more meditative than the others. Mythological accounts of Chiron usually speak of his wisdom. Nessus would be, then, the lieutenant carrying out orders, and he could easily represent man's violence against his neighbor through the story of his attempt to rape Deianira. Might Pholus be the blasphemer of the gods, the man who once entertained Hercules and met his death by dropping one of Hercules' poisoned arrows on his foot?

As Virgil argues with Chiron over safe conduct for himself and Dante, he points out that Dante is still alive, and alludes to Beatrice as having interrupted her singing of the alleluia when she requested his help in guiding Dante. The words that Virgil uses with *il gran Chirone* are almost the same as those he used with Charon, the ferryman-guardian of canto 3. The will of Heaven is a continually repeated motif in the *Inferno*.

Nessus, called *il gran Centauro*, points out to the two travelers examples of tyrants such as Alexander (probably Alexander the Great) and Azzolino; murderers such as Guy de Montfort; and finally Attila, "a scourge on earth," and two ruthless highwaymen of Dante's day. We are doubtless intended to infer from the last line of the canto,

> Poi si rivolse e ripassossi 'l guazzo
> [then he turned back, and passed the ford again]

that Nessus, during his final words to Dante and Virgil, has landed the poets on the opposite shore and returned to his post.

The poets are now on the edge of the forest, the second *girone*, which they enter before Nessus has had time to return to his original position, as we learn in the first line of canto 13.

Principal Signs and Symbols

The images of violence (sins of the lion) in canto 12:

1. *The Minotaur (il Minotauro,* called *l'infamia di Creti):* the demon-guardian of the seventh circle, who has the body of a man and the head of a bull. The sins of violence would seem to be related to the sins of bestiality.

2. *The centaurs (i Centauri):* half man, half horse, guardians of murderers and tyrants. They appear less violent than the Minotaur, more disciplined, more wise.

3. *The Phlegethon (il Flegetonte)* or "river of blood" *(la riviera del sangue),* goes around the whole of the seventh circle and marks the first of its three divisions. It contains the sinners who did violence to their fellow men, causing blood to flow, and are now immersed in boiling blood.

4. The tyrants named in lines 106–38:

Alexander, possibly Alexander the Great;

Dionysius, possibly Dionysius the Elder, tyrant of Syracuse;

Azzolino, Ghibelline son-in-law of Frederick II;

Obizzo II d'Este, marquis of Ferrara, Guelf nobleman. He was murdered by his son (although this is not certain). Dante uses the word *figliastro* in line 112 (stepson), probably to point out the unnatural nature of the crime;

The heart they venerate: Prince Henry, nephew to the king of England, was murdered by Guy, son of Simon de Montfort;

Attila, king of the Huns;

Pyrrhus, probably king of Epirus;

Sextus, probably younger son of Pompey the Great;

Rinier da Corneto, a robber-baron of Dante's day;

Rinier Pazzo, robber-baron of the Pazzi family.

CANTO

13

The Suicides: Pier della Vigna

THIS CANTO is one of the most memorable of the *Inferno* in the awesome scene it depicts, in its moving dialogue between Dante and Pier della Vigna, and in its treatment of the act of suicide.

Saint Augustine and the church fathers considered suicide equivalent to murder. They were severe in their judgment of this act, which they defined as a crime of insubordination in which a person cuts short, by an act of will, the life span allotted by God. For the early Christian theologians, the one excusable case of suicide is a direct command from Heaven. Samson, for example, destroyed himself in accordance with the will of God. A modern reader recalls Baudelaire's discussion of suicide in his essay *"Le Dandy,"* where he applauds the act of suicide from the philosophical viewpoint of the stoics, and calls it the one sacrament of stoicism.

After the blood river of the first *girone,* the reigning motif of the second "round" of the seventh circle is the forest, called in line 2 *il bosco,* the usual modern Italian word. The forest of line 2 in the opening canto, the *selva oscura,* is used in canto 13 in lines 106–7 (*la mesta selva*—the sad wood), and a second time in line 124. Italian editors tend to refer to this episode as *la selva dolorosa* (the doleful wood), and we will find that expression in canto 14, line 10.

Three times in the second tercet, in the rhythm of anaphora, the negative quality of the dismal wood is stressed: *"no* green, *no* smooth branches, *no* apples." Harpies make their nests in the gnarled warped branches. They are obscene figures, traditionally foreboders of despair, with wings, human faces and necks,

clawed feet, and feathered bellies. They utter cries as they sit on
the trees and devour the withered leaves and branches. This first
movement of the canto comes to a climax with Virgil's words in
lines 17–19.

> sappi che se' nel secondo girone,
>   ...e sarai, mentre
> che tu verrai ne l'orribil sabbione.
> [know that you are in the second round,
>   and shall be, until
> you come to the horrid sand.]

In the river of blood, the damned had done violence to others,
but those among the forest scene did violence to themselves, and
Dante makes this act of suicide a deeper crime than the previous
one. In it a closer relationship is destroyed: the relationship of a
person to himself. The grimness of the place, this *bosco* or *selva*,
is so designed and described as to suggest the state of mind, the
deep despair, that was able to produce it. Violence is shown first
in the river, then in the wood, and finally, on the sand. They are
three successive sites which are related to one another in Dante's
mind. Commentators have endlessly disagreed and argued with
the poet on the ordering of the sins in his *Inferno* and on their
punishments, but in so doing they tend to lose the poem. We are
in the Hell of Dante's mind and imagination, and it is only right,
if we are studying his work, to submit our mind and imagination
to his.

Dante underscores the uncanniness of this forest scene. A tree
here holds a person's soul, and is able to moan, bleed, and speak,
but not to move. Thus Dante hears wailings, looks about him, and
sees no one. At first he believes the wailing comes from people
hiding behind the stumps of the trees. Then, at Virgil's sugges-
tion, Dante breaks off a twig. This initiates a spectacular scene in
which Dante follows quite closely an episode in Virgil in which
Aeneas meets Polydorus (*Aeneid* 3). In breaking off the twig,
Dante has unwittingly given pain to Pier della Vigna. The first
part of the dialogue between Dante and Pier is here condensed
into three tercets, lines 31–39. "Why do you tear me?" is Pier's
first question, and he ends this opening conversation with the
startling revelation:

> Uomini fummo, e or siam fatti sterpi [13:37]
> [we were men once, and are now turned to trees]

Probably of humble origin, Pier della Vigna, who died in
1249, was one of the truly learned men of his day. He studied at
Bologna, and was recommended to Frederick II by the archbishop of Palermo, and gradually became the most intimate adviser of the emperor. He was envied by others at the court who
circulated charges against him, principally accusations that he
was wealthier than the emperor, and that he had revealed secrets
to the pope. Inclined by nature to be over-suspicious, Frederick
had Pier thrown into prison and put his eyes out. There, according to one of the accounts, he beat his dead against the wall of the
dungeon and thus killed himself.

Four cases of suidice are named in canto 13, and all occurred in
Dante's own time. Of the four, only Pier della Vigna's is important, and Dante's strong sympathy with him is obvious. Pier was
a poet as well, and Dante had known during his own life the envy
from which the Sicilian poet had suffered.

Pier never names himself in his talk with Dante and Virgil. He
is concerned with honoring Frederick, with expressing his love
for the emperor, and with rehabilitating his own good name.
Dante had already placed Frederick among the archheretics in
canto 10 (lines 118–20), but he admired the emperor as prince,
poet, as patron of the arts, and as a great Ghibelline. He writes
the episode on Pier as if it were an elegy on the theme of a man's
loyalty and fidelity to his emperor, and on the suffering caused
by false accusation and dishonor. The adviser-poet is punished
in the *Inferno* as a suicide and not as a traitor. The sin of
treachery, which was the formal accusation against Pier della
Vigna, is punished in the ninth and lowest circle.

The moral question raised by the act of suicide, provided a
person's mind is sound, might be put this way: will one submit
to chastisement and misfortune or take one's life? As Pier relates
his story, we are at the court of Frederick, probably in Sicily
rather than at Naples. He describes himself at the highest point
of his power:

> Io son colui che tenni ambo le chiavi
> del cor di Federigo [13:58–59]
> [I am the one who held both keys
> of Frederick's heart]

The "two keys" might well be the two judgments of mercy and
punishment which Pier would suggest to the emperor when con-
sulted about any given cause. Pier's patron, of course, was Saint

Peter, who holds the two keys of Heaven (mercy) and Hell (punishment). Unable to bear the dishonor brought to his name or his condition as a blinded prisoner, he killed himself. In Dante's Hell one matter weighs heavily on him: the accusation of treachery. Pier is the third movingly sympathetic case we meet in the *Inferno*. As with Francesca (canto 5) and Farinata (canto 10), Dante has chosen in Pier della Vigna a figure sympathetic to him, thereby emphasizing the inexorable nature of God's law. Through Dante's eyes, we see in Pier a loyal courtly figure, a spirit still devoted to the man who wronged him.

We see him also as the poet, especially in three lines of the canto, where the thought is expressed in elaborate and somewhat strained speech. The rhetorical term "conceit" is usually applied to these lines. The French term "preciosity" might be used, or, more simply, we might view them as an artificial turn of language. In the first of the lines Dante expresses his bewilderment at the beginning of the canto. "I think that he [Virgil] thought I was thinking" (the voices they heard come from people hiding):

Cred'ïo ch'ei credette ch'io credesse [13:25]

A heavy line, one almost humorous in its use of three tenses of the verb *credere*. The other two lines are spoken by Pier in the sketch of his fall he gives to Dante. He has just said that envy "inflamed" all minds against him, and using the verb *infiammare*. Then, in line 67, he plays on this word in saying that "those inflamed so inflamed Augustus" (he uses the name Augustus to refer to Frederick):

e li 'nfiammati infiammar sì Augusto

A few lines later (13:72), in the richest of the three, he plays on the word "just" referring to his suicide. Although he was a just man, his mind made him unjust to himself:

ingiusto fece me contra me giusto.

This particular line summarizes succinctly the reason for the orthodox judgment on suicide. In order to commit the act of suicide, a man becomes two persons, one strong and forceful enough to commit the act against the other more passive person. Thus suicide may be considered an act of violence punishable in the seventh circle.

"I never broke faith with my lord," is the moving message that Pier asks Dante to take back to the world with him. The voice

becomes silent, and Dante feels such pity in his heart that he
cannot continue speaking but asks Virgil to inquire into the
means by which the spirits come to this dismal wood. It is one of
the moments in the journey when Dante realizes that his very
thoughts and questions are known to Virgil. The Latin poet is,
momentarily at least, Dante's other self.

Virgil asks the question, and Pier answers him briefly by saying that at death the soul is sent down by Minos to this seventh
region and falls into the wood, although no particular place has
been chosen for it. It takes root where it falls and shoots up into a
plant, *come gran di spelta* (13:99, "like grain of spelt"). Like
many seeds, spelt sends up first a single shoot, then many.

A plant cannot kill itself, and yet the plants in Dante's dismal
wood have blood, sensations, and language. There is a direct
literary source for this metamorphosis of a man into a tree. In
book 3 of the *Aeneid*, Aeneas breaks a twig and the branch bleeds
and speaks and warns Aeneas to flee. The twig in Virgil's poem
was Polydorus, who was not a suicide and who had committed
no moral offense. Dante gives this transformation an ethical
meaning.

These monstrous plants are associated with monstrous animals:
Harpies that feed on the leaves, thus giving pain to the spirits and
at the same time opening up "windows," through which the
suicides' pain is heard:

fanno dolore, e al dolor fenestra [13:102]
[they give pain, and to the pain an outlet]

Again, in answer to Virgil's question, Pier graphically describes
what will happen to the suicides at the Last Judgment. Like the
others, they will return to earth and recover their bodies, but will
then drag the bodies back to the wood and hang them on their
trees. The spirits will thus continue being punished for having
denied the use of their bodies.

A brief and very violent scene follows the words of Pier della
Vigna. Two naked spirits rush through the wood pursued by
black dogs. These are the profligate, who had been more violent
in their destruction of earthly goods than the spendthrifts of the
fourth circle. The ravenous dogs would seem to dramatize the
violence perpetrated by these two spirits, one a Sienese, Lano,
and the other a Paduan, Giacomo da Sant'Andrea.

The final image of the canto is that of another suicide, an unknown Florentine who hanged himself in his own house. This
spirit speaks of Florence ironically when he says that Mars, the

god of war, not John the Baptist, remains the true guardian spirit of Florence. He predicts that the god of war will give the Florentines yet more trouble. Florence became a Christian city in the fourth century. Pagan Florence held Mars as a patron and had erected a temple to him. The unnamed spirit who speaks to the travelers (15:137–51) refers to the statue of Mars that had fallen into the Arno when Attila destroyed Florence. This actually never happened and here Dante confuses the name Attila with Totilla. The cause of the continuing strife in the city is this offense given the pagan god of war.

The punishment of Pier is summarized in the phrase in line 87 where he is called an "incarcerated spirit" (*spirito incarcerato*). It is the punishment of immobility, the familiar dream and nightmare experience when one cannot move, or move fast enough, to escape a pursuer. This experience of extreme frustration is often accompanied by a metamorphosis, as it is in canto 130. In a milder form it occurs each morning as we awaken and have to rediscover our identity and remember where and who we are.

Freud has studied this will of the subconscious to being about a metamorphosis. When such a change is accompanied by an immobilization, Freud calls it the instinct for death, a desire to return to the inorganic. Pier della Vigna, appearing to us as a plant in canto 13,is not unlike Gregor Samsa, who is changed into a bug in Kafka's *Metamorphosis,* or Winnie, who is immersed up to her neck in a mound of earth in Beckett's play *Oh! les beaux jours.*

Leo Spitzer has made a striking comment on Dante's two gestures at the beginning and at the end of the canto. His first gesture, that of breaking off a twig, inflicts pain on Pier (although the *un poco* in *porsi la mano un poco*—"I stretched out my hand a little"—indicates hesitation on Dante's part). At the end of the canto, Dante's gathering up of leaves for the anonymous suicide, to place them at the foot of his tree, is interpreted by the German scholar as an act of atonement.

Principal Signs and Symbols

1. *The wood of the suicides (il bosco):* a place where everything is negative (*non* begins verses 1, 4, and 7), dense, and dismal. It is the second round (*girone*) of the seventh circle.

2. *The Harpies (le Arpie):* huge birds with the heads of hags.

When Aeneas and his companions came to the Strophades Islands (to which the Harpies had been banished), the Harpies devoured and defiled their food. (*Aeneid* 3:209 ff.) They represent the will to destruction.

3. *Bleeding trees:* the suicides here have no resemblance to their bodies. This round continues the blood imagery of the first round.

4. *Pier della Vigna:* at one time the most trusted minister of Frederick II. Dante gives to Pier the poetic language for which he was known as a poet of the Sicilian School (see lines 68–72).

5. *The profligates:* men who dissipated their wealth through lust for disorder and the desire to destroy. They rush through the wood, pursued by bitches (13:115–21). The violence of these sinners distinguishes them from the spendthrifts of the fourth circle (canto 7).

6. *The anonymous Florentine who hanged himself* (13:151): the historian Benvenuto names several Florentines who hanged themselves about Dante's time.

CANTO

14

The Sandy Plain: Third *Girone* of the Violent

IT IS INDEED a ritual gesture that opens this canto, proving that Dante did answer the request of the anonymous Florentine spirit:

> raunai le fronde sparte
> e rende'le a colui ch'era già fioco. [14:2–3]
> [I gathered up the scattered leaves,
> and gave them back to him who was already hoarse.]

This canto provides the transition from the second to the third *girone* where the violent are punished. It falls between two very dramatic cantos, the thirteenth, marked by the figure of Pier della Vigna, and the 15th, dominated by Brunetto Latini. By comparison with them canto 14 seems quieter, more prosaic perhaps, and yet it is filled with important details and the figure illustrating blasphemy against God. Such a pause is necessary for the reader both psychologically and aesthetically.

After the river scene (*la riviera*) and the wood (*il bosco*), we come on to a plain, *una landa* (14:8), that is, the landscape of a moor or a heath. A few lines later (14:13), it is called *una rena arida* ("dry sand"). Such a plain prohibits all growth of plants, and this would seem to be analogous to the act of sodomy that denies conception, whether it be between male and male or male and female.

When the full punishment becomes clear to Dante, he is shocked by it and exclaims: *O vendetta di Dio* (14:16, "O vengeance of God"). He reminds us that all the souls in Hell are naked, but in this case the nudity increases the suffering because over all the sandy plain flakes of fire rain down continually. Three groups of sinners are distinguished in this third *girone*, and each one is characterized by a verb describing a different posture. In the first group (14:22), it is *giacere* (to lie): these spirits are lying supine on the ground. In the second (14:23), it is *sedere* (to sit): these are sitting crouched. In the third (14:24), it is *andare* (to go): these spirits are ceaselessly moving about.

Dante asks about one of the sinners, a "great" spirit, *quel grande* (14:46), who seems to scorn the fire. He appears stretched or contorted, and the rainfall does not ripen him:

la pioggia non par che 'l maturi [14:48]

Before Virgil names him, this powerful-looking spirit answers Dante with a sentence of exceptional pride: "What I was living, that am I dead."

Qual io fui vivo, tal son morto. [14:51]

He follows this with a curse addressed to Jove which, if paraphrased, might read thus: "No matter how many thunderbolts you hurl at me, you will never get me!"

Loud and voluble is this Capaneus, one of the seven kings who assaulted Thebes, who in Hell, stretched out on his back under flakes of fire, continues to curse God. We associate blasphemy with Christianity, but Dante has perhaps wisely chosen a figure from classical poetry as an example of a blasphemer. It would have been more than scandalous in Dante's Christian world to hear a contemporary figure speaking in this way. There are other instances in the *Commedia*, comparable to that of Capaneus, of aesthetic softening. The mythical Capaneus, in his physical strength, energy, and madness, would appear to be the offspring of the race of giants that attempted to scale Heaven.

When Virgil calls the sin of Capaneus *superbia* ("pride," 14:64), Dante's reader tends to recall the figure of Farinata in canto 10, but actually these two figures are far apart in the manifestation of their pride. Farinata made no reference to his suffering, and preferred to speak with Dante about Florence. His was an austere greatness. Capaneo is boastful, vain, and loquacious. Virgil concludes the brief passage by pointing out that the real torment of Capaneus is his rage rather than the torture by fire.

The two poets continue their way without speaking, and come

to a place where a small river gushes out from the wood. Its redness makes Dante shudder. This is a tributary of the Phlegethon, the river of blood. The rest of the canto is given over to Virgil's explanation of the rivers of Hell and his answers to Dante's questions concerning them.

Commentators on the *Divine Comedy* have raised endless problems connected with these rivers. What is certain in Dante's conception is the fact that they derive from our world. The four rivers in the *Inferno*, Acheron, Styx, Phlegethon, and Cocytus (at the bottom of Hell), are not really rivers; they are circular bodies of water. We would call them stagnant water. *La palude* ("marsh"), used to describe the Styx in canto 7 (7:106), is accurate. The rivulet (*fiumicello*, 14:77) in the present canto makes a channel over the hot sand.

When Dante asks about the source of the infernal rivers, Virgil explains that the tears of Time form these rivers for the punishment of the guilty. The image described, the image of Time, is colossal, and is derived from both Hebrew and Greek writings. The arialike beginning of Virgil's speech speaks of the island of Crete, a waste land in the middle of the sea:

> In mezzo mar siede un paese guasto,
> ...che s'appella Creta [14:94–95]
> [In the middle of the sea lies a waste land
> which is named Crete]

Within Mount Ida, on the island, stands erect a great old man (*un gran veglio*, 14:103) whose back is toward Damiata (Damietta) and who looks toward Rome.

Both Dante and Virgil looked upon Crete as the middle ground between Europe and Asia, and considered it the primeval source of the Romans. The Damietta mentioned in the text would represent Egypt or Palestine, that is, the East, whereas Rome would of course represent the West. Dante envisages this huge image of Time as including the three epochs of civilization: Oriental, Greco-Roman, and Christian.

The statue is made of five materials: gold (head), silver (arms and breast), brass (abdomen), iron (the lower part), and baked clay (the right foot.) The image of this statue comes from the second chapter of Daniel and is usually interpreted allegorically as the four degenerating periods of history, to be followed, however, by the fifth, for Christ and his Church will not pass away. The four ages of man are listed in book 1 of Ovid's *Metamor-*

phoses. This statue in the middle of the civilized world looks from the old civilization of Damietta (the East) to the new civilization of Rome (the West).

The name of Crete, with all its mythical and historical associations, dominates the latter part of the canto. Its mythical King Minos has already been given a key role in the *Inferno.* The Cretan king, alluded to in line 95, during whose reign the world was chaste, is Saturn, a very ancient Roman god. The Romans identified Saturn with Chronos, believed to be the father of Jupiter (or Zeus). And thus Zeus-Jupiter was believed to have been born in Crete.

Dante's reasons for this discussion of the Old Man of Crete is to explain the rivers of Hell. No tears flow from the head of the statue. But the statue, in its deepest symbolic sense, embodies the total idea of the *Inferno*: a wicked act is converted through Time into the means of its punishment. The Acheron surrounds the upper edge of Hell. The Styx encircles the city of Dis. The Phlegethon is the boiling blood of murderers and tyrants in the seventh circle. Cocytus is the frozen lake at the bottom of Hell, containing the traitors.

It would be natural for Dante to ask Virgil about the Lethe (14:130–32) because the ancient authors traditionally included it among the five rivers of Hades. Virgil explains that the Lethe is not in Hell because it is the river of forgetfulness. In Dante's conception, each soul in Hell is tormented by the remembrance of his sin. This is clearly said by Francesca in canto 5: "There is no greater grief than that of remembering happiness in misery" (5:121–23) After the experience of Purgatory, souls are washed of their remembrance of sin in the Lethe.

This mythological episode of Crete and *il gran veglio* is carefully and somewhat mysteriously expounded by Virgil in his role as teacher, and he makes as clear as possible the parts of his lesson that he understands. He provides an interlude separating blasphemy (the perversion of the heart we see in Capaneus) from sodomy (the perversion of the senses we will see in Brunetto Lantini).

Principal Signs and Symbols

1. *The plain (la landa)* or *wasteland of sand (un' arena arida)*: in this third *girone*, the image of sand represents sterility, and the

shades here from three groups: blasphemers (supine), usurers (crouching) and sodomites (ever walking).

2. *Capaneus*, the example of blasphemer, is the image of pride, more obdurate than Farinata. Statius describes him as blaspheming against Jove who struck him with a thunderbolt.

3. *Crete* (*Creta*), the wasteland in the middle of the sea, was the birthplace of Trojan civilization. Trojan Aeneas was found of Rome. Crete is also the center of the known world. In Mount Ida Dante places the statue of the Old Man of Crete (*il gran veglio di Creta*). The symbolism of the Old Man is drawn from Daniel II and from Ovid's *Metamorphoses* (1:89ff.)

4. *Lethe,* the river of forgetfulness, is placed by Dante at the top of Purgatory (see *Puratorio* 28:25ff.).

CANTO

15

The Sodomites: Brunetto Latini
(Eliot's "Little Gidding")

THE POETS CROSS the burning sand by walking on a dike that banks the Phlegethon, and Dante compares the dike to those built in Flanders to keep out the sea. Wissant, a harbor city, and Bruges, a center of trade with Italy in the Middle Ages, are specifically named. The Paduans also built embankments along the river Brenta to prevent spring floods when melted snow from the mountains swelled its waters. In the text God is referred to as the "master" (or "engineer," 15:12), who constructed the walls of the dike in this third *girone* of the violent souls.

Dante sees coming toward him, hurrying close to the bank, a troop of shades that eye him and Virgil with marked curiosity. A metaphor is developed to emphasize the piercing look the sodomites give the two travelers. They knit up their brows and squint hard as an old tailor might squint at his needle's eye. The intensity of their gaze and their ceaseless running reflect both the act of men appraising other men on earth as possible sexual partners and the fruitlessness of the exertion of running. Canto 5 (the lustful) and canto 15 (the sodomites) present parallels, especially in the aimless drifting through the air of the *lussuriosi* and the perpetual hastening of the *sodomiti,* and even more notably in Dante's tone of sympathy and respect. Both Francesca and Brunetto are exceptionally revered by the poet.

"Sodomy" is not an accurate term, but it is the word used by Dante to designate all the physical forms of homosexual activity. In all the manifestations of sensuality, whether it be gluttony, as in the case of Ciacco, or sexual love between a man and a woman, as with Francesca and Paolo, or sex between men, as with

Brunetto Latini in canto 15 and the trio of Florentine men in canto 16, Dante expresses no ethical abhorrence. These sins are chiefly physical and do not destroy the individual. They leave the character of both man and woman intact. The dialogue in cantos 15 and 16 will stress politics as Dante mutes the moral implications.

Brunetto Latini, who dominates canto 15, was a leading figure in Florence in the generation just before Dante's. He was born about 1220 and became distinguished for his culture and erudition. His profession as a notary gave him the title *ser*, a word derived from *signore*. He was also a vigorous member of the Guelf party. When serving as ambassador at the court of Castille, he learned in 1260 of the overthrow of the Guelfs at Montaperti. As a result of that political change, he went to Paris where he wrote an encyclopedic work in French called *Le livre du trésor*. Later he wrote in Italian a shorter didactic version of the work entitled the *Tesoretto*. At the end of the canto, which is the end of his speech to Dante, he refers to this work as *il mio Tesor* (15:119). After the overthrow of the Ghibellines in 1266, he returned to Florence and there occupied several public offices in which he was honored until his death in 1294.

There seems to be no other document, save canto 15, referring to the friendship between Dante and Brunetto. In his role as teacher he lectured in Florence on Latin composition, but is is not known whether Dante was present at those meetings. Some historians claim that he introduced the subject we would today call political science.

No other text of the day has come to light in which Brunetto Latini is accused of sodomy. Others in the thirteenth century must have known about this reputation, because it is inconceivable that Dante would have invented it in order to have this particular punishment illustrated by a celebrated and revered figure. Dante may have exaggerated somewhat in his poem the relationship between pupil and teacher, disciple and poet. This meeting in Hell is charged with such highly emotional overtones that it seems almost a page of autobiography. As he has already done in the cases of Francesca and Pier della Vigna, Dante chooses here a figure of notable intellectual and moral qualities in order to stress the harsh doctrine that a single fault, unexpiated at the end of a person's life, is sufficient to damn him.

The lesson is one of a strong contrast between the noble dignity of a man, revealed in his words to Dante, and the weakness of his sin, emphasized at the end of the canto when Brunetto has to run like a racer to catch up with his companions. In order to stress the swiftness of Brunetto's running, and possibly to prepare the athletic scene in the next canto, Dante compares Brunetto to the winner in an annual race held on the first Sunday of Lent in Verona during the thirteenth century, in which the winner was awarded a green cloth (*il drappo verde*, 15:122). The participants in the race also ran naked, as does Brunetto Latini in the infernal race. Thus athleticism opens and concludes canto 15, and the dialogue between the younger and the older poet is an interruption in the running that might cause additional punishment for Brunetto.

This encounter takes place as the two men walk together, Dante on the dike and Brunetto Latini on the plain below. With the two thus placed, Brunetto, when he recognizes Dante, takes hold of the hem of Dante's gown. His opening words, *Qual maraviglia!* (15:24, "What a wonder!", or as we might translate them, "How marvellous!"), are an exclamation that might easily be interpreted as an example of affected speech.

The three tercets that follow these words (15:25–33), contain two strong moments of pathos, one evoked by Dante, and the other by Brunetto. When Dante bends down to look closely at the "baked" features of the figure who pulled his gown, he recognizes Brunetto and says five words, framed as a question that summarizes the tragedy of damnation and the poet's emotional concern for this spirit:

> Siete voi qui, ser Brunetto?

The line will always remain slightly ambiguous. Is the emphasis on *voi* ("Are *you* here, ser Brunetto?") or is it on *qui* ("Are you *here*?")?

The normal Italian accentuation would fall on the end of the question and would therefore stress *qui*, "here," or "this place among the sodomites." If it falls on *voi*, Dante is emphasizing his surprise at finding such an esteemed figure as Brunetto among the sodomites. This is the third and last time in Hell that Dante uses the formal *voi*, rather than the informal *tu* with the spirits of Hell. In canto 10 he used *voi* in addressing Farinata, thus showing respect for his exceptional qualities of military leadership, and he uses it as well to Cavalcante Cavancanti in order to express the high esteem he had for his best friend's father.

In order to speak together, even briefly, Brunetto indicates the manner in which they must walk. The spirit has to continue enduring the punishment of the fire and remain on the sandy plain, while Dante, above him, has to keep his head bent down. It is a posture of reverence, and Dante so names it in line 45. Then, in answer to Brunetto's question as to why he is in Hell, Dante sketchily reviews his poem, referring to his having lost his way "in the clear life" (*in la vita serena*, 15:49), to Virgil's coming, and to his present pilgrimage on his way home (*a ca*, 15:54; *ca=casa*) or his return to God.

In the closely woven lines of the tercets following line 54, a series of relationships binding the younger to the older man is revealed in which the role of Brunetto as teacher-inspirer is combined with a prophecy of Dante's poetic genius, set against the background of a troubled, strife-ridden Florence. Brunetto first speaks as an inhabitant of Hell who is endowed with visionary powers. "If you follow your star, you cannot fail to reach a glorious haven." These words could apply to both Dante's spiritual and poetic attainments. But immediately Brunetto reminds Dante of the two irreconcilable parts of the Florentine make-up: the Fiesolans (or the Etruscans), a malignant folk who, coming down from the hill just outside of Florence, did not mix easily with the old Romans of the city. The men from Fiesole were like "bitter berries" among the "sweet figs," Dante's metaphor for the original Romans who settled Florence.

The poet's invective is strong at this point when he calls the people of Florence "avaricious, envious, and proud": *gent' è avara, invidiosa e superba* (15:8). The hardness of the Fiesolans, like the moutain and the rock from which they descended to the city, might account for the hardness of exile imposed on both Brunetto Latini and Dante Alighieri. Fiesolans and Romans, like the Guelfs and Ghibellines who divide the city, will both hunger for Dante when the poet is famous and honored. The image of the bitter sorb trees (*il lazzi sorbi*, 15:65) is renewed in the sustained metaphor of the "plant" containing the holy seed of the Romans which must not be touched by The Fiesolan beasts (15:73–78).

These wise and forceful words of Brunetto turn our attention to history and prophecy, and make us forget Brunetto's posture of humiliation, the body flaked with flames. Dante's grateful reply is equally strong and personal as he designates himself the pupil, the poet and the man devoted to the love of Beatrice, who will guide him in the future. Again, in this reference to the lady who will explicate his texts, Dante is reviewing the sources and the

reason for his poem. A half-submerged and mysterious relationship between Beatrice and Brunetto must exist in Dante's
mind. Fire falling from above is an archetypal image for many
experiences: the purifying fire of love, the punishing fire of sin,
the illuminating fire of understanding.

In a few lines just prior to this specific reference to Beatrice,
Dante, in his speech to Brunetto, alludes to his love for his
teacher in words that are as deeply moving as any in the *Divine
Comedy*. In his heart and his memory he holds the beloved, kind,
and paternal image of Brunetto:

> ed or m'accora,
> la cara e buona imagine paterna
> di voi [15:82–84]
>> [and now goes to my heart
> the dear and kind paternal image
> of you]

These lines of Dante's memory for a man held in his heart culmi-
nate in a line of supreme acknowledgment:

> quando nel mondo ad ora ad ora
> m'insegnavate come l'uom s'etterna [15:84–85]
> [when in the world, hour by hour,
> you taught me how man makes himself eternal]

To no one else in all of Hell, not even to Virgil, does Dante speak
with such fervor. This phrase, *come l'uom s'eterna*, is so marvel-
ously ambiguous that one wants to apply it simultaneously to the
eternal soul of Dante, guided and protected by Beatrice in
Heaven, and to the creative mind of Dante the poet, in debt to all
the poets who preceded him as represented by the single figure
of Brunetto Latini.

One senses the interplay of feeling in this scene between the
humiliated master and the honored pupil, as one senses the cor-
diality in the tone of the two speakers, which contrasts so strik-
ingly with the region where the meeting takes place. Even
Brunetto Latini's invective against Florence is turned into a
loving eulogy of Dante. He implies that Dante is too good for the
distraught city. Although he commends his *Tesoro* to Dante in
line 119, we realize that Brunetto is that type of writer who derives his immortality from his pupil.

In accordance with his custom, Dante asks the names of the
most noted sodomites. Brunetto names only three, and describes

the group with whom he runs as *cherci* and *litterati grandi e di gran fama* (15:106–7), "clerics" and "well-known men of letters." This is meant to designate a category of men who typically indulge in homosexual practice, a speculative type of man: members of the clergy, writers, students. Centuries after Dante, Marcel Proust will list in *Sodome et Gomorrhe* comparable segments of modern society. Today, a half-century after Proust's novel, sociologists and pyschologists would not confine the homosexual to any given profession. And even Dante, in the following canto, will broaden the temperament and professional activities of the homosexual. Brunetto might well have represented for Dante, in a strictly spiritual sense, that type of Christian who outwardly shows conformity to religion and who is inwardly heathen in culture and temperament.

T. S. Eliot, in "Little Gidding," the last of the *Four Quartets*, draws heavily on Dante's meeting with Brunetto Latini. Part 2 of the quartet is an episode describing a particular moment in time that appears to the modern poet as eternal. Eliot uses a modified *terza rima* in the prosody of part 2 and deliberately proposes a form that is a near equivalent to a canto.

The scene comes after an air raid over London during World War II when Eliot was in the fire-spotting service. The fire falling from Heaven, both literal and metaphorical, unites at least four moments in history and literature: the fire falling on Sodom and Gomorrah in Genesis 18, fire from airplanes falling over Paris during World War I in Proust's *Le temps retrouvé*, fire from planes over London in "Little Gidding," and fire falling on the sodomites in Dante's *Inferno*.

There are several almost literally translated phrases from canto 15 used in the Eliot poem. The difficulty of seeing in the darkness,

> In the uncertain hour before the morning

recalls Dante's

> each look at us as in the evening men look
> at one another under a new moon.

> The dark dove with the flickering tongue

is of course an airplane with its machine gun, and it corresponds to the

> dilated flakes of fire falling slowly over the sand

in canto 15, lines 28–29. Eliot then describes a hurrying figure in the dark:

> I met one walking, loitering and hurried
> As if blown towards me

and in the next few lines Eliot uses specific words from Dante: "I fixed (*ficcai*) upon the down-turned face (*la sua faccia*), and "brown baked features" (*lo cotto aspetto*). When Eliot speaks to this "familiar compound ghost, he uses the same words that Dante used to Brunetto Latini: "What! are *you* here?" With this dramatic question of discovery in a London street, a duality between centuries is established: Eliot and Dante, pupil and master, poet and ghost. Time is both past and present. We are in the seventh circle of the *Inferno*, and we are in the hell of wartime England. Eliot's line,

> We trod the pavement in a dead patrol

is both literal and evocative of *la landa* and the dead souls in the third *girone*.

"Little Gidding" gives us a picture of this present world of suffering, and the *Inferno* gives us the world of suffering beyond and outside of time. But Eliot is also referring to the world beyond time, and Dante is also referring to this world here below. Both Eliot and Dante in their respective passages bear testimony to their belief that each poet is all poets, and each moment is eternity.

Virgil? He speaks only once, near the end of the canto, in order to give brief approval to the exchange of words. Dante still refers to him with the familiar *lo mio maestro* (15:97), but Virgil is here only one of the many poets in Dante, and Brunetto Latini has taken his place—momentarily—as he has taken the place—momentarily—of Beatrice. The real Beatrice is established in Heaven, and the real Brunetto is a poet damned in Hell. But they are the two beloved figures who teach Dante the way to eternity. And Dante's poem is precisely that way along which he is being led by Virgil.

Principal Signs and Symbols

1. *Sodomites*: in addition to those spirits who practiced sodomy, Dante probably includes here spirits whose vices were

extreme in damaging the powers of the body: drug addicts and alcoholics. To the more gentle souls, such as Brunetto, should be added the stronger, more athletic types, such as the soldiers in canto 16.

2. The literal *wandering* or *running* of these spirits (15:16, 122) seems related to the lustful blow about by the wind in canto 5.

3. *Ser Brunetto*: Messer Brunetto Latini (1220–94), Florentine Guelf, statesman, writer, and notary. When Brunetto asks who Virgil is (15:48), Dante does not answer, possibly in order not to offend Brunetto by naming a second guide or teacher.

4. *The fame of being blind (Vecchia fama nel mondo li chiama orbi:* "Old report on earth proclaims them blind" (15:67). The Florentines, half Fiesolan and half Roman, were proverbially called "blind Florentines" probably because of these two strains Dante describes.

5. *Francesco d'Accorso,* 1225–93 (15:110): a Florentine lawyer who lectured at the University of Bologna and at Oxford.

6. *Andrea dei Mozzi* (15:110–14): from a White Guelf family in Florence, was bishop of Florence from 1287–95. In line 112 *servo de'servi* ("servant of servants") refers to Pope Boniface VIII who transferred Andrea dei Mozzi from Florence to Vicenza in 1295.

7. *Verona* (15:122): this famous race in Verona, held on the first Sunday of Lent, announces the athletic images of the next canto.

CANTO

16

The Wheel of the Three Florentines
Dante's Cord

USUALLY AT THE BEGINNING of a canto Dante begins a new song or *canzone* almost as if he were taking a new breath in order to initiate a new aspect of his great theme of perdition and salvation. But canto 16 is very much a continuation of the dramatic fifteenth canto. Dante is on the same path in the third *girone* and following his guide. He is far enough along to hear the crimson stream of the Phlegethon falling into the next circle. Another troop of spirits appears under the burning rain, and three shades move out from the troop in order to speak to Dante and Virgil. This second episode of the sodomites is related to Brunetto's appearance and related as well to the sins of the city, specifically of Florence.

The drama of Brunetto Latini is still in our minds, but even more than the drama, we still remember the extreme sympathy which Dante extends to the sinner, as well as the debt Dante acknowledges and the studies in human relations, in human nature, which each of the major Dantean encounters provides. With Francesca it was the expression of love we followed, with Filippo Argenti it was rage, with Farinata it was the pride of heresy, with Pier della Vigna it was suicide, with Brunetto Latini it was the plight of the homosexual and also the role of the creative artist. Brunetto talked with Dante during a moment when he transcended his plight, and Dante's reverence during that moment certainly expressed a longing that things might be different. We readers of the *Inferno* profit the most from Brunetto's lesson to Dante on how to bring human nature, through study and the composition of a poem, into communication with the spirits of the past.

Between cantos 16 and 17 we observe the punishment of three sins of violence: blasphemy, sodomy, and usury, in that order. The sinners in these *gironi* have done violence to God, to nature, and to nature and art. This classification would appear to represent in Dante's eyes an infernal progress. Is it possible to justify the theory that the sodomite is less guilty than the usurer? Commentators in the nineteenth century in particular, when sodomy was an unmentionable sin, argued against this classification. In that century banking had grown into an admired art that concealed practices that might be considered usurious.

For Dante, these three forms of sin turn man against God, who is the means of life itself. We should not forget that for Dante there were two major characters or forces in the unfolding of his life: a woman and a city, Beatrice and Florence. When a man acts against both woman and the city, the supernatural and the natural life of his soul is endangered. It is not too difficult to follow what was probably Dante's reason for his classification: the belief that what sodomy was with regard to Beatrice, usury was with regard to the city of Florence.

The sin of Francesca and Paolo was as much a sin against the law of the city as it was a moral sin in their own lives. Farinata without any question loves his city of Florence, but Dante presents him as a man who loved his political party more passionately than he did his city. The usurers are about to be presented to us as men who in the practice of their business derived private profit from the city. Dante does have a well-thought-out conception of infernal progress and it behooves us, if we wish to enjoy his poem, to accept his classifications—otherwise we will lose the work.

Beatrice is not merely the girl from the Portinari family whom Dante had met, she is every woman who has been loved with total devotion. And Brunetto Latini is not merely the notary of Florence, who must have been known in his own day as a sodomite, he is all the poets who inspire and teach a given poet, and who guide him in his vocation in the city of men. Before the beginning of canto 16, Dante clearly establishes his respect and admiration for Brunetto (as he does in the *Vita nuova* for Beatrice), as well as his duty to express such a debt (15:86–87). The poet's love for Beatrice and his loyalty to Brunetto Latini are both necessary to the life of the city. Brunetto is damned, but Dante's art derives at least in part from Brunetto. In the brief phrase *come l'uom s'eterna,* Dante honors the function of the poet and acknowledges his derivation. He is more loyal to Brunetto than Peter was to Christ, when the apostle said: "I do not know the man."

The image of the wheel dominates the opening section of canto 16. Three eminent Florentines who recognize Dante by his dress leave the troop of sodomites and come toward Dante and Virgil. The Latin poet recommends them as deserving of courtesy. Dante is pained by the sight of the wounds caused by the burning of their bodies, and he weeps. As they approach, they form themselves into a wheel

fenno una rota di sè tutti e trei [16:21]

and circle about Dante. He thinks first of athletes sparring naked with one another as he watches them. This wheel formation permits each in turn to look at and speak to Dante. By moving continuously they avoid some of the flakes, and they would be unable to stand still under the fire. The well-chosen image of the wheel indicates that these sinners have no rest within or without. Thus joined together, they have more stability than they would have if detached from one another.

These spirits were not scholars or clerics in the world, but warriors and statesmen, strong, active, publicly-minded men. Dante goes to some pains to indicate that no one temperament and no one profession characterizes the sodomite. The spokesman of the three Florentines, Rusticucci, implies that the harshness of his wife's character drove him into the practice of sodomy. He names himself and the other two: Guido Guerra, a zealous Guelf, and Tegghiaio Aldobrandi, a Guelf leader of the Adimari family. Already in the circle of the gluttons, Dante had asked Ciacco for news of Tegghiaio and Rusticucci. He is moved to join them down below on the plain, but cannot because of the fire. He tells them that he too is a Florentine and knows of their deeds. And once again, in one terzina, he summarizes his journey for these spirts. He has to leave the "gall" of Hell (*lo fele*) and reach the "center" (the center of the earth or Cocytus) before attaining the "sweet apples" (*dolci pomi*) of Heaven promised by his guide (16:61–63)

The exchange of words is brief and concerns Florence. Dante is the accuser here when he speaks of the decay of the city. These words on the waywardness of Florence end the passage, as the three spirits break their wheel formation and flee. They disappear in less time than it takes to say "amen."

The three Florentines are more dimly drawn than Brunetto. After a hasty greeting, a polite request, and a word of farewell, the encounter is over. The word *cortesia*, in line 67, used by Jacopo Rusticucci when he asks if there is still "courtesy" in Florence, best characterizes the entire episode. It is a rich word that has about it a cluster of meanings: nobility of character, graciousness, refinement, politeness. Dante and the three sodomites in their wheel show reverence for one another, a mutual *cortesia*.

Before even thinking of the usurers, who will not appear until the next canto, Dante receives a series of new and strong impressions after the trio of Florentines vanish from sight. He hears the cataract of the Phlegethon falling with a roar into the eighth circle. The first line of the canto uses the noun *rimbombo* in speaking of "the resounding of the water," and it returns one hundred lines later as a verb: "that river resounds," *quel fiume rimbomba*.

The final passage begins at line 106:

> Io aveva una corda cinta.
> [I had a cord girt round me.]

Virgil asks Dante to unloosen the cord. He takes it and throws it into the abyss. Dante takes this to be a signal for some help by means of which they may descend into the eighth circle. The last lines of the canto relate the poet's amazement at the sight of a wondrous figure (*una figura meravigliosa*, 16:131–32) who seems to be swimming upwards through the air. The monster will be named and described in canto 17.

There had been no previous allusion to this cord, although Dante claims, in line 108, that he had hoped at one time to catch with it the "leopard with the painted skin" (*la lonza alla pelle dipinta*). This is certainly the leopard of canto 1, who is described there as *leggiera e presta, alla gaietta pelle ("light and nimble, with a gay skin."*) (Can the symbol mean that he has now passed beyond the sins of incontinence (leopard) and the sins of violence (lion) and has come to the sins of fraud and malice (wolf)? The symbolism of the cord remains uncertain. Some commentators believe that it is proof that Dante belonged to the Franciscan Order and became an apostate monk. In speaking

directly to the reader, Dante, in line 128, for the first time names
his poem: *di questa comedìa* (the medieval accent was on the *i*,
whereas today it falls on the second syllable).

Principal Signs and Symbols

1. *The wheel* (*la rota*, 16:21): this turning wheel of the three
Florentine men may symbolize sexual acts as well as enable the
shades to remain abreast of Dante. The virile tone of Rusticucci's
speech (16:28–45) is very different from Brunetto's in canto 15.

2. *Not contempt but sorrow* (*non dispetto ma doglia*, 16:52):
once again Dante's feelings for the sinners are made clear.

3. *The sudden gains* (*i subiti guadagni*, 16:77): to this sudden
wealth of the Florentines, Dante seems to attribute the decay of
Florence. In line 9, he uses the term *nostra terra prava* (our
perverse land).

4. *That river* (*quel fiume*, 16:94): called today the Montone,
was once called the Acquacheta (16:97). It rises in the Etruscan
Alps and falls into the Adriatic.

5. *A rope* (*una corda*, 16:106–8): this rope girdle, used as a
signal, has puzzled commentators because of its relationship to
the leopard (*la lonza*, 16:108). Yet it is the wolf's power rather
than the leopard's that extends over this last region of Hell that
Dante is about to enter.

CANTO

17

Geryon; the Usurers;
the Descent to the Eighth Circle

THIS CANTO, clearly divided into three parts, begins with the image of fraud in the monster Geryon (17:1–30), continues with a brief passage on the usurers (17:31–75) of the seventh circle, and ends with the dramatic descent into the eighth circle (17:76–136). Canto 17 marks the transition from violence to fraud. The usurers in the last round of the violent are in Dante's mind unquestionably related to the fraudulent, and before we see them, we read the awesome description of "the beast with the pointed tail":

Ecco la fiera con la coda aguzza [17:1]

The canto opens with this arialike line. As Dante presents him, Geryon (*Gerione*) is the picture of fraud (*imagine di froda*, 17:7). In Greek mythology, Geryon was a king of Spain who was slain by Hercules. In the eighth book of the *Aeneid*, Virgil pictures him as a monster with three bodies. He stands for fraud because of a medieval tradition according to which Geryon attracted strangers into his power and then killed them.

Dante also demonizes him, possibly basing his description on the ninth chapter of Revelation. He is an important symbol for the entire eighth circle with its ten divisions, its ten *bolge* or ditches. The Minotaur at the beginning of the seventh circle and Geryon at the beginning of the eighth depict in their gothicized monstrousness the sins of violence and fraud. Dante gives Geryon a triune nature: the face of a just man, the body of a reptile, and the hairy paws of a beast. Eden's serpent is in Dante's Geryon, that serpent who spoke to Eve the greatest word of fraud: "ye shall be as gods knowing good and evil."

As Virgil goes off to parley with Geryon, who is stretched out on the edge of the abyss, he urges Dante to talk with the usurers sitting on the burning sand trying as best they can to ward off with their hands the flakes of fire. They resemble dogs in summer who with snout or paw try to fend off fleas and flies. They are the last of the violent. In canto II there had been a short study of the subject, and commentators have often wondered about the strong condemnation of usury in the poem. Dante does not recognize any of the usurers. From the neck of each hangs a kind of pouch or money bag bearing an armorial impress indicating his family and name. The color and armorial signs of three are described, and from these indications scholars have tried to discover the specific names. The spirits are crouched shapes on the sand. Their bodies have taken on the form of lumps of metal.

The art of the usurer is to cause money to breed money. It is the sterility of this practice that Dante obviously wants us to feel. Usury is the sin against industry and art, or, in Dante's stronger words, against nature and God. In today's world, usury has been replaced by monopoly. In this brief scene, Dante is merely the observer. He does not speak to any spirit.

The dramatic part of canto 17 in which the monster Geryon plays an important and practicable role, fills almost the latter half. Dante turns away from the usurers to find Virgil already seated on the haunch of the animal. From here to the end of the canto, Virgil and Dante represent very opposing states of mind. Virgil is serene and sure of himself in this descent on the back of Geryon, whereas Dante is terrified, first at the need to mount in front of Virgil, and then even more terrified as the descent begins. Virgil places Dante in front of him so that the monster's tail will not injure the poet. Once Dante is in place, Virgil clasps him in his arms and holds him up. He has already said that Geryon is the stair by which they must descend.

The take-off is given in detail: Virgil orders the descent to begin, advising Geryon that the circles he makes in the air be large. Geryon stretches out his tail like an eel and gathers in his paws. Dante's fear of falling is such that he recalls two classical allusions to legendary falls from the great height. Phaeton, son of Apollo, was allowed to drive the chariot of the sun for one day, and, inexperienced, scorched a part of the heavens. To save the earth from being burned, Jupiter killed Phaeton with a thunderbolt. Icarus, too, met disaster in his flight when the wax of his wings melted from the heat of the sun. These two examples are in Dante's mind as the monster swims slowly downward. Water imagery is used at the beginning and at the end of the canto. The roaring of the whirlpool below does not alleviate Dante's terror.

Geryon is compared to a falcon who cannot capture the bird he was released to catch, and who, when called back to earth, is weary and sullen. When Geryon sets the two poets down, he gives Dante this impression of scorn and quiet anger. But as soon as he is relieved of his burden, "he bounds off like an arrow from the string":

si dileguò come da corda cocca. [17:135]

The two elements of air and water are everywhere in the canto. Air is the space through which the poets descend to the eighth circle, and it was the space through which Phaeton and Icarus fell to their death. The continuous sound of falling water joins with the visual impression of Geryon swimming upward from below when he is called by the signal of the cord, and this image of swimming through water changes during the descent when Geryon appears as a great bird, a falcon called down after a useless hunt in the sky. Once relieved of his burden at the bottom of the abyss, the image of Geryon changes once again into an arrow to indicate the speed with which he takes off after his mission has been carried out. We have thus seen the man-reptile-animal-monster compared to a fish, a boat, a bird, and an arrow. Little wonder that Dante's terror grows throughout the canto as he tries to cast the unfamiliar into something known.

This particular canto provides a very elaborate use of the phenomenon of gravity. The river and the waterfalls are seeking the bottom, just as the Geryon-falcon is forced to obey and descend. This is the entire experience of Dante's Hell, one of an ever-deepening evil. Both the nature of the *Inferno,* and the fatality of Dante's journey, the need to reach the bottom of Hell, or the center of the earth, are recalled here. The two friends of truth ride on the back of the monster imaging fraud, whose tail links the two sins of violence and fraud. In the Middle Ages the two mythic figures of Phaeton and Icarus, in their fall to earth from a great height, were interpreted as examples of pride. Behind them one senses the archetypal imge of Lucifer's fall from highest Heaven.

Virgil is the active supervisor throughout the canto. As Dante's fear grows, Virgil's counsel multiplies. He directs the movements of his protégé, and he encourages his flagging spirits. He embraces Dante throughout the slow descent. His equanimity reassures the reader that all is planned and that all will be well at the end.

Principal Signs and Symbols

1. *Geryon* (*Gerione*): personifies fraud. In mythology he was a monster killed by Hercules (one of his twelve labors). Dante gives him three natures: human (his face), bestial (his paws), and reptile (his tail). This may be an adaptation from Revelation 9:7–11) or a perversion of the Holy Trinity.

2. *Usurers*: those using violence against nature, and against art derived from nature. Unrecognizable, they look at the ground. The proverb "making money breeds money" would indicate how the usurers make fertile what by nature is sterile. This might be considered the opposite of the sodomites' sin.

3. *The pouch* (*la tasca*) around each sinner's neck (17:55):

1. "Yellow pouch with blue lion": the Gianfigliacci family of Florence (17:59–60).

2. "The red pouch with white goose": the Ubbriachi family (Ghibelline) of Florence (17:62–63).

3. "The blue pregnant sow": the Scrovegni family of Padua (17:64).

4. Vitaliano dei Vitaliani was a Paduan (17:68).

5. The Paduan who speaks (17:64–76) is a fifth usurer.

4. *Phaeton* (*Feton*): son of Apollo, he was unable to control the chariot of the sun, scorched the part of the sky we call the Milky Way. Jupiter killed him with a thunderbolt (17:107).

5. *Icarus* (*Icaro*): son of Daedalus, he flew too high with wings fashioned by his father, and plunged to his death in the Aegean Sea when the sun melted the wax of his wings (17:109).

CANTO

18

Malebolge: The Panders and Seducers
(First *Bolgia*)
The Flatterers (Second *Bolgia*)

A SOLEMN LINE opens the introduction to the eighth circle, which is called *Malebolge* or "evil ditches":

> Luogo è in inferno detto Malebolge
> [there is a place in Hell called *Malebolge*]

As Dante descends on the back of Geryon, he sees and carefully observes the shape of the lowest part of Hell. The general image he uses is that of a "well," (*un pozzo,* 18:5—a word used as the name of a character in Samuel Beckett's play *Waiting for Godot*). If we summarized the description of the first twenty-one lines, we might call *Malebolge* a series of ten circular pits, carved in the rock and bridged by spurs of stone.

Most of the canto is given over to the first chasm or ditch, inhabited by panders and lying seducers (18:22–99). Briefly at the end of the canto, we see the second *bolgia,* where the flatterers are punished.

As in the upper circle of incontinence, we find here at the beginning of *Malebolge* a sexual image. Two sets of sinners, *i ruffiani* (panders) and *i seduttori* (seducers) are moving fast in opposite directions. This recalls the opposing movements of the avaricious and the prodigals in the fourth circle. The sinners of the first *bolgia* run continually, not because of a wind storm as in the second circle, but because of the lashing of whips administered by devils. The two classes of pimps and seducers are together in the one *bolgia* because both, in the practice of their sin, undermined the honor of women, the pimps for money (again,

this class recalls the *avari*) and the seducers for self-indulgence
and gratification (this recalls the *prodighi*). Both pander and
seducer use their intelligence to make gain of what they destroy
or dishonor. From this point on in Hell, all human relationships
begin to appear perverted or falsified.

Dante first fixes his attention on the panders (procurers, pimps,
go-betweens) because he sees them whipped by horned demons:
vidi i demon cornuti (18:35). This is the only place in the *Inferno*
where demons have horns. *Un cornuto* is the Italian word for the
French *cocu* and the English cuckold. Tradition has it that horns
grow out the the heads of husbands whose wives had been unfaithful. The sexual overtones are strong in this canto, where the
poet emphasizes the nudity of the sinners (*erano ignudi i peccatori*, 18:24) because of which the scourging would be more
painful. He also emphasizes the large number of sinners who in
their double march in opposite directions recall a scene in Rome
during the Jubilee year of 1299–1300, when the crowds were so
huge that a barrier was erected along the bridge of Sant' Angelo,
so that the pilgrims going to and from St. Peter's might pass in
opposite directions.

Dante recognizes one of the procurers, who tries to hide by
lowering his face. Addressing him by his name, Venedico Caccianemico, Dante asks him what brought him to this particular
place. This man, whose father had been head of the Guelfs in
Bologna, came from a well known Bolognese family. He had
acted as procurer for his own sister when he gave her to the
marquis of Este. Dante has chosen here an extreme case of pan-
dering. As a demon lashes Venedico with a whip, Dante lashes
out against Bologna. He knew the city (he had probably studied
at the university), and he knew that the practice of pimping was
widespread, largely because of the thousands of male students
living in the one community. Bologna is one of the five or six
Italian cities associated in Dante's mind with a particular sin, the
others being Pisa, Genoa, Siena, Lucca, and Florence.

Onely one procurer is named and addressed, and only one
seducer of women is named but not spoken to. Virgil points him
out:

> guarda quel grande che viene [18:83]
> [look at that great soul who comes]

It is the Greek hero Jason, famous as a seducer, who met,
seduced, and abandoned the strongest woman on Lemnos, an
island inhabited by fierce women. Whereas the Greeks tended to

applaud Jason for his triumphs in the art of seduction, Dante punishes him in Hell. After the episode of Lemnos, Jason sailed from Colchis where he won the golden fleece and where he seduced Medea. Later he abandoned her for Creusa. Dante shows some admiration for Jason's courage and counsel (*per cor e per senno*, 18:86), but he spends more time listing his sexual infidelities. After the meeting with Brunetto Latini, the poet tends to emphasize the specific fault rather than the nobler aspects of the sinner's character.

The last thirty-six lines of the canto describe the second *bolgia*, the repulsive plight of flatterers who are immersed in excrement. Dante recognizes one man from Lucca who acknowledges the innumerable flatteries his tongue had spoken. Then Virgil points out the prostitute Thaïs and quotes a word she used to her client, an instance Dante uses as an example of flattery. The word *putana*, applied to Thaïs in line 133, is still a very strong word for prostitute in Italian. This Thaïs is not the famous courtesan of Athens, but a character in Terence's play *Eunuchus*. When in the play the lover asks Thaïs "Do you thank me?" she answers *"Meravigliose"* (marvellously), as Dante mentions in line 135. Cicero in *De amicitia* quotes this answer as an example of flattery. Dante doubtless found it there rather than in Terence.

The word Dante uses for "flatteries" is *le lusinghe* (18:125), where it is spoken by Alessio of Lucca. There are no devils in this second *bolgia*. The punishment of the flatterers is the stench and the filth of the ditch. In this way the offensiveness of flattery is portrayed. We think easily today of flattering courtiers, and, more seriously, of demagogues who flatter the people, the voters, with their speeches.

The curious word Dante uses to illustrate flattery, *meravigliose*, is an extravagance of speech, a word used falsely by Thaïs, and used moreover in her profession for gain. In today's world the excessive claims of advertisement and commercials might be comparable. The first two *bolge* punish deceit, and especially, considering the examples given, malicious deceit that is carried out for personal gain. *Merda* (18:116) as the punishment is Dante's way of saying that flattery is unfruitful excrement. With other words than those of flattery, a man's sentiment could be expressed truly. Accuracy is all important in mathematics and architecture, for example, but it is also important in matters of the heart and of the spirit, in love, in philosophy, in morality, in the writing of a novel.

Thaïs is the last character in Hell whose image is sexual. Cantos

2, 5, and 18 represent a descent from the loftiest to the lowest. Canto 2 gives us the image of Beatrice's intercession, of love far more purified than it was even in *La vita nuova*. Canto 5 is the picture of Francesca's sexual love, warm, tender, but unwise, and the cause of tragic death. Thaïs in canto 18 is the image of sex without love, and Dante accentuates its filthiness. Each of the feminine figures plays a dual role: Beatrice as the beloved and as the spiritual guide; Francesca as lover and adultress; Thaïs as prostitute and flatterer. The few lines given to Thaïs make her the fraudulent in love, the one who in carrying out her profession of sex has totally perverted the meaning of love.

The word *meravigliose* is in the next-to-last line of the canto. The final line is a brief, almost curt warning by Virgil. He says in effect to Dante, let us be satisfied with what we have viewed, let us look no longer on this scene:

E quinci sien le nostre viste sazie.
[And herewith let our view be sated.]

This is Virgil the doctor speaking: part psychologist, part theologian. His lesson is unequivocal. We might become involved morbidly, even sexually, in such a scene. Dante, with his strong voyeurism, displays this tendency. At times he is fascinated by what he sees, and at other times he shows impulses of cruelty toward the sinners. Virgil is there to correct such human weaknesses in the poet.

Aquinas taught that free will in man has built the ethical institutions of the world in order to protect the free will of all men. These ethical institutions are the family, the rituals of society, the laws of the state, and the Church. Dante knew, in accordance with the teaching of Aquinas, that in the free will of man lies the opposite possibility. The huge subject of fraud, treated in the ten *bolge* of the eighth circle, is not a physical power but an intellectual power that undermines free will in someone else. By the cunning and the deception of one person, the free will in another may be lost. The eighth circle receives the longest treatment of sin in the *Inferno* because it is the study of how general confidence between individuals is destroyed. The ninth circle punishes those sinners who have destroyed a very special kind of confidence, such as that found in friendship, kinship, discipleship. The eighth and ninth circles are closely related.

The ten ditches of *Malebolge* occupy thirteen cantos. What is common to the sins of this circle? We will follow in the gradual development of the sin of fraud or malice the ways in which a person or an institution is perverted from its truth by an individual's untruth. In each case the sinner is a deceiver.

Principal Signs and Symbols

1. *Malebolge:* the Italian *bolgia* means a trench in the ground or a large bag or pouch. Dante puns on the two meanings "evil pits" and "evil pouches." There is no English word that combines the two. *Malebolge* is also the eighth circle, with its ten *bolge,* series of trenches with immense spurs of rock forming bridges over the trenches. *Malebolge* is the image of the city and the disintegration of every relationship: personal, social, public. All the means of exchange between two persons are falsified. We are in the circle of fraud or malice, the sins of the wolf.

2. *The first bolgia:* it has two classes of sinners: pimps who are walking toward Dante, and seducers who walk in the same direction with Dante and Virgil. Attention is paid to the Bolognese Guelf Venedico Caccianemico who was procurer for his sister, giving her to the marquis of Este, and to the seducer Jason, leader of the Argonauts, who seduced the daughter of the king of Lemnos.

3. *The second bolgia:* flatterers, represented especially by Thaïs, a character in a play of Terence, whose reply to her lover is for Dante the prostitution of words.

4. *Ma che ti mena a sì pungenti salse?* (but what brings you to such a biting pickle? 18:51): *salse* means "sauce" but it is also the name of a place near Bologna where criminals were flogged and killed. Is Dante punning on *salse?* Probably.

CANTO

19

The Simonists: The Three Popes
(Third *Bolgia*)

MORE HATEFUL to Dante than panders and seducers are the sinners of the third *bolgia:* the simonists or simoniacs. Their name comes from the man's name that Dante invokes in the opening line:

> O Simon mago, o miseri seguaci
> [O Simon Magus, O wretched followers]

This is Simon of Samaria who was cursed by Saint Peter (Acts 8) because he believed that the gifts of the Holy Spirit might be bought with money. Ever since the first century, when Saint Peter rebuked Simon, the curse has been heard throughout the history of the Church. The sin of simony, by which a finite value is believed capable of purchasing an infinite value, has continually plagued the Roman Church.

This canto on simony is closely related to the preceding canto in which the honor of a woman is bartered for money. Here the Church, traditionally called "the bride of Christ," is prostituted for gold and silver: *per oro e per argento* (19:4). It was also believed that Simon of Samaria used sorcery.

The relationship of the sin to its punishment is brilliantly worked out in this third *bolgia.* The simonists are "pouched" head down in pockets of the rock. In life they had reversed the order of things by subordinating spiritual to material values. The soles of the feet of the sinners are uppermost and seem to Dante to be on fire. Flames, like oil, move back and forth on the outer surface of their soles. The canto thus begins in anger, with the words uttered by Dante because of his disgust with the corrupt clergy and especially with the corrupt papacy. The popes of Rome are clearly designated and reproved in canto 19.

Since all priests have been consecrated, the sacraments they administer are valid. This remains doctrinally sound even if the priests are unholy men. Simoniac priests are those who traffic in the sacraments and offices of the Church by selling them for personal gain. The image of a prostitute profiting from sex, which we saw in canto 18, is reproduced in the chief simonist of canto 19, but the sinner is no longer a woman. It is a pope. And the pope is prostituting a feminine figure, namely the Church, the "bride of Christ."

The gradation of sins is carefully determined in the opening ditches of *Malebolge*. The first two *bolge*, treated in one canto, punish sexual sins connected with money; the third *bolgia* punishes simony, or the sale of holy things; the fifth *bolgia* punishes barratry which is secular simony, corruption in government or administrative posts, or what is sometimes called graft. Between the third and fifth *bolge*, we find the soothsayers. Soothsaying and fortune-telling also are related to spiritual matters and money. Dante's attitude varies considerably as he passes from one ditch to another. He is more the observer and commentator in the first two *bolge*. In the presence of Jason the seducer Dante feels some admiration as he remembers Jason the navigator and hero of the golden fleece. In the third *bolgia* he is angry and shows full moral outrage. This tension loosens in the fifth *bolgia* of the barrators, where the tone is overtly comical. With the soothsayers in the fourth *bolgia* the tone is more nostalgic as the poet evokes historical and mythical characters. With the pimps and prostitutes, with the flatterers and with the spiritual adulterers, the simonists, Dante's tone is fairly austere. It becomes relaxed in the fifth ditch.

As Dante looks at the holes in the third *bolgia*, he is reminded of an episode in his own life that had taken place in the Baptistery of Florence, originally called the Church of Saint John the Baptist. An affectionate phrase is used by the poet in line 17:

nel mio bel San Giovanni

This Baptistery stands today beside the cathedral of Florence, Santa Maria del Fiore (usually called the *Duomo*). Dante himself was baptized in the *Batistero*.

At that time there was a large number of baptismal fonts sur-

rounded by stone compartments or holes in which the priests
stood to protect themselves from the jostling of the crowds on
days when many babies were being baptized at once. One day a
boy was caught in one of the holes, and in order to release him,
Dante had to break a part of the stone. The poet may have been
called a destroyer of church property in committing an act of
sacrilege. It would seem that Dante wished to exonerate himself
and set the record straight in the brief passage of lines 16–21.

As Dante watches the quivering of sinners' legs, he notices one
spirit whose legs quiver more than the others and asks Virgil who
he is. The poet is led to the lower bank where his eyes are on a
level with the groin of the spirit. The head and torso of the sinner
are out of sight in the hole. Dante describes his stance as that of a
priest listening to the confession of a murderer. At one time in
Florence a murderer was staked in the ground alive and then the
hole was filled in.

> Io stava come 'l frate che confessa
> lo perfido assessin [19:49–50]
> [I stood, like the friar who is confessing
> a treacherous assassin]

Dante bends down to hear the spirit as a priest had to bend down
to hear the last words of the condemned assassin.

At this point, in a most ingenious manner, Dante announces
the damnation of his archenemy, Pope Boniface VIII. He asks
the spirit, whom he calls a "stake," to speak. The spirit, Pope
Nicholas III, who had died in 1280, believes the one speaking to
him is Boniface, and is puzzled because Boniface is not due in
Hell until 1303, and it is now 1300. Virgil urges Dante to name
himself and clear up the misunderstanding. When that is done,
the spirit then says he once wore the great mantle—meaning the
papal mantle—and that he was the son of the she-bear. Orsa, the
word for she-bear, indicates that Nicholas is of the Orsini family.
The confession of his guilt is made in just a few words. To advance the "whelps" (orsatti) of his family, he says, "I pursed
wealth above and myself here below":

> e veramente fui figliuol de l'orsa,
> cupido sì, per avanzar li orsatti,
> che sù l'avere, e qui me misi in borsa [19:70–72]
> [and truthfully I was a son of the she-bear,
> so eager to advance the whelps,
> that I pursed wealth above, and pursed myself here]

By enriching his nephews (*nipoti*), Nicholas III committed simony, and this act has been called ever since "nepotism," the granting of privileges or the showing of favoritism to members of one's family.

Line 72 is exceptional for its ellipsis and image. *Sù*, "up above," *misi l'avere in borsa*, "I put a fortune in a purse," *e qui*, "and here," *me misi in borsa*, "I put myself into a purse." By acquiring money (and giving it to members of his family), Nicholas is saying that he placed himself in this particular predicament in the third ditch. But Dante is less interested in attacking Nicholas than he is in attacking Boniface, who reigned from 1294 to 1303. Nicholas names another successor, Clement V, the first pope at Avignon, also known for simony. All three simoniac popes will eventually be staked head first in the same hole. Boniface VIII belonged to the Caetani family, as noble a family as the Orsinis. He was still living in 1300, his Jubilee year. In this passage Dante is careful to restrain his words, probably through reverence for the high office of the papacy.

Simony has been one of the most painful trials for the Church of Rome. A church building must be cared for and priests must live. It is often difficult to know where simony begins in the distribution of church money, and certainly throughout the history of the Church, it has differed according to time and place and clergy.

Dante accuses three popes of his own day, and yet the tone of the canto is not irreverent. Because it is 1300 when Dante makes his journey, Boniface and Clement are not yet in Hell. Prophecy is in the scene as well as tragedy. This Orsini, Nicholas III names himself to Dante, confesses his guilt and describes his punishment. He practiced simony for his family's sake and not for his own.

Dante uses the device of the prophetic power of spirits in Hell by having Nicholas prophesy and then by continuing this tone as he himself speaks in a discourse of severe reproof that begins with line 88, and develops into a lofty diatribe of judgment that is partly historical and partly theological. By giving a picture of the primitive Church, Dante, using two striking examples from the activities of Saint Peter, shows how the sin of simony has in the past been avoided. When Christ gave the keys of the kingdom to Peter, he did not ask for money. And when Peter chose Matthias to take the place of Judas, he did not ask for money. Dante concludes with words addressed to Nicholas:

Però ti sta, ché tu se' ben punito [19:97]
[stay here, for you are justly punished]

Five lines later, Dante again addresses Nicholas, again using
tu, when he says:

la reverenza de le somme chiavi
che tu tenesti [19:101–2]
[the reverence for the great keys you held]

and then, two lines later, in line 104, he attacks all the popes by
using *la vostra avarizia*, "your avarice," in the plural form.

The condemnation of simony grows increasingly more severe
as the poet next refers to the Apocalypse and to the Church as the
great whore of Babylon. He compares the popes' desire for gold
to the Jews worshiping the golden calf. Dante's crescendoing
vehemence ends with his cry *Ahi Constantin* (19:115) and his
reference to the donation or dowry of Constantine in 313. In this
document, which today is believed a forgery, Constantine, the
first Christian emperor, gave the pope temporal power over Italy.
Dante obviously deplored the act, which he believed resulted in
a decline of the emperor's authority and in the beginning of
ecclesiastical corruption.

In the canto itself there are two reactions to Dante's outcry.
Through anger or shame Nicholas shakes his feet more violently
than before. Virgil, in the expression on his face, shows con-
tented satisfaction as if he were teacher or father, and is delighted with the words of his pupil or son. These are "true
words" (*parole vere*, 19:122) that have been expressed, and in
recognition of them, Virgil takes Dante into his arms, clasps him
tightly and helps him to the crossway from the fourth to the fifth
rampart. It would be a difficult passage even for mountain goats,
and Virgil shows himself physically able with his strength and
nimbleness to carry Dante and set him down in view of the next
valley. During the last thirteen lines of the canto, Virgil returns
to the foreground in his role as loving guide. The words
soavemente and *soave* are used in verses 130 and 131: gentleness
and gratitude impell Virgil to reward his exchange.

Not since cantos 1 and 2 have we seen Virgil so explicitly the
poet and glorifier of the Roman Empire. In canto 19 he rejoices
that his pupil is able to denounce the simoniacal worldliness of
the papacy. The passage illuminates Dante's principal political
theory that an even balance between imperial and papal forces

would assure peace in the world. That plan was the utopia of the fourteenth century, and Dante was its chief interpreter. The practice of simony involved the alienation of the Empire for the profit of the Church. The temporal sovereignty of the popes was therefore the cause of the ills suffered by the church and the threat to the souls of believers.

Principal Signs and Symbols

1. *Simony:* the sin of simoniacs or simonists, is especially the sale of ecclesiastical offices or the sale of the sacraments. For example, a mercenary marriage is the sale of a sacrament. Money associated with a "pouch" is underscored here in the image of the fiery pockets in the rock where the sinners are place head downwards. These sinners have prostituted the things of God for silver and gold (*per oro e per argento* in line 4 links simony with the flattery of the whore Thaïs in canto 17).

2. *Simon the magician* (*Simon mago*) gave his name to the sin. He believed he could purchase the power of the Holy Spirit (Acts 8:9–24).

3. *"The soles of every sinner's feet were on fire"* (19:25): the perversion of baptism. Rather than the head baptized with water, the feet are baptized with oil and fire.

4. Nicholas III *"weeps with his legs"* (19:45): the word *zanca*, "leg" or "shank," is also used for the legs of Lucifer in the last canto of the *Inferno* (34:79).

5. *The Evangelist* (*il Vangelista*, 19:106): Saint John the Evangelist relating his vision in Revelation 17. The "seven heads" and the "ten horns" (*le sette teste ... e ... le dieci corna*) of lines 109–10, are usually interpreted as the seven sacraments and the ten commandments.

6. *Constantine* (19:115): emperor of Rome from 306–37, adopted Christianity as the state religion, and this made it possible for the Church to claim temporal power which, according to Dante, led to political and ecclesiastical evils.

7. In canto 34, when Dante looks up to see the legs of Lucifer, one may remember the legs of Nicholas. Nicholas's sin was defrauding the Church and Lucifer's was defrauding God.

CANTO

20

The Diviners: Tiresias (Fourth *Bolgia*)

As with the simonists, Dante demonstrates strong disapproval and even loathing for the diviners and sorcerers who inhabit the fourth *bolgia*. He must have known that during the Middle Ages Virgil was sometimes thought to have been a magician. There is even some reason to believe that Dante himself was accused of dealing in the black arts. His energetic reproving of soothsayers in canto 20 might be explained in part by his desire to dispel all doubts concerning Virgil and himself.

It is an unusual canto in that no sinner speaks in it. The poet calls up legends and mysterious characters from both antiquity and modern times. Most readers will remember from this canto the story of Tiresias and the strange account of the origin of Mantua. There is even a slightly comic note as the end in the reference to Asdente.

From the arch of the bridge to which Virgil has carried him, Dante now looks down at this new world of augurs and sorcerers. The sinners walk at a very slow pace, weeping, silent, and with their necks fully twisted around so that there is an opposition between their forward movement and their backward vision. The picture is one of the most striking examples of the appropriateness of the sin to its punishment. If a man knows his future, his actions in the present will be impeded. His knowledge may paralyze his body.

Dante is so moved by this picture of men and women whose faces are turned around and whose tears bathe their buttocks, that he himself weeps. This punishment for soothsaying would

appear to be Dante's own invention. There is no source in
Homer or Virgil, and just a faint hint of it in the Old Testament
where we read: "I am the Lord that turneth the wise man backward, and maketh their knowledge foolish" (Isaiah 44:25).

Dante's weeping (*Certo io piangeva*, 20:25) is immediately
chided by Virgil: "Are you a fool?" The word used by Virgil for
fool, *sciocco*, is still used in Italy today. In a masterly line of
ellipsis and double meaning, comparable to the *borsa* line in the
preceding canto, Virgil explains his rebuke:

Qui vive la pietà quand'è ben morta [20:38]

Only by giving its double meaning to *pietà* can the line be fully
understood. "Piety" and "pity" are both in *pietà*. The line might
be paraphrased thus: "Here piety (to God) lives, when pity (to
man) is dead." If you feel and show pity for the sinners, Virgil is
saying to Dante, you are questioning the justice of God.

This line is referred to by Samuel Beckett in his short story
"Dante and the lobster," where the hero Belacqua Shuah worries
about its implications and the entire problem of God's mercy.

Virgil then begins to point out some of the ancient seers and
soothsayers. Because of his appearance in Greek tragedy, the
best known today is Tiresias, seer and prophet of Thebes. In
book 3 of Ovid's *Metamorphoses*, we can read the full story of
Tiresias, who as a boy found two serpents twined together. When
he struck them to separate them, he was changed into a girl.
Seven years later he found the same serpents, struck them again,
and recovered his manhood. When Jupiter and Juno argued over
which sex has the greater pleasure in love-making, they turned to
Tiresias to settle the question for them. When he replied that it
was the woman, Juno struck and blinded him. As a recompense,
Jupiter gave him his gift of prophecy. There were many Greek
and Roman soothsayers, but Dante most certainly believed that
true prophecy belonged to the early Hebraic and Christian
epochs.

Lines 57 to 99 provide a detailed account of the origins of the
city of Mantua, home of Virgil. This passage would seem to be
Dante's invention. In the text it is spoken by Virgil. He relates
the story of Manto, the daughter of Tiresias. A sorceress, she
chose a spot that seemed suitable for the practice of her arts at
some distance from towns and dwellings. Manto did not literally
found Mantua, but lived and died on its future site. The name of
the city occurs in line 93: *Mantova*, which is near Milano, capital

of Lombardy in the north. Here *Mantova*, or *Mantua*, as we say in English, is described as an island in a marsh, and bears some resemblance with the infernal city of Dis. It is believed Dante drew features of the landscape of his underworld from this district of Italy. The epithet *il Mantovano*, an inhabitant of Mantua, was used in canto 2, line 58, for Virgil. The word is still used in Italy to designate the Latin poet. Dante tells us, insisting that this is the true story, that the city of Mantua was built over the dead bones of Manto and her ministers:

> Fer la città sopra quell'ossa morte [20:91]
> [They built the city over those dead bones]

The last thirty lines of the canto are given over to other more recent soothsayers. Michael Scott, for example, was a magician and occultist, and the astrologer of Frederick II.

The absence of any speech on the part of the sinners places the emphasis in the canto on the idea of soothsaying and on Dante's theory that to sell the mind of God for money is a worse offense than simony and is therefore placed lower in Hell.

Prophecy is a true gift, but charlatans pretend to be prophets and exploit a gift they do not possess. Witches are now called fortune-tellers and their art thrives on credulity. In Dante's scheme, soothsaying follows the prostitution of language, the speech of flatterers and seducers, and the prostitution of the Church in simony. Soothsaying is the prostitution of God's mind because God knows the future. In those periods when religion is discredited, men turn to wizards and false prophets, to astrologers and spiritualists. In Dante's image, the twisted organism is the result of the twisting of the future. He weeps at the physical contortion of the human body.

Virgil, after condemning Dante's weakness, offers an abundance of special explanations and examples. His eloquence is in marked contrast with the silent spectacle the two poets watch. The reader is drawn away from the gruesome sight in order to follow legends and historical data. It is a vanished world of magic that Virgil evokes.

In this lesson of the fourth *bolgia*, is Dante condemning all the efforts of man to look into the future? If that were true, he would be condemning his own poem. These particular sinners are a medley of magicians, thaumaturgists or workers of miracles, of heathen prophets, of medieval soothsayers and fortune tellers. The connection between this fourth *bolgia* and the preceding

one is in the name of Simon Magus, the opening words of canto
19, *O Simon mago*—"simony" and "magic." The man himself
was an unimportant magician or prestidigitator, but there is a
deep and involved connection between simony and magic.

There is a belief, especially prevalent in the Middle Ages, that
the "mysteries" of the Church have their counterpart in magical
rites that are controlled by Satan. When mass is celebrated by an
excommunicated priest, the sacrament is valid but the ceremony
then becomes comparable to a rite of witchcraft. One of the oldest names for the devil is "God's ape" or "wonder-worker."

Divination is traditionally forbidden because it looks into the
future in order to see what is in God's mind. The divinity of God
is, of course, a basic dogma, but divination or the guessing of
what God knows is going to happen, is a serious error of pride.
When this divination or guess-work is sold for money, it becomes, in Dante's scheme, a darker form of simony.

And yet there is a universal element in the future that man is
able to know and should know and utilize for the help that
knowledge will bring. To prophesy a famine, for example, or
report weather, or foretell the results a neglect of ecology will
bring about, is to do good to humanity.

The story of Mantua's foundation has been criticized by some
commentators as being a digression. But in telling the story Virgil obviously wishes to correct errors or beliefs of the past, and he
gives a conscientious account of what he presents as truth. This
offsets the elements of wizardry and hocus-pocus that the canto
contains.

This fourth *bolgia* of the soothsayers marks a turning point in
Dante's voyage because it is the last moment of pity for the
damned on the part of Dante. The *pietà* line (20:28), spoken by
Virgil, stresses the advice that pity is out of place in Hell. A sinful
act is the breaking of a spiritual law. It is the scheme of the poem
to demonstrate to Dante the justice of God, and thus in canto 20
Virgil's eloquence is in strong contrast with the speechless suffering of the soothsayers. It is true, however, that Virgil did not
accuse Dante's expression of feeling when he was with
Francesca, Ciacco, Pier della Vigna, and Brunetto Latini. Here,
with Tiresias, Manto, and Michael Scott, theology is stressed.
The mention of philtres and mommets (herbs and images) in line
123 is a reference to dangerous magical arts. Philtres were used
to obtain power over the will of others, and waxen images were
pierced to bring about the death of the victim.

The last seven lines of the canto make an important allusion to time in the world of men. During the night preceding Good Friday 1300, the moon was full, and now Dante is describing the setting of the moon. "Cain with his thorns" (*Caino e le spine*, 10:126) is the "man in the moon," when the moon is seen to appear with a lantern and a thorn bush. The time now in the narrative would be early Saturday morning.

Principal Signs and Symbols

1. *Sorcery:* the art that takes over God's knowledge of the future. The twisted nature of magic is in the punishment of the sorcerers. Behind this sin lies the misuse of knowledge and psychic power.

2. *Amphiaraus* (20:34): one of the seven kings who waged war on Thebes. He was the prophet of Argos and foresaw his own death and hid. His wife betrayed him to Polynices, and when fleeing from the Theban prince, he was swallowed up by an earthquake. (Statius, *Thebaid*, 7, 8).

> Anfïarao? perché lasci la guerra? [20:34]
> [Amphiaraus? why do you leave the war?]

3. *Tiresias:* prophet and soothsayer of Thebes. When Juno blinded him, Jupiter in compensation gave him the gift of prophecy.

> Vedi Tiresia, che mutò sembiante [v. 40]
> [see Tiresias who changed his appearance]

4. *Manto* (20:55): daughter of Tiresias. There is reference to the founding of Mantua by Manto in *Aeneid* 10:198–200.

5. *Mantua* (*Mantova*, 20:93): this long account, given by Virgil, of the founding of Mantua (20:61–99) emphasizes the truth of the account to offset any imputation of sorcery.

CANTO

21

The Barrators (Fifth *Bolgia*)
Note on Beckett's "Malacoda"

BELOW THE SIMONISTS and the sorcerers are the barrators of the fifth *bolgia*, and in them the organism of the state or the city is shown to be unhealthy. What simonists are to the Church, barrators are to the state, because they traffic in offices of the state. After mistreatment of things of God, we come to mistreatment of the things of Caesar. By placing barrators lower than simonists, Dante is implying that the selling of the things of Caesar is a worse sin than the selling of the things of God.

The state, like the Church, in Dante's philosophy, derives its authority from God. The state, represented by the emperor, head of the natural order of man, lies at a deeper level than the Church, represented by the pope, head of the spiritual order of man. According to this theory, it is necessary first to be honest about worldly riches; from that discipline, one can learn to be honest about spiritual riches. A saying of Christ is often called upon to justify this theory: "If a man love not his brother whom he has seen, how shall he love God whom he has not seen?"

The fifth bolgia occupies cantos 21, 22, and the first fifty-seven lines of 23. Barratry, in the form of a complex comedy, is therefore the most elaborate drama or episode in the *Inferno*. In order to announce the new tone of this *bolgia*, Dante uses, in the second line of the canto, the word *comedia* in speaking of his entire poem. At the end of the preceding canto, in line 113, Virgil referred to his poem as a *tragedìa*. The two words are defined by Dante in his *De vulgari eloquentia* and in his letter to Can

136

Grande. By "tragedy" he means a poem whose action ends in disaster and whose style is elevated, whereas by "comedy" he means a narrative poem ending happily whose style is less lofty and more colloquial. The fifth *bolgia* illustrates the theory of a literary genre in which the element of the grotesque will be pushed very far.

The words "barratry" and "barrator" have gone out of use in English, and have been replaced by "graft" and "grafter" or "swindler," if the swindle is associated with public offices. *La barratteria*, then, is prostitution of the state. *Il barrattiere* is the barrator, a word derived from the Old French *barater* meaning "to deceive." *Le baratin* is modern French for voluminous speech intended to trick the listener. The word "graft" comes from a Greek word, and is used especially in America.

The means by which barrators are punished is boiling pitch. Dante uses two words for pitch: *la pegola*, an older word (21:17), and *la pece* (21:8) which is still in use. Dante had doubtless seen the pitch used to caulk ships in Venice in the Arsenal, an important shipyard in the Middle Ages when Venice was a great sea power. The characteristic of pitch is to glue or vitiate or entangle whatever comes in contact with it. It is dark and tenacious (*tenace* is used in line 8). Our word "viscous" is in the word *inviscava* in line 18, and connotes an evil, base substance as well as something that is adhesive.

The greater complexity of barratry is evident when it is contrasted with simony and divination. An act of simony corrupts the priest or the bishop, but it does not corrupt the parishioners or the members of the diocese. Divination is harmful to the diviner or the soothsayer, but it is not harmful to God. Each simonist in canto 19 in punished individually in a hole (*borsa*), and each diviner in canto 20 walks with his neck twisted. Barratry, comparable to the nature of pitch, contaminates the entire city or the entire civil institution. The very associative principle by which a city is governed has been perverted. The darkness of the place (*oscura* is in line 6) is appropriate because barrators are compelled to hide as they carry out their actions in the dark. In the fifth *bolgia*, they are hidden under the pitch, as they once hid behind their evil plottings.

The barrators are punished not only by the pitch but also by demons on the banks who tear them with hooks if they emerge from the pitch farther than they are allowed. These demons are

winged, black, with sharp shoulders, and they carry hooks with
them with which to carry out their torment. The scene is comparable in a general sense to canto 12 where tyrants and murderers
are plunged into boiling blood and watched over by centaurs
armed with arrows and who keep sinners at their proper depth.
The demons of the fifth *bolgia* are more vicious, more sadistic,
and more comical. They are the chief objects of interest in the
barratry scene as they harass and clown, and they add to the
Inferno a lesson in demonology reminiscent of the fallen angels
at the entrance of Dis (canto 8) and the many centaurs in the
realm of violence (canto 12). The scene here is not classical, not
comparable to other episodes in which we saw one monster at a
time. It is gothic, medieval, grotesque, northern.

As the drama unfolds in its several parts, we will see the sinners tormented and the tormentors tricked. In the spectacle of
evil undoing itself, we witness a demonstration of the absurd and
the farcical. Three sets of characters are clearly delineated: the
demons, the damned, and the onlookers, Virgil and Dante, and
all three sets play equally important parts.

Canto 21 is quite evenly divided into two parts, forming the
first two acts of the entire episode. The first (21:1–57) is the
prelude to all the action of the three cantos. Dante and Virgil
appear on the bridge, and, looking down into the scene below
them, watch a black demon (21:29) carrying a senator of Lucca on
his high sharp shoulders. The senator has evidently just died and
is being assigned to his place in the pitch. Dante thus castigates
Lucca, a city close to Florence in Tuscany, for her barratry.
"Everyone there is a barrator," we read in line 41: *ognuom v'è
barattier,* "except Bonturo," *fuor che Bonturo.* This last phrase
is ironical because Bonturo was known as the leading barrator of
the city.

After the demon hurls the senator into the pitch, he scampers
up the cliff to keep watch, as if he were a dog following a thief.
The sinner rises to the surface "bent up" (*convolto,* 21:46), as if in
an attitude of prayer. This posture of seeming piety calls forth
from the demon a scathing remark: "There is no place here for the
Sacred Face." The reference is to an ancient image of Christ
venerated in the cathedral of Lucca. The demon continues to
taunt the senator by saying that in the Serchio, the river of Lucca,
one swims differently than in the pitch. He calls on the other
demons, using the term *Malebranche* or "evil claws," to keep the
sinners thrust under the pitch. With more than a hundred prongs,

the demons mangle and drag the senator, and Dante compares their action to that of the vassals of a cook who, with hooks, keep the large mass of meat in the middle of the boiler as it cooks.

In the second scene (21:58–139), first Virgil and then Dante comes into play. Virgil goes down among the devils to parley with them, as Dante, more terrified than he usually is, hides behind a rock. The devils rush on Virgil like a whirlwind (*con quella tempesta*, 21:67), and Virgil, the man of courage, stops them, asks for passage to the sixth *bolgia*, and once again, argues that it is the will of Heaven that he show the way to Dante. The devils call on Malacoda ("evil tail"), their leader and the subtlest member of their gang. In Malacoda we will see, although it is not evident here, the working of fraud, because he points out a bridge for the two travelers to take, and since all the bridges are broken, he is pointing out the way to nowhere.

Before this lie is spoken by the head-demon Malacoda (21:110), one of the devils threatens to nick Dante on his rump, and Malacoda turns on him quickly with the words:

Posa, posa, Scarmiglione! [21:105]

which might be translated, "quiet, quiet," or even "down, down," a term we might use in speaking to a dog.

There is a roll-call of all the demons chosen to escort Dante and Virgil, ten names in all, each of which is ludicrous in sound, and vaguely meaningful: Alichino, Calcabrina, Draghignazzo, Ciriatto, Graffiacane. The threat of Scarmiglione terrifies Dante all the more. He suggests to Virgil that they proceed alone, but the grotesque squad of demons is ready, *la decina*, the "decury" of ten devils. Each of them makes a signal to their leader, a noise made by pressing the tongue against the teeth, and Malacoda answers with a fart: "he made of his rump a trumpet." This final line of the canto is, according to Italian scholars, the one remembered best by Italian school boys.

Principal Signs and Symbols

1. *Pitch* (*pegola*, 21:17; *pece*, 21:8): activity around the vat of pitch initiates a new kind of satire unlike anything else in the *Commedia*. Since the dealings of barrators are secret, they are plunged into the boiling pitch which sticks to them, as money once stuck to their hands.

2. *Malebranche* (evil claws): the demons of the fifth *bolgia* who oversee the punishment.

3. *Cooks* (*cuochi*, 21:55): the devils are called cooks and this image of cooking continues in the subsequent canto.

4. *Malacoda* (evil tail): almost to be a reproduction of Geryon. Here are possible translations of the names of the ten devils:

Alichino: stoop-wing;
Calcabrina: snow trampler;
Cagnazzo: harrow hound;
Barbariccia: curly beard;
Libicocco: libbicock;
Draghignazzo: dragonel;
Ciriatto: boar-tusk;
Graffiacane: scratch dog;
Farfarello: hell bat;
Rubicante: red nose.

Note on Beckett's "Malacoda"

In a group of thirteen poems, called *Echo's Bones*, written by Samuel Beckett between 1933 and 1935, Dante's presence is felt quite distinctly in at least four of the poems, especially in the one given the title "Malacoda." In the *Inferno*, Malacoda is the leader of an infernal procession, both terrifying (to Dante) and comical (to the reader). In Beckett's poem, Malacoda is an undertaker's assistant who comes three times into a home, presumably Beckett's, in order, first, to take the measurements for a coffin for the deceased husband, and second, to place the body in the coffin, and on the third trip, to cover the coffin.

Malacoda is here the leader of another kind of procession to the world of the dead. Whereas Dante's procession takes place within that world of the dead (although organized for a man still living, for the voyager Dante Alghieri), Beckett's procession is organized in this world in order to conduct a man who has died into the other world of eternity. Malacoda, as his name indicates, presides over the tail end of a life.

In canto 21 Virgil never forgets that his mission as guide through Hell is divinely instituted. Similarly, strong sentiments are evident in Beckett's poem, in the observant calm of the narrator who may be the son of the dead man, and in the grief of the widow whom the narrator wishes to protect from Malacoda and from the coffin-funeral preparations.

The original Virgil, Dante, and Malacoda are all reduplicated in Beckett's "Malacoda." The humor, the scariness and the solemnity of cantos 21 and 22 are present as well. The most notable trait relating the Italian episode to Beckett's poem is a deep sense of eeriness and unreality. In Dante the sufferers are dipped in pitch and clawed by demons. Their human form is mangled and disguised by a viscous covering. In Beckett's poem, the living—the narrator, the mother, and perhaps the undertaker's assistant—are overcome not only by grief but by their momentary proximity to a body no longer totally human. The deceased man in his home is already undergoing a physical change and thereby extending to the living a lesson on human frailty, on the transformation of a body that is the negation of the body, and that will cause the modern poet to terminate his poem with the monosyllable *nay*. The funeral arrangements would seem to be preparing a voyage, but in reality there will be no voyage, there will be nothing. The word *nay* is the final line and is detached from the three stanzas. It succinctly negates what the poem builds up in the mind of the reader.

The voyage-archetype is the basis of the *Divine Comedy*. It is the primordial structure of the work and one of the explanations for the appeal the poem has exerted through the centuries. The richness, the dramatic intensity, and the endless variety of the episodes in the one hundred cantos are held together and justified by the voyage through the three realms of the other world. "Malacoda" is the earliest of Beckett's texts in which the voyage archetype is behind the poem's concept but in which the impossibility of its achievement is the sense of the poem.

As the original Malacoda and his companion devils, the *Malebranche,* supervised the sinners in the afterworld, so the undertaker's assistant in the first stanza measures the body for the coffin. In the vestibule he appears "knee deep in the lilies," as Malacoda might sink knee deep in the pitch if he fell into it (as some of his fellow devils actually do in Dante's scene). The assistant is there "to measure this incorruptible." In this one theological word, "incorruptible," there is condensed the reason for funeral preparations in the real world, and the reason for the literary allusions to Dante, even if it is the *Inferno,* because all three parts of the *Divine Comedy* are founded on the belief in the

corporeal incorruptibility of man. The gross line associated with
Dante's Malacoda is muted in Beckett's, literally muted in
sound, and linguistically muted in an exaggerated choice of
words:

>that felts his perineum mutes his signal.

In the second stanza the name Malacoda is not used, but the
descriptive word "ungulata," referring to animals, turns him into
a devilish form:

>to coffin
>with assistant ungulata

The third stanza terminates the funeral preparations and gives
a eulogy of the dead man, and a new reference to the fifth *bolgia*
is fused with a transformation of the soul. The undertaker says to
his assistant:

>stay Scarmilion stay stay

which in line 105 of canto 21 is:

>posa, posa, Scarmiglione.

Then, with the line

>lay this Huysum on the box

Malacoda asks his assistant to lessen the pain of the closing of the
coffin by placing on it a painting of flowers. Jan van Huysum was
a painter of flowers in Holland in the eighteenth century. Finally
the word "imago" is used to replace the dead man:

>mind the imago it is he

The image of the deceased will remain in the mind of the narrator (and of the widow) long after the actual death. The perpetuation of the dead is thus assured, as the perpetuation of a
flower is assured in a painting.

The unreality of the human body, which might be considered
the theme behind the themes in "Malacoda," will continue to
obsess Beckett's mind. In most of his subsequent writings he
asks in various ways the same question: What can be saved from
this unreality? Is the artist the only one able to salvage something from this ambiguity of life leading to death, and of death
leading to life, to which Dante's poem testifies?

CANTO

22

The Barrators (Fifth *Bolgia*)

THE GROTESQUERIE of the sinners in the pitch continues in canto 22, when at the very beginning Dante compares Malacoda's signal (canto 21) to military signals the poet himself had witnessed in the battle of Campaldino (1289) where the Aretines were defeated by Florentine and Luccan troops.

Dante and Virgil move on with the ten demons:

Noi andavam con li dieci demoni [22:13]

The playful atmosphere is sustained and recreated by such a phrase as "in church with saints and in the tavern with guzzlers":

ne la chiesa
coi santi, e in taverna coi ghittoni. [22:14–15]

This statement by Dante indicates the involvement and the participation of all the figures present in the scene.

The third set of characters, the sinners in the pitch, now emerge more prominently. As their backs appear just above the surface, Danto compares them to dolphins joyously cavorting in the sea. Within the space of very few lines, Dante compares the grafters to dolphins (22:19), frogs (22:25–33), an otter (33:36), a mouse (22:58), and a wild duck (22:130).

If at first the sinners appear to be dolphins, as soon as the demon-leader Barbariccia approaches, the one who is called in line 94 *il gran proposto*, "the great marshall," the grafters all dive below quicker than a flash of lightning (22:24). It is then, with their snouts showing out of the pitch, that Dante compares

143

them to frogs at the edge of the water of a ditch that all dive
below at the approach of a stranger. The drama begins when one
sinner (one frog) remains above too long and is clawed out by the
demon called Graffiacane (scratch-dog). When he is held up on
Graffiacane's hook, he resembles an otter (*una lontra*, 22:36).

Dante is curious to know who he is and asks Virgil to inquire.
As the demon flays him, the barrator identifies himself as a
Navarrese. He is sometimes identified as Ciampolo, a man who
took to barratry in the service of King Thibault of Navarre. As he
speaks, another demon, Ciriatto, rips him with his tusk. The
scene becomes more savage as it becomes more complicated.

Ciampolo (if that is his name) says that he has left below in the
pitch Fra Gomita, an Italian barrator who was talking with Don
Michele Zanche. This man, a Sardinian friar, had indulged in the
sale of private offices and was hanged for his crime. Michele
Zanche may have been governor of Logodoro, a district on the
island of Sardinia. He was attached to Enzo, king of Sardinia, the
natural son of Frederick II, who was murdered by his son-in-law
Branca d'Oria (a figure who will appear in canto 33).

The first lie spoken in the *bolgia* of barratry was Malacoda's,
when he described a fallen bridge as one suitable for use in
crossing to the next *bolgia* (21:112–14). The second lie is that of
the barrator Ciampolo; it becomes the means by which he
escapes the claws of the demons bent on torturing him. If the
demons are willing to hide, he promises to whistle and call up
from below seven of his colleagues, Tuscans and Lombards, to
provide entertainment for the demons. He promises a new kind
of sport for them, a *nuovo ludo* (22:118).

This is the first time in the *Inferno* that we watch a sinner
performing the very sin that had assigned him his place in Hell.
When Ciampolo first speaks, we have to believe that he gives
truthful facts about his life. He then speaks a falsehood which is
believed, although the devil Alichino is suspicious of this plot
designed to trick the barrators. This hesitation on the part of
Alichino adds to the complexity of the ruse, in which the de-
ceivers are deceived and the demons of fraud are outwitted.

As soon as the demons hide, Ciampolo, who has been watching
for his chance, dives down out of sight in the pitch. Alichino flies
after him, but too late to catch him. The poet compares the
winged demon to a falcon diving through the air after a duck
(*anitra*, 22:130) that escapes. The defeated falcon returns up into
the higher air, angry. Calcabrina, furious at the trick that has

been perpetrated on the *Malebranche*, flies after Alichino. They collide over the pitch, claw each other, and finally drop down into the boiling pond. There they separate because of the heat, but they are unable to rise. The pitch has clogged their wings. Virgil and Dante leave the scene just as Barbariccia sends out four of the fiends with their hooks and rescue the limed pair.

This ending of canto 22 focuses on two escapes. We see one of the sinners eluding his tormentors by means of a lie. It is an example of fraud deceiving the punishers of fraud. And then we see the quiet, almost sly escape of the two travelers, who choose a moment when the demons are embroiled in their own quarrel.

The reader of cantos 21 and 22 follows the action, which is violent and slapstick, without always realizing that the four types of actors in this sadistic farce are four distinct comic types. The demons are coarse, realistically portrayed with their wings and hooks, and they are cruel. The barrators are endlessly terrified in their beglued state, and try endlessly to emerge from the pitch and at the same time to avoid the hooks of the demons. They are scorned and abused, comic in their resemblance to frogs and otters. Dante, in his extreme terror as he hides and shrinks, is comic too, comic against his will. Virgil, in very strong contrast with Dante, preserves his dignity, but we are able to smile at his seriousness as it is thrown against such a rich canvas of gothic demon-monstrousness. The comedy rises out of the swift moving action that combines all four types of characters.

For the tastes of some readers, the humor of these two cantos, including the first part of canto 23, is too elaborate and too sadistic. They may easily feel that the ethical keynote of the poem has been lost. As in a Fellini film where the monstrousness of a given scene may be so concentrated that it appears too detachable from the film as a whole, so here in the fifth *bolgia* Dante crowds horror on horror. It may be argued that the poet wishes to make clear that all sense of pity in him has disappeared. Dante's last moment of pious reverence among the damned was in the fourth bolgia, among the soothsayers, the moment preceding Virgil's *pietà* line. There is hardly any noble moment between the barratry *bolgia* and the tenth *bolgia*. In the eighth circle with Ulysses, and in the ninth circle with Ugolino, there is a sense of nobility in the sinner and a fleeting, almost subtle sense of pity in Dante.

Principal Signs and Symbols

1. The *military scene* (22:1–12) refers to the battle of Campaldino (1289), in which Dante had been present, and had seen the Guelfs (Florence) defeat the Ghibellines (Arezzo).

2. *With bells* (*con campane*, 22:7): each Italian city had a *carroccio* (war-chariot), serving as a rallying point in battle, provided with a bell.

3. *Of the good king Thibault* (*del buon re Tebaldo*, 22:52): this is Count Thibault V of Champagne, who was king of Navarre from 1253 to 1270.

4. *Latium* (22:65): Dante never uses the word "Italian," but speaks of Tuscans or Lombards (22:99) and others in the north and *Latini* (Latians) in the south.

5. The *second lie* of cantos 21 and 22 (22:97–132): we infer there is constant interplay of grotesque activity between demons and sinners in the fifth *bolgia*. Trickery and cruelty are prominent.

CANTO

23

Dante Rescued from the Fifth *Bolgia*
The Hypocrites (Sixth *Bolgia*)

THE FINALE to the drama of the demons unfolds during the first fifty-seven lines of the new canto. The two travelers walk one behind the other, silent and unaccompanied as if they were *frati minor* (23:3), that is, Franciscan monks in an attitude of humility. This solemn parade is in contrast to that of the ten demons (*i dieci demoni*) at the beginning (22:23) of canto 22. Because of what he has just witnessed, Dante is reminded of the fable of the mouse and the frog which is that of a deceiver caught by his own trick.

A mouse (*topo*) wants to cross a body of water. A frog (*rana*) suggests that they bind their legs together. Then once in the water, the frog begins to sink. But he is seen by a hawk who swoops down and carries off both mouse and frog. The Navarrese Ciampolo would correspond to the frog, Alichino to the mouse, and Calcabrina to the hawk. But no such exact comparison is satisfactory. The fable is not in Aesop, as Dante says, but many years after Dante's time it was put into French verse by La Fontaine, and appears in the fourth book of *Fables* (11).

This fable, once remembered, also brings to Dante's mind the danger that he and Virgil are in from the now irate *Malebranche*. Using the image of a mirror, Virgil says that his feelings are a perfect reflection of Dante's. He catches hold of Dante—like a mother who, waking up and finding the house on fire, seizes her son and escapes—rushes to the edge of the bank, and slides down the rocky slope into the sixth *bolgia* "more swift than water shooting through a spout to turn a mill-wheel" (23:96–97). At that moment the *Malebranche* reach the top of the bank but cannot go farther because they are confined to their own ditch.

And thus the comedy comes to a close, with the appropriately farcical action of Virgil clutching Dante and sliding on his back down a rock away from the devils. Here the grotesque almost becomes a caricature of itself. It is the kind of scene illustrating a medieval gothic bent in Dante that we associate with mystery plays, puppet shows, and Italian pantomime. The spirit of the episode is northern-teutonic, and not in the least classical. The name Calcabrina, for example, means "snow-trampler." Since barratry is political prostitution, one can easily draw a parallel between such scenes as those of the fifth *bolgia* and the fight for offices that took place so often between Guelfs and Ghibellines, and between *Neri* and *Bianchi*. Even Dante himself was accused of barratry when he held the offiice of prior of Florence.

When Dante and Virgil come in sight of the hypocrites of the sixth *bolgia*, we return to ethical characterization, to sentiments that arise out of the confusion of ethics and religion, and also to the recent history of Florence. A feeling of hatred stirred in Dante's heart in the third *bolgia* of the simonists. He wept out of a sense of pity as he watched the twisted heads of the soothsayers in the fourth *bolgia*. The terror he felt in the fifth *bolgia* is almost forgotten by the reader or almost dissolved in laughter over the trick of Ciampolo and the beglued wings of Calcabrina and Alichino.

But Dante's mood changes in the remaining ditches of the eighth circle. He begins now to feel less sympathy and less anger. As he describes what he sees, the pictures become clearer and more objective. By the time we reach the ninth circle, Dante's delineations have cooled down, appropriately, for the entrance into the realm of ice, and the poetry moves close to the style of mere reporting. The din and violence of the fifth *bolgia* tended to diminish the ethical emphasis. With the hypocrites the moral meaning of the poem recovers its urgency.

In Hell the hypocrites are known and recognized by their outward appearance. The skill with which they once kept their false natures turned toward the world is now gone. Here each of them groans under a heavy mantle of lead and moves slowly, laboriously. They are not important in the poem as hypocrites, but their condition is important because all their movements are impeded. No real progress, either physical or spiritual, is possible to them.

The opening line (23:58) is solemn, slow, and inspired by Scripture:

Là giù trovammo una gente dipinta
[there below we found a painted people]

This recalls the passage from Matthew 23:27: "Woe unto you, scribes and Pharisees, hypocrites! for ye are like unto whited sepulchres, which indeed appear beautiful outward, but are within full of dead men's bones, and of all uncleanness."

No monster guards the hypocrites and no element of nature punishes them. The symbolism is obviously in their appearance: the lead cloaks that cover them and the slowness of their gait. In the world they presented a false appearance. Their hypocrisy is of the religious sort, and the religious hypocrite pretends to be what he is not.

Religious hypocrisy is referred to in the opening passage, in which Dante points out the "deep hoods" (*cappucci bassi*, 23:61) on the cloaks of the sinners, similar to those worn by "monks in Cologne." Some editors read Cluny for Cologne, and believe the reference is to the Benedictine monks, well known for the elegance of the habit they wore. Outwardly the cloaks of Dante's hypocrites are gilded and shiny, but within they are of lead so heavy that Frederick's lead is straw by comparison (Frederick II punished traitors by having them placed in cloaks of lead which were then melted over a fire).

The brief description of the punishment is concluded in a striking slow line in which the "o" is a heavy prolonged sound:

O in eterno faticoso manto! [23:67]
[O weary mantle for eternity!]

The word "hypocrite" comes from the Greek word meaning "actor," a man who by profession affects virtues and vices he does not have. The fraud of the sixth *bolgia* is the pretence to goodness.

Dante, as usual, is eager to speak with the sinners and discover one he might recognize. Two of the sinners, who, because of Dante's Tuscan dialect seem intent upon speaking, are surprised that Dante, by the action of his throat (*a l'atto de la gola*, 23:88), appears to be a living man. One of the two asks him who he is, and Dante's answer states his birthplace as Florence. Dante acknowledges he is still alive:

I' fui nato e cresciuto
sovra '1 bel fiume d'Arno a la gran villa,
e son col corpo ch'i' ho sempre avuto. [23:
[I was born and grew
on Arno's beautiful river in the great city
and I am with the body I have always had.]

In answer, the two spirits identify themselves as "jovial friars
and Bolognese" (*Frati godenti . . . e Bolognesi*, 23:103) named
Catalano and Loderingo. Dante would have been familiar with
the peace-making effort these two men represented. The Order
of the *Cavalieri di Beata Santa Maria* or *Frati Gaudenti*, as they
were called, was founded in Bologna in 1261, for the reconciliation of enemies and for the protection of the weak and poor. The
rules were so liberal, and the organization so poorly run, that the
members were called "Jovial Friars." Catalano, a Guelf, and
Loderingo, a Ghibelline, were jointly elected to the office of
Podestà (mayor) of Florence, in order to help reconcile the two
political parties. In their speech to Dante the friars refer to the
Gardingo (23:108), the name given to the part of Florence around
the Palazzo Vecchio where the palace of the Uberti family, leaders of the Florentine Ghibelline party, was destroyed in 1266.

Dante begins to speak (*O frati, i vostri mali . . .*) (Oh friars,
your woes' 23:109), but he breaks off because of a strange spectacle. He sees the shade of the crucified Caiaphas upon the ground.
The other hypocrites are obliged to trample him under foot.
Caiaphas, the high priest of the Jews who is associated with the
crucifixion of Christ, is crucified in Hell and bears the weight of
all the hypocrisy of that region. The punishment is an extreme
example in the *Inferno* of retaliation. The moral or tropological
meaning of the spectacle is clearly indicated. Caiaphas is the
type of man who sacrifices his inner truth for expediency, thus he
is exiled from truth and condemned to suffering. In John 11,
Caiaphas states that it is better for a man to die than for an entire
nation to be destroyed. Other council members, including
Annas, Caiaphas' father-in-law (23:121) suffer in the same way in
the sixth *bolgia*. These men are both hypocrites and evil coun-
celors. Virgil's amazement is best explained by the unusual nature of the retaliation in this awesome picture of crucifixion.

Virgil, when he sees that no unbroken bridge exists, realizes
Malacoda's lie, and thus the action of the fifth *bolgia* and that of
the sixth come to an end in the same passage. Dante is here

pointing out the close relationship between barratry and hypocrisy, calling the devil, in the words of the friar, "the father of all lies" (*padre di menzogna*, 23:144). Malacoda and the *Malebranche* deceived Virgil and Dante. The Navarrese Ciampolo deceived the *Malebranche* by saying he would call up new sinners out of the pitch to be tormented by the demons. And finally, the sin of hypocrisy is presented as being the reflection of all deceptions and all lies.

The heavy monotony of the hypocrites, their sad weariness and their slow gait, are in strong contrast to the comedy of action in the barratry *bolge*. We remember the earlier contrast between the "noble castle" (*nobile castello*, 4;106) of the great spirits in limbo and the winds of the second circle where the *lussuriosi* are punished. The *Inferno* contains more differences of tone and movement than either the *Purgatorio* or the *Paradiso*. Even if in Dante's scheme hypocrites are more sinful than pimps, seducers, simonists, magicians, and barrators, Dante does not manifest any scorn in the sixth *bolgia*. He, as the traveler, seems to reflect some of the fatigue and melancholy of the canto. When the sinners ask Dante to tell them who he is, they use the same phrase that Farinata did in the tenth canto: *O Tosco* (23:91; 10:22), but the tone in which they speak is more prayerful than Farinata's was, and Dante immediately thinks of Florence and the Arno.

The main tone of this canto is audible in the adjective "sad," as it applies to the hypocrites, *ipocriti tristi* (23:92) recalling the passage in Matthew 6:16: "When ye fast, be not, as the hypocrites, of a sad countenance: for they disfigure their faces that they may appear unto men to fast."

If memories of Florence fill Dante's heart at the end of the canto, Virgil, leading the way out of the sixth *bolgia*, shows anger on his face. *Ira* (23:146) is a strong word, and Virgil reveals this sign of indignation somewhat unexpectedly. A devil has duped him, and now a hypocrite has just pointed out the trick and set him right. Does his anger stem from a sense of weakness? Has he forgotten the divine protection promised him in his role of guide?

Principal Signs and Symbols

1. *The Franciscans* (*frati minor*, 23:3) walk in a single file almost as the hypocrites will walk later in the canto. The clothing of the hypocrites is like that of monks.

2. *The monks in Cologne* (*Li monaci in Cologna*, 23:63): (some editors believe Cologne is Cluny) were famous for the elegance and fullness of their robes.

3. *Leaden cloaks* (gilded without, 23:64–65): the hypocrites make a brilliant show. "Hypocrite" comes from the Greek *hypokrinesthai*, "to answer" or "act on the stage."

4. *Catalano de' Malavolti* and *Loderingo degli Andalò* (23:103–8): both from Bologna, were elected jointly to the office of mayor (*podestà*) in Florence. Their brief term of office was characterized by an anti-Ghibelline rising in which the palaces of the Uberti, in the Gardingo, were burned.

5. *Caiaphas:* high priest and one of the evil counselors who judged Christ. Dante calls them "the seed of evil for all Jews" in line 123:

che fu per li Giudei mala sementa.

CANTO

24

The Difficulty in Reaching the Seventh *Bolgia*
The Thieves: Vanni Fucci

THE SEVENTH DITCH of *Malebolge,* in which thieves are punished, is described in cantos 24 and 25. Taken together, the two cantos display a unity of action and thought. The drama in them that unfolds before Virgil and Dante is so spectacular that it may remind us of the struggle between the barrators and the demons. But in the seventh *bolgia* the sinners are continually changed into serpents and then changed again into human form. The thieves of the *Inferno* are thus related to Satan, the serpent whose first great act of thievery in the Garden of Eden precipitated the Fall.

In Genesis we read: "The Serpent was more subtle than any beast of the field." The Latin word *subtilis* means "finely woven," or, by extension, "ingenious." It is an important adjective, and designates Satan as the perpetrator of the original fraud by which the race of man lost its innocence. To this biblical reference Dante adds a description of the serpent lands of Africa: Libya, the lands near the Red Sea, Ethiopia, and Arabia (24:85). The five types of reptilian monsters listed in lines 85–87 are in the ninth book of Lucan's *Pharsalia:* chelydri, jaculi, pareae, cenchres, amphisbaena. Some of their characteristics used by Dante were first described by Lucan. We remember that in canto 4 Lucan is for Dante one of the leading poets of the world.

Dante's picture of the thieves is dominated by the principle of transformation, and here the source unquestionably is the fourth book of Ovid's *Metamorphoses.* In this *bolgia* of the thieves Hebraic and classical souces are beautifully fused.

153

The main action of canto 24 is preceded by an unusually long prelude (24:1–60). It is a striking passage in itself, but commentators tend to ask whether it is connected closely enough to the drama that follows to justify its length. The first part of the prelude is a prolonged simile occupying seven tercets (lines 1–21). The personal terrors Dante has just experienced are maintained by Virgil's expression of anger and bewilderment. But change takes place in Virgil when he reaches the shattered bridge. His face changes then, and the look of serenity on it (*quel piglio / dolce*, 24:20–21) reminds Dante of Virgil's sudden appearance at the foot of the mountain in canto 1. The word *così*, "thus," in line 16, that announces the simile comes at the end of the picture of a countryside in early spring covered with frost which, when the peasant (*lo villanello*) sees it in the early morning, is discouraged, and goes back into his house. A few minutes later, on his return outside, he finds that the surface of the earth has changed. It is no longer white with frost. He takes up his staff and chases his lambs out into the fields.

Despite its length and elaborateness, there is a notable connection between the seasonal change in the country scene and the sudden transformation we are to see in the forms of the thieves. The simile of the melting frost is the preparation for the canto's action, and it also serves to underscore the change of attitude in the two poets.

There are several examples of "equivocal rhyme" in the passage, two words spelled the same, that rhyme with each other, have different meanings, and that seem to represent a metamorphosis: *che si faccia*, in line 11, for example (*faccia* comes from *fare*, "to do"), and *aver cangiata faccia*, in line 13 (*faccia* here means "face").

The second part of the prelude (24:22–60) is the arduous climb from the bottom of the sixth *bolgia* to the arch of the seventh. Virgil takes Dante from behind and pushes him up the ascent, urging Dante to throw off all weakness. He exhorts him by saying that only by exertion can a man deserve renown (*fama*, 24:48). When Virgil states in line 55 that "steeper stairs will have to be climbed,"

Più lunga scala convien che si saglia

he may be referring to the ascent up Lucifer's legs (canto 34) or even to the steep ascent to Purgatory. Before Dante can be reunited with Beatrice, an active work of purgation will have to be accomplished. The necessary moral effort implicit in the entire *Divina Commedia* is here restated, and Dante is heartened by his leader's words, as he says to Virgil:

Va, ch'i' son forte e ardito. [24:60]
[Go on, for I am strong and confident.]

The two poets make their way up the cliff, and, once on the ridge of the arch, they can look down into the darkness of the *bolgia*. It is a vast den of serpents where terrified sinners run about naked. Before the poet describes the spectacle of the thieves, he refers to the three great deserts which surround Egypt: Libya, Ethiopia, and Arabia.

Dante sees thieves with their hands bound behind them with snakes as if they were cords, or knotted in front. The distinctive characteristic of the *bolgia* is in this first picture: men and serpents are one, and yet they are two. Because of its flexibility (its "subtlety"), the serpent can bend itself into many forms. Dante in his vision and interpretation is saying that the thief also is serpentine—both externally and internally.

Beginning with line 97, two fairly distinct acts unfold before the eyes of Virgil and Dante. Each act has specific characters, and each one is divided into three stages.

In stage 1 (24:97–120) we see a serpent spring on a thief and transfix him at his neck. The spirit takes fire and drops down into ashes. The ashes then reunite and the body assumes its former shape. Immediately Dante introduces a comparison with the phoenix (*la fenice*, 24:107), the oriental symbol of immortality in which the body, when it vanishes, is remade by the soul. The entire *Commedia* is based on the belief that the soul is never annihilated, and after death takes on a new body. At this particular point in the *Inferno*, coming so soon after the caricature of the crucifixion in the presentation of Caiaphas, the phoenix appears as a travesty of the resurrection.

The phoenix is alluded to by many classical and medieval writers. Undoubtedly Dante drew upon the fifteenth book of Ovid's *Metamorphoses* for the story. In its five-hundredth year the phoenix builds its nest with the branches, roots, and leaves of aromatic plants, such as spikenard and myrrh. Then, covering itself with these, it turns to the rays of the sun, and flaps its wings so vigorously that it kindles its nest, in such a way that the bird is consumed.

Before we learn the name of the thief, Dante describes the

bewilderment he feels at the painful metamorphosis he has watched. At the same time he marvels at the power of God (*O potenza di Dio*, 24:119) that has ordained such an act of punishment. When Virgil asks the spirit his name, he replies:

Io piovvi di Toscana [24:122]
[I rained from Tuscany]

and forthrightly calls himself a beast, and names his city, Pistoia, "A fitting den for myself":

Pistoia mi fu degna tana [24:126]

The last part of the canto (24:127–51) is a moving clash of personalities between Dante and the thief Vanni Fucci. Dante had known him as "a man of blood and rage," and urges his guide to find out the specific sin that caused him to be plunged ("rained") into the seventh *bolgia*. The depth of the ditch, indicating the seriousness of the sin, is emphasized in the story of Vanni Fucci. He is pained at being found in Hell by Dante, and he sets about to pain Dante with the dismal news of future Florentine politics.

Vanni Fucci robbed the church of San Zeno of its sacred furniture. He is a leading example of a sinner who is not contrite, who shows no trace of repentance and whose suffering in Hell increases his bitterness. He was a Black Guelf from Pistoia who hated Dante, a White Guelf from Tuscany. The canto ends with Vanni's prophecy. The *Neri* (or Blacks) with be expelled from Pistoia, and the *Bianchi* (or Whites) will be driven from Florence. "Piceno's field" (*campo Piceno*, 24:148) is probably the battle in which the *Neri* of Florence and Lucca, under the command of Moroëllo Malaspina (the "stack of vapor"), Lord of Lumigiana in the Valdimigra, captured the *Bianchi* of Serravalle.

The action of the violent and fraudulent Vanni Fucci continues in the next canto.

Principal Signs and Symbols

1. *The youthful year* (*il giovanetto anno*, 24:1): the long introduction (24:1–18) describes the change from winter to spring, and aptly serves as a preparation for the metamorphoses of the thieves in this canto and in canto 25. Both Dante and Virgil also

undergo a change as they recover from terror (Dante) and Malacoda's lie (Virgil).

2. *At the foot of the mountain* (*a piè del monte*, 24:21): a reference to canto 1.

3. *A longer ladder must be climbed* (*più lunga scala convien che si saglia*, 24:55): the stairway or ladder image may refer to Lucifer's legs (canto 34) or the steep ascent to Purgatory, or even, here, the spur of rock between two *bolge*.

4. *Heliotrope* (*elitropia*, 24:93): here, a stone which had the power of making its wearer invisible.

5. *The phoenix* (*la fenice*, 24:107): its characteristics were described by Ovid and Brunetto Latini. Dante compares the metamorphosis of the phoenix to that of Vanni Fucci, a Black Guelf from Pistoia who stole a church treasure.

6. *Pistoia* (24:126): thought of as the birthplace of the feud between the Blacks and Whites.

7. *Thieves* (*ladri*) the word thief (*ladro*) is not used until line 6 of canto 25. Dante emphasizes the similarity between a serpent and a thief. Because the thief steals another man's goods, here in the seventh ditch he is robbed of his appearance.

CANTO

25

The Thieves (Seventh *Bolgia*)

AFTER WE SENSE the violence of Vanni Fucci's temperament, and after learning of the violence of his thievery, we witness at the beginning of canto 25 an act of violence which he directs at God. He shapes his fists into figs and raises them to God:

> Togli, Dio, ch'a te le squadro! [25:3]
> [Take them, God, for I aim them at you!]

The curse is as deliberately vulgar as the spirit could make it. Whereas *il fico* is the word for "fig" in Italian, *la fica* (pl. *le fiche*, used in the line), is an obscene term for the vagina. The gesture is especially familiar in southern Europe. The thumb, placed between the first two fingers, is intended to mimic the sexual act.

In this spectacle of invective against God, Vanni Fucci, on the score of violence, is comparable to Capaneus, who appeared in the third *girone* of the seventh circle. He is the third example of excessive pride in the *Inferno*. The first, Farinata, in canto 10, desplays a sullen kind of haughtiness as he rises above his burning tomb. Capaneus, in canto 14, continues to jeer and hurl defiant cries at God. Vanni Fucci, in cantos 24 and 25, distinguishes himself by his obscenity. Dante himself, in lines 13–15, called Vanni Fucci the proudest spirit he has encountered, prouder even than Capaneus.

At the end of the curse, one snake coils about the sinner's neck, and a second snake ties his arms together and rivets him in front. The action of the first snake stops the speech of Vanni Fucci, and the action of the second puts an end to his gestures. Dante's

159

reaction to this assault of the snakes is one of relief. He now looks upon the serpents as his friends: *mi fuor le serpi amiche* (25:4). As the poet castigates Pistoia, he speaks of the city's "evil seed," or criminal ancestry, which is probably a reference to the legend that Pistoia was founded by the remnants of Cataline's army.

As Vanni Fucci flees from the immediate scene, he is pursued by Cacus, called here a centaur, but who was in Greek mythology a monster-giant noted for his thefts of Hercules' oxen. In Virgil's poem, Cacus is called "semihuman," and this may have suggested to Dante the image of a centaur. Other centaurs, called here "brethren of Cacus," serve as guards in the first *girone* of the seventh circle (canto 12). To his crime of bloodshed, Cacus added theft, and is thus placed here in the seventh *bolgia*. As he rushes by, Dante sees that the horse-part of him, his haunch, is covered with snakes, and a fire-spitting dragon hangs over his shoulders. It is implied that Cacus will follow Vanni Fucci, and when the contact is made, the sinner will again fall to ashes, dying and yet unable to die.

Thus Cacus serves here as an example of both sinner and punisher. The large number of snakes on the back of Cacus reminds Dante of a region near the sea, Maremma (25:19, a corruption of *maritima*). This low-lying part of Tuscany was once infested with snakes.

After the Vanni Fucci episode, Dante observes during the rest of the canto (25:34–151) a far more complex drama of transformations. Five Florentine nobles figure in the scene. With some difficulty Dante discovers their names. Three of them appear first in human form, and two appear already changed into reptiles.

The three spirits (*tre spiriti*, 25:35) are Agnello dei Brunelleschi, of a Ghibelline family, Buoso degli Abati (later mentioned in canto 30) and Puccio Sciancato (the "lame") dei Galigai (named in line 148). The *serpente of* line 50 is Cianfa dei Donati, who merges with Agnello. The *serpentello* of line 83 is Francesco dei Cavalcanti who takes on Buoso's human shape, while Buoso turns into a serpent.

At the beginning of the passage, Dante uses three successive similes to explain the snake-drama in which the sinners fuse with another form and thus undo themselves: "ivy" (*ellera*, 25:58), rooted to oak; "hot wax" (*calda cera*, 25:61) that sticks; and "paper" (*lo papiro*, 25:65) that changes color when it burns. In life these thieves made no distinction between what was theirs and what was someone else's, and therefore in Hell they cannot call their bodies or their personalities their own. The canto is a parody of that type of change through which a body fluctuates and is lost.

In a slightly boastful way, Dante compares this art of reciprocal transformation (a man becoming a snake and a snake becoming a man) with the more simple art of Lucan (*Pharasalia*, book 9) and Ovid (*Metamorphoses*, book 4) in which a one-way transformation is described. Dante is shocked by what he sees, and there is some confusion—deliberately planned, it seems—over the identity of the Florentine thieves. Only one of the original three thieves, Puccio Sciancato, does not assume a new shape. A Ghibelline of the Galigai family, he was exiled from Florence in 1268.

The last line of the canto refers to Francesco dei Cavalcanti, who was killed by the inhabitants of Gaville, a village in the upper Arno valley. Gaville mourns, says Dante, because its inhabitants were slain in revenge by the Cavalcanti family.

If, in the barrators' *bolgia*, the grotesque dominates, here with the thieves the drama is pushed to the repulsive. The oldest existing illustrations of the *Inferno* are by Botticelli, and these, in their faithfulness to the text, emphasize the repulsiveness of the punishment.

Roman law, which Dante doubtless had in mind as he composed this canto, distinguishes three species of theft. The most serious is the stealing of sacred things, which is different from the theft of secular objects. Vanni Fucci, who robbed holy things from a sacristy (probably jewels and furniture), is the offender in this category. The next most serious act is the theft of public property, for which Cianfa and Agnello were accused. The last category is the theft of privately owned objects and property.

The city of Florence figures strongly in canto 25. The dominant image of change and interchange accentuates the central temptation and perversion of the city. Without our being aware of it, we accept Florence, through its forceful reiteration throughout the *Divine Comedy*, not only as a literal city in Tuscany, the birthplace of Dante Alighieri, but also as the microcosm of the Empire. The moral meaning of the city is strongly apparent in all the cantos in which Florence figures, because the city can survive only if the moral code is defended and protected and followed. The five Florentines of canto 25 are in Hell precisely because of their infidelity to the moral life of the city. And finally, in this fourfold interpretation, Florence is anagogical in its spiritual relationship to the Divine City, the City of God.

The deep pitlike setting of the seventh *bolgia*, its many

characters, and the extraordinary metamorphoses which take place there, vividly illustrate the life of the poem that Dante recreates over and over. Human pathos and suffering are embodied in the characters of the various scenes, but also in the travelers who descend from circle to circle. In cantos 24 and 25, Virgil's reaction to the thieves is not stressed, but Dante's reaction is important. In many different ways Dante reacts through the poem to the reality of God's punishment. Whereas he did not endorse Francesca's punishment, here he does endorse the serpents and calls them his friends.

At times he is emotionally drawn into the life of the lost souls: in cantos 5 (Francesca), 10 (Farinata), 13 (Pier della Vigna), 15 (Brunetto Latini), 26 (Ulysses), and such moments in the poem are movingly remembered. But with the thieves, at the end of canto 25 (lines 142–44), he seems to apologize for the writing of his work:

> e qui mi scusi
> la novità se fior la penna abborra.
> [and here let the novelty
> excuse me, if my pen wanders a bit]

In the words immediately preceding these lines, and joined with them, Dante has succinctly described the entire scene:

> Così vid'io la settima zavorra
> mutar e trasmutare [25:142–43]
> [thus I saw the seventh ballast
> change and rechange]

This word *zavorra*, meaning "ballast" or "cargo," which helps to steady a ship, is a prelude to the imagery of the sea and to Ulysses' ship in the next canto.

The substance of canto 25 emerges from the change of man into a snake, and this metamorphosis is closely related to the sin of thieving. We observe thieves stealing their shape from one another, and we realize this act of stealing is also the punishment. The canto is a brilliant example of *contrapasso* or retaliation. In life these men were rebels against the institution of property. We have to infer that they stole less from a love of money than from a hatred of the law. This hatred would explain the bestial nature of the thief which Dante wants us to feel. The incredible and the horrible aspects of the sin are thus made more visible.

In the long passage in which Buoso and Francesco exchange bodies (25:91–138), Dante's manner of speech is that of a story-teller, bent on holding and horrifying his reader. He is almost pretending to be immune to the sin and its punishment. It is a report of what he sees and differs from passages in which he is emotionally involved. The mood of this canto offended Goethe and Manzoni, who found it to be the expression of fanaticism rather than of ethical hatred.

Principal Signs and Symbols

1. *Pistoia* (25:10–12): a city possibly founded by remnants of Cataline's army.

2. *He who fell at Thebes down from the walls* (*quel che cade a Tebe giù da' muri*, 25:15): this reference is to Capaneus (see canto 14). Capaneus and Vanni Fucci both continue to blaspheme God in Hell.

3. *Maremma* (25:19–20): a swamp on the coast of Tuscany, infested with snakes.

4. *Cacus* (25:25): here described as a centaur. He was a monster living in a cave beneath Mount Aventino, a famous thief of the region.

5. The five Florentines punished in this circle are:

(a) *Agnello* (of the Brunelleschi family, a Ghibelline). He appears as a man and merges with Cianfa.

(b) *Buoso degli Abati* (possibly *Buoso dei Donati*). He appears as a man and changes shape with Francesco de' Cavalcanti.

(c) *Puccio dei Galigai*, called the "lame" (*Sciancato.*) He does not change.

(d) *Francesco de' Cavalcanti*, who takes on Buoso's shape after he appears first as a four-legged lizard.

(e) *Cianfa de' Donati*, a six-legged monster who is merged with Agnello.

CANTO

26

The Evil Counselors: Ulysses and Diomedes
(Eighth *Bolgia*)

WHEREAS CANTO 25 closes on a quiet note with the identification of the fifth Florentine thief, canto 26 opens with a cry, an ironic salute to Florence:

> Godi, Fiorenza
> [Be joyful, Florence]

It is the invective, or rather the reproach of a man who loves his city and knows that the city is doomed. He sees the city in the form of a bird spreading its wings over sea and land and spreading its name through all of Hell. It is an ironic image of the city's greatness. Dante's voice speaks the opening tercet in an outburst that is high and loud. In this context, Florence prefigures the appearance of Lucifer's wings in canto 34, and more immediately announces Ulysses' mad flight over the sea in which the oars of the boat appear as wings:

> de' remi facemmo ali al folle volo [26:125]
> [of oars we made wings for the foolish flight]

This opening image, related to the vast space of the sea and the vastness of the navigator's ambition, sustains the entire canto. And it also announces, even in the opening tercet, the tragedy of this ambition whereby the name of Florence is seen to plunge through all of Hell (*per lo 'inferno*, 26:3).

Then, without any transition, Dante gathers up the movement of greatness and breadth, combines it with the tragedy of the five thieves of Florence he has just left, and directs it toward himself:

"shame comes to me" (*mi vien vergogna,* 26:5). This is one of the five or six cantos of the *Inferno* in which Dante's personal feelings are strongest. Nowhere in his writings is his relationship to Florence more movingly stated.

The reference in this early passage to Prato and to what seems to be a prophesied curse on the city is not totally clear. Pope Benedict XI sent Cardinal Nicholas of Prato to Florence in 1304 for the purpose of reconciling the opposing political factions. Unsuccessful in his endeavor, he placed a curse on the city, and various disasters happening to the city shortly thereafter were attributed to the curse of the Church. Another interpretation sees Prato, a small Tuscan town, as representing several towns which were soon to rebel against Florentine rule.

This introduction to the big scenes of the eighth *bolgia* is devoted to an elaborate analysis of Dante's feelings: his love for Florence and his shame over the waywardness of his city. Virgil serves merely as guide at this point, helping Dante physically by pulling him up over the stone stairs. When the poet came into full sight of the *bolgia,* he was overcome by sorrow, which still sweeps over him in waves when he remembers the scene:

> Allor mi dolsi e ora mi ridolgio [26:19]
> [then I sorrowed, and now I sorrow again]

What he sees taxes his power to describe: a tableau of fireflies such as a peasant can see in his valley in the summer at twilight.

This simile refers to the flames of the eighth *bolgia,* and each flame conceals an evil counselor. Since their tongues spoke deceit when they were men on the earth, a flame is the only tongue they have now. Dante calls to mind the Old Testament story of Elisha, who saw Elijah carried up to heaven in a chariot of fire and who was made fun of by children. As a punishment for this mockery, the children were devoured by bears (2 Kings 2.) The flames are so numerous, and the sight so overwhelming, that Dante has to hold on to a rock to avoid collapsing. Virgil explains that the spirits are within the flames.

> catun si fascia di quel ch'elli è inceso. [26:48]
> [each one swathes himself with that which burns him]

One of the flames appears divided, and Dante asks the question that by now we have come to expect: "Who is in that fire?" Its divided form reminds the poet of the funeral pyre of Eteocles and Polynices, the two sons of Oedipus. Virgil answers: "Ulysses and Diomedes." With this discovery we move into the story of the foremost evil counselor in Dante's poem and the narrative of his death.

In line 63 the Palladium is referred to as being the secret source (in Ulysses' case) of the sin punished in the eighth *bolgia*. The Palladium was the sacred statue of the goddess Athena, which, as long as it remained in Troy, guaranteed the safety of the city. Ulysses and Diomedes stole it, and this theft led to the victory of the Greeks over the Trojans. The wooden horse, constructed by the Greeks outside the city of Troy, and offered to the city, was the pretended atonement for the Palladium.

Dante's eagerness to talk with Ulysses is explained by his belief that the fall of Troy was directly connected with the founding of Italy. This would also be in the mind of Virgil. Ulysses was, of course, the central figure in the Trojan War, and Diomedes, another major figure, was closely associated with the exploits of Ulysses. The ambush of the horse (*l'agguato del caval*, 26:59), the most famous of the deceits and evil counsels of Ulysses, was in Dante's words the "doom by which the noble seed of the Romans came forth" (26:58–59). The fall of Troy led to the journey of Aeneas and his followers ("noble seed"), which was undertaken in order to establish a new nation in Italy, destined to become the heart of the Roman Empire.

Dante insists on his fervent desire to speak with Ulysses, but Virgil, while applauding Dante's desire, comes to the forefront in the action of the canto and initiates the dialogue by saying that since Ulysses and Diomedes were Greek, they might scorn the speech of the Italian poet. So Virgil, author of the *Aeneid*, asks Ulysses the leading question concerning where and how he died. It might, of course, be argued that Dante had as much claim as Virgil in this encounter. He was a descendent of the Romans, and the Romans were the offspring of Aeneas, and therefore belonged to the lineage of Troy. Since Ulysses and Diomedes were the conquerors of Troy, the confrontation is highly dramatic and deserves the long introduction.

Thus Virgil says: "let me speak" (*Lascia parlare a me*, 26:73), and Dante tells us: "I heard him speak *in questa forma*" (26:78), a phrase usually translated "in this manner." The phrase may be more meaningfully construed as "with this form of words," or "with this formula." Virgil, after all, is on a heaven-appointed mission, and Dante may be using the word *forma* as synonymous with "conjuration." Theologically, Virgil is in favor with God, although he is not in the grace of Christ. In framing his question, Virgil refers to the "high verses" he wrote (*li alti versi,* 26:82), thereby reminding Ulysses and Diomedes of his merit in sustaining the memory of them in the world of men.

It is just past the middle of the canto when "the greater horn of the ancient flame began to shake itself" (26:85–86) and speak. The voice of Ulysses plunges immediately into a narrative which is best described as a myth. Traditionally, a myth is a story that joins thought with vision, and thus brings about a correspondence between the mental or intellectual apparatus and the world of the senses. It is a natural and familiar operation of the human mind, and in its highest forms is both philosophical and poetic. It bears relationship with all forms of art because it is willed and controlled by the creative spirit.

The modern writer tends to begin with an idea or a concept for which he then discovers an image or a myth. Albert Camus, for example, began with the idea of the vanity or absurdity of human effort, and then used as illustration the myth of Sisyphus and his rock in Hell. André Gide, in order to convey one of his basic precepts, made use of the parable of the prodigal son. Mallarmé, in one of his sonnets on the subject of poetic impotence, describes a swan whose wings are caught in a frozen lake.

Dante as the type of older writer usually begins with the figure or the image or the myth, and then discovers behind it the idea. Beatrice is first a Florentine girl, and only later becomes synonymous with love and salvation. Virgil is in the first canto the great Latin poet, and then in subsequent cantos gradually grows into the example of guide and human wisdom. Ulysses, king of Ithaca and conqueror of Troy, becomes for Dante the ambitious explorer-navigator whose odyssey was not a homecoming.

In the epics of Homer, Odysseus (Ulysses) is the warrior, a wise, courageous man, resourceful and skillful, whose elaborate deceits are made to appear masterly. Dante inherited more immediately the medieval picture of Ulysses, taken from the writings of Virgil and another Latin poet of the first century, Statius. Here is the warrior, successful in combat because of his lies, deceit, and cunning. He is the navigator in search of adventures rather than the husband and father impatient to return home.

In the eighth *bolgia,* Ulysses and Diomedes are one flame

because they were united in life in their exploits and in the practice of deceptions. Thus they are forever united in their punishment. Dante is eager to learn the manner of Ulysses' death. Homer, Virgil, and Statius make no mention of Ulysses' death. In the usual narrative, he returns to Ithaca after his adventures and there the story leaves him in the midst of his family. What we read in the second half of canto 26 is doubtless the invention of the Italian poet.

Ulysses speaks first of his appetite for knowledge. His eagerness to learn is made to appear universal, heroic, and even inhuman. This hero is not held back by any of the more human ties: love for his son Telemachus, reverence for his aged father Laertes, or conjugal love for Penelope. His "ardor" is his overwhelming desire to learn of human vices and human worth. Dante translated the central drive in his Ulysses with this word, *ardore*, which also connotes the flame of punishment. So, rather than turning toward Ithaca, Ulysses turns his boat toward the deep open sea:

> ma misi me per l'alto mare aperto [26:100]
> [but I put forth on the deep open sea]

Ulysses and his small band of men sail past Spain, Morocco, Sardinia, and finally the pillars of Hercules, which we call the Straits of Gibraltar, and which was regarded as the western limit of the habitable world.

In the words Ulysses addresses to his men, he is made to appear as an evil counselor, urging them to learn with him more of the world than is allowed to be known. This immense tragedy Dante tells in thirteen lines (26:130–42). After five months of navigation on the great ocean (*alto passo*, which might be translated as "highway of the deep," 26:132), Ulysses and his crew sighted land. It appeared as a mountain, dark in the distance. The men were gladdened by such a promise, but immediately a tempest rose up from the land, whirled the ship around three times, and then drew it down, prow first, "as it pleased Another" (*com' altrui piacque*) until the sea closed over it.

Behind the tragedy of the whirlwind scene is the tragedy of Ulysses, adventurer of knowledge, a Faustian character, having the courage of the most intrepid voyagers. Dante's Ulysses saw what no man had seen. The same thought is expressed in Rimbaud's poem on the sea, *Le bateau ivre*":

J'ai vu ce que l'homme a cru voir.
[I saw what man believed he saw.]

This thirst for knowledge makes Ulysses into a heroic figure for our age, but Ulysses was punished by God, the "other" designated by the word *altrui*. Dante is Ulysses in this canto, aspiring to know the life of the other world, and in a sense, Dante is punishing himself for writing such a poem as the *Inferno*. It is forbidden for human eyes to see the mountain of Purgatory. That in itself would be a sign that Dante is condemning a part of himself. In the figure of Ulysses he presents a man whose thirst for knowledge exceeded his love for his family and his duty to his people and city.

After the sinking of Ulysses' boat, the sea stretches out again flat and peaceful. This is one of the many water images in the *Inferno*. Does this cool liquid image, this voyage of Ulysses with its salt breath of the open sea, tell us something about sin? Ulysses is presented to us here as a counselor of madness, of human folly. He uses his mind in order to undo the minds of other men concerning some important issue. Dante is deliberately transforming the Greek legend of Ulysses. We should not forget that Dante had the Roman prejudice against Greece in its conflict with Troy. Aeneas was Virgil's hero, and Aeneas was Trojan. Because of Dante's loyalty to Virgil, Aeneas remained a protoype for Dante. The Christian poet in canto 26, as he has already done on so many occasions, sets about to demonize a famous figure, in this case the hero of Greek cunning.

Dante's reconstruction of the end of the *Odyssey* would seem to indicate that he believed the Greek world ended with the beginning of the Christian world. Ulysses and his men, just prior to their death, receive a sign of redemption in the sight of a distant mountain—a moment of hope, followed by tragedy, similar to the moment when Moses approached the Promised Land and yet was unable to enter it.

For Dante, Ulysses was the plotter and intriguer who enjoyed this activity for its own sake. He turned Machiavellianism into a fine art. Ulysses' audacity is judged as sinful, and here Dante follows the Church in teaching that there are limits to human knowledge, that modesty and humility are more to be praised than knowledge, or at least a vain exhibition of knowledge. The *turbo* ("whirlwind") in canto 26 is presented as a force of nature carrying out God's decree. And yet the passage is not without a

hint of Dante's admiration for the greatness of Ulysses' attitude
and understanding. He condemns in a doctrinal sense, but his
personal feelings of sympathy for the sinner are also in evidence.

Theologically, he is concerned with the intellect's boundless
appetite. Because of false counsel, the spirits in the eighth *bolgia*
"have lost the good of the intellect" (*hanno perduto il ben de
l'intelletto*, 3:18). Dante here forcibly reminds us that the world
is not governed by the human mind, but by the unknowable
mind of God. The spirit of Ulysses, wrapped in a flame for all
eternity, is isolated from all that surrounds him, as Ulysses the
daring navigator fell out of touch with all intimate human relationships.

The central word is "the tongue," *la lingua*, spoken by Virgil
when he says to Dante,

> ma fa che la tua lingua si sostegna. [26:72]
> [but see that your tongue refrain]

On the literal level, it refers to Dante's impatient speech. Behind
the *lingua* is the argumentative speech of Ulysses that convinced
his men to accompany him on his mad mission. And visually, of
course, it is the tongue of fire, the flame enveloping the spirit.

Francesca's lust in the second circle was that of the senses, and
Ulysses' lust in the eighth circle is that of the intellect. Both the
woman and the man speak of their lust as moving toward a climax
and a catastrophe. Dante's moods, which change four or five
times during canto 26, are behind this story of catastrophe. His
anger over Florence in the first line of the canto turns to grief, a
feeling the shame for his city. Then with the image of the
valley sparkling with fireflies, the mood is one of pastoral serenity. This gives way to excitement over the possibility of hearing
Ulysses, and finally, we come to understand Dante's attitude of
total receptiveness at the end of the canto as he listens to the
words of Ulysses.

The image of the mountain seen by Ulysses and his men is a
link between the *Inferno* and the *Paradiso*. In canto 27 of the
Paradiso, Beatrice recalls Ulysses' voyage with the phrase "*il
varco folle d'Ulisso*" [the mad passage of Ulysses]. It is perhaps
significant that the tale told in the eighth *bolgia* of the eighth
circle of Hell is remembered in the eighth heaven of Paradise,
in lines 82–83.

This Dantean Ulysses, the seeker after knowledge, is a radical
change from the Homeric aspect of Ulysses. This tradition is

continued in the nineteenth century, in Tennyson's "Ulysses," and in the twentieth century, in the long work of the Greek poet Kazantzakis, *The Odyssey, a Modern Sequel.* On a smaller scale the Dantean Ulysses is also visible in the work of two other modern Greek poets, Seferis and Cavafy. Whereas the Ulysses/ Bloom in Joyce's novel is home-bound and life-accepting, Kazantzakis's hero is outward-bound and life-abandoning.

Principal Signs and Symbols

1. *Evil counselors:* in contrast to the real thieves of the seventh *bolgia,* the evil counselors (those who advise fraud) are spiritual thieves who drain men of their integrity.

2. The *flames* of the punishment not only torment the sinners, but also conceal them.

3. *Ulysses* and *Diomedes* (26:55–56): joined here because they fought against Troy. This recalls the union of Paolo and Francesca in canto 5.

4. *The ambush of the horse* (*l'agguato del caval,* 26:59): this stratagem allowed the Greek soldiers to be smuggled into Troy, where they then sacked the city. . . .

5. *They might scorn your words* (*ei sarebbero schivi, forse del tuo detto,* 26:74–75): this is a puzzle—why Virgil does not allow Dante to speak to Ulysses and Diomedes. A possible explanation is that Dante, an Italian, is a descendent of the ancient Trojans.

6. *The voyage of Ulysses* (26:90–142): one of the most admirable of the *Inferno,* it has no classical source, and would seem to be Dante's invention. Tennyson used it in his poem "Ulysses."

7. *A mountain* (*una montagna,* 26:133): presumably the mountain which first was the Earthly Paradise, and which, after Christ's descent into Hell, became the mountain of Purgatory, rising from the sea in the southern hemisphere, opposite Jerusalem.

CANTO

27

The Evil Counselors: Guido da Montefeltro
(Eighth *Bolgia;* Eliot's "Prufrock")

The eighth ditch holds two sinners in extreme situations. One is from the ancient world: Ulysses in canto 26; the other is modern: Guido da Montefeltro in canto 27. The former is related to the state or the government of men, the latter to the Church. The Church and state are the two institutions whose rulers are the most exposed to, the most vulnerable to, evil counsel. Taken together, the two cantos present a striking dual pattern: pagan and Christian, ancient and modern, mythical and historical, one representing the state, and the other the Church.

In his new canto, Dante is the natural interviewer, since he is dealing with a fellow countryman. Guido da Montefeltro was a count and the Ghibelline leader whom Villani called "the wisest and subtlest man of war of his time in all Italy." He was indeed famous for his valor and wisdom, for his courtesy and for his skill in strategy, because of which he was called "the fox" (*volpe,* 27:75). Because of his fame in the fourteenth century, Dante does not feel the need to name him in canto 27, in which we can read a fairly full account of his history. Guido da Montefeltro was first a soldier, then he became a monk, and finally at the end of his career, an evil counselor to Pope Boniface VIII, whom Dante looked upon as the Antichrist.

At Guido's request, Dante gives a picture of conditions in Romagna:

> dimmi se i Romagnuoli han pace o guerra [27:28]
> [tell me if the Romagnols have peace or war]

Dante's words, as he describes Romagna under various petty tyrants, are brief, concrete with the names of nobles, rivers, and events, and sadly nostalgic (27:37–55). Romagna was a papal state in the north east, on the Adriatic. What Ghibelline Guido da Montefeltro had been for Romagna, Farinata, another Ghibelline, had been for Tuscany. After Dante tells of the dissensions in some of the great cities of Romagna, such as Ravenna (27:40), Guido begins his personal story with a line that summarizes his career as the soldier and monk:

> Io fui uom d'arme, e poi fui cordigliero [27:67]
> [I was a man of arms, and then became a Franciscan friar]

Guido explains that this dramatic change, a seeming act of contrition, was offset by the strong will of Pope Boniface VIII (*il gran prete*, "the great priest," 27:70) who led him back to his first sins. What were these sins? They were deeds, says Guido, not of the lion, as one might expect from a soldier, but of the fox:

> l'opere mie
> non furon leonine, ma di volpe [27:74–75]
> [my deeds
> were not those of the lion, but of the fox]

Like Ulysses, Guido became learned in the "wiles and covert ways" he used, but unlike Ulysses, he is ashamed and attains a degree of greatness through what he has suffered.

Why did Pope Boniface turn to Guido da Montefeltro? Quite simply because of the man's world renowned skill in deceit. Boniface VIII, scornfully called by Dante "prince of the new Pharisees" in line 85, was in open conflict with the Colonna family, who lived near the Latern Palace, the papal residence. This family, excommunicated by Boniface, took refuge in their fortress at Palestrina, twenty-five miles east of Rome (Palestrina was at that time called Penestrino). Guido, in his role as papal adviser, counseled that an amnesty should be offered the Colonnas. But when the family surrendered on those conditions in 1298, their fortress-castle was destroyed.

At first, when Boniface asked for counsel, Guido kept silent. But when the pope promised to absolve him, Guido agreed to give counsel, saying in short: "Promise to pay, but don't pay." Since Guido showed no repentance, he could not be absolved, even by a pope.

Although this story of evil counsel was not invented by Dante, the struggle between Heaven and Hell for Guido's soul was (the episode is told in lines 112–26). Dante imagines that at Guido's death, Saint Francis came for his soul. At the same time a black cherub claimed the soul for his menials, on the grounds of the fraudulent counsel. The cherub was a good logician, proving that the devil keeps his accounts better than do men.

This particular story emphasizes the church doctrine that the eternal fate of a soul depends on its intrinsic condition at the moment of death. Although absolved by a pope, Guido had not genuinely repented of his deed, and therefore the absolution was invalid.

In the *Convivio* (4:28), Dante looks upon Guido da Montefeltro as a morally great man. Canto 27 seems to contradict this, but at least Dante gives his account a pathos in which a fallen great man laments the errors of his life. Guido is reluctant to tell his story. His abiding wish in Hell is to be forgotten in the world. There is a nobility in this wish that helps elevate Guido to a position only slightly inferior to that of Ulysses. For the sake of completeness, possibly, Dante wanted an Italian Ulysses for this *bolgia*. In terms of his feelings and his insights, Guido appears nobler and greater than Ulysses. And his agony is shown to be deeper than Ulysses' agony.

Because of T. S. Eliot's use of lines 61–66 as the epigraph to "The Love Song of J. Alfred Prufrock," the passage, spoken by Guido, has been closely examined in our day. When Dante asks the sinner who he is, Guido's flame speaks, and argues that since no one ever returns to the world alive from Hell, he will agree to speak because he has no fear of his infamy being related to the living.

Guido's initial error is believing that Dante is a spirit and not a living man. The reader is more accustomed to hearing spirits in Hell express a wish to be remembered on earth. The last to express this hope were the three noble Florentines in canto 16, the sodomites who made themselves into a wheel. In the circles of incontinence and violence, the shades want to be remembered, but in the two circles of fraud, they want concealment and oblivion.

Eliot's poem is often interpreted as a series of contrasts between time present and time past. Throughout the *Inferno*, the attitude of the sinners toward the past is a principal subject. The present is criticized in "Prufrock" by the characters' attitudes toward the past. The women who come and go are not in the least awed by Michelangelo. Prufrock himself, who epitomizes the present, is in a condition of acute social fright, a condition not unlike that of the damned in Dante's Hell. When he says he is Lazarus come back from the dead to tell all, we can easily see behind Prufrock the figure of Montefeltro, who does exactly that. Guido tells all to Dante, as Prufrock tells all to his two selves, the private and the public: "let us go . . . "

Both the story of Guido da Montefeltro and his name are related to Eliot's title. Consider the relation between the names Montefeltro and Prufrock. *Feltro* means "felt" or "filter," and comes from the Latin *feltrum*. Felt is used as a filter of liquids. *Monte* is "mountain" or "rock." "Filter" can also mean "philter" (*philtre*), a love potion, as in the Tristan story.

The episode told by Guido in canto 27 concerns his putting his Church to the proof. He advised the evil Boniface to deceive and destroy the Colonnas, and relied on the pope's power to grant absolution. Prufrock, whose evil counsel is to himself (if we interpret the opening line this way), is able to speak only by way of soliloquy:

> Let us go then, you and I,
> When the evening is spread out against the sky . . .

"You and I": the "you" is probably the public personality of Prufrock. The "I" would be the thinking, sensitive character. These two selves, the two *moi* of Bergson, are engaged in a debate similar to the "body and soul" debate, so popular in the Middle Ages.

The epigraph from canto 27 expands on Prufrock's frustration: he is in Hell, and Hell is static, unchanging. Guido is in Hell because of his active evil in the world. Prufrock is in hell even though he was never actively evil. His resemblance to Guido is therefore as ironic as the references in the poem to Hamlet and the decapitated John the Baptist. But is is also accurate because both Guido and Prufrock abused their intellects. Prufrock speaks in the form of a soliloquy because he habitually channels his intellect into profitless fantasy and daydreams. Prufrock's personal tragedy is his conviction that love is beyond achievement, that it is limited by desire. His loveless fate has been decided by his age, his shyness, and even by his unromantic sounding name.

The bankerlike, Anglo-Saxon J. Alfred has a ring to it far different from the Italian Guido, although Alfred and Guido have some similarity in sound.

Thus we surmise that Prufrock is living a kind of death. He speaks to us as Montefeltro speaks to Dante. Whereas Guido speaks because he believes there will be no infamy related about him on earth, Prufrock does not fear infamy. Modern man, as he appears in our literature, has learned the habit of making a public confession to anyone who will listen. He has encouraged in himself a strong masochistic tendency to belittle himself. "Prufrock" takes its place beside later works of confession such as Camus's *L'etranger*, Roth's *Portnoy's Complaint*, and Walker Percy's *Lancelot*.

Principal Signs and Symbols

1. *The Sicilian bull* (*il bue cicilian*, 27:7): a bronze bull made by Perillus for Phalaris, the Sicilian tyrant. Victims were roasted alive inside in bull, and their cries were supposed to resemble a bull roaring. Perillus himself was the first victim.

2. *Guido da Montefeltro* (27:29): the great Ghibelline leader (1223–98) of Bologna and Romagna. Montefeltro is a region between Urbino and Mount Coronaro. As a soldier Guido was famous for his military skill and especially for his foxlike strategies. In 1298 he entered the Franciscan Order. The story of his advice to Boniface VIII is in Villani's *Chronicles*.

3. *Verruchio* (27:46–48): the castle inhabited by the lords of Rimini. Malatesta and his son Malatestino of Rimini were called mastiffs or hounds because of their cruelty. They were called the "old" and "new" mastiffs respectively. In 1295 Malatesta captured Montagna de' Parcitati, head of the Ghibelline party, who was later murdered in prison by Malatestino.

4. *Cordigliero* (27:67) or *cordelier:* a friar wearing the cord of the Franciscan Order.

5. The high priest (*il gran prete*, 27:70): Pope Boniface VIII.

6. 27:85–90: this passage refers to the long feud between Boniface ("the prince of the new Pharisees") and the Colonna family, who lived near the Lateran palace, residence of the pope. Boniface launched his crusade, not against Saracens and Jews (27:87), but against Christians.

7. 27:108–9: "Father, since you cleanse me of that sin": but a man cannot be absolved of a sin before he commits it.

CANTO

28

The Sowers of Discord: Bertrand de Born
(Ninth *Bolgia*)

THE NINTH DITCH of *Malebolge* is the subject of canto 28, and Dante approaches the horrors of its particular punishment with grave misgivings. Even "with words set free" (*con parole sciolte,* 28:1), who could relate the spectacle of these sowers of discord? The ninth *bolgia* is filled with schismatics. The image of schism comes from a passage in the first letter to the Corinthians, chapter 12, in which Saint Paul speaks of the oneness of spirit and the diversity of gifts. All members of the new Church should work together, he says, "so that there be no schism in the body."

As the schismatics had split an institution's body when they were in the world, so now in Hell their bodies are cut and sliced. The idea of body is both institutional and personal. Whereas the evil counselors of the eighth ditch assailed the head of an institution, the schismatics of the ninth ditch mutilate the institution itself.

Thus the imagery of the new canto is that of mutilation. Dante derives most of his images from medicine and war. In four of the opening tercets (28:7–18), the poet, dwelling on the battlefields of Apulia, infernalizes the hospital and the activity of surgeons after the bloody fights. Apulia, or Puglia as it is called today, is in the southeastern part of Italy. The first reference is the long war between Samnites and the Romans (343–290 B.C.). The second is to the Second Punic War (218–201 B.C.) in which Hannibal's armies were so successful against Rome that after the battle of the Cannae, the Carthagenians gathered three bushels of gold rings taken from the fingers of dead Romans. The third battle centers on Robert Guiscard, a Norman adventurer who in the eleventh century won control of the most of southern Italy. There he fought the schismatic Greeks and the Saracens on behalf of the Church between 1059 and 1080. In the *Paradiso* (18:48) he is assigned to the Heaven of Mars among the warriors for the Faith. There is then a reference to the pass of Ceperano, where the Apulian barons, under Manfred, deserted and allowed Charles d'Anjou through to defeat Manfred at Benevento in 1266. Finally, we learn that at Tagliacozzo, Charles d'Anjou defeated Manfred's nephew, Conradin, by a strtagem whereby he allowed most of his army to retreat, and then, with reserve troops, demolished the enemy who had set out in search of plunder.

This condensed but very impressive list of battles is the prelude to the appearance of the first schismatic: Mohammed, founder of Islam in the seventh century, and the revered leader of the Arab world. Dante, in keeping with medieval opinion, looked on Mohammed as the religious figure who perpetrated the greatest schism in the Christian world. In canto 28 (lines 22–51) he is seen ripped open from chin to crotch for having divided the body of Christ. In another sense this would be the rent between the East and West.

Four classes of schismatics are found here in the ninth *bolgia:*

1. Among those who introduced discord and division in the Church are Mohammed and his son-in-law Ali, who succeeded Mohammed (although not immediately). Ali, who is cleft from the chin to the forelock, is pointed out to Dante by Mohammed. There is also a curious reference to Fra Dolcino, not yet dead. He was a monk and the leader of a heretical sect condemned by Pope Clement V in 1305. This sect preached the common holding of property and the sharing of women. In the hills of Novara the followers of Fra Dolcino withstood the soldiers of the pope for a year; most of them finally starved to death. Mohammed and Dolcino held similar views on marriage and women.

2. Pier della Medicina, mutilated by having his throat pierced, his nose cut off up to the eyebrows, and one ear severed, is typical of the schismatics who divided the state (28:64–75). Medicina, the seat of his family, is east of Bologna. The members of this family were driven from Romagna in 1287, after which Pier succeeded in his intrigues in Romagna and in setting the houses of Malatesta and Polenta against each other. In his words to Dante, he speaks of the towns of Vercelli and Marcabò which designate the west and east points of Romagna. Malatestino of

Rimini, one-eyed in Hell, is also among the sowers of discord in the state. He invited two French noblemen to a conference at La Cattolica, on the Adriatic, and had them drowned off the headland of Focara, famous for its dangerous winds. The last example of a schismatic against the state is Curio, who joined Caesar's party after serving under Pompey. When Caesar hesitated to cross the Rubicon at a point near Rimini where the river empties into the Adriatic, Curio convinced him to cross and to march on Rome. At that time the Rubicon marked the boundary between Gaul and the Roman republic. Caesar's decision to cross the river brought on the Roman civil war.

3. A third type of schismatic is the man who divides a community, here represented by Mosca dei Lamberti. In Hell his two hands have been cut off. As he raises the stumps, blood drips down and smears his face. The important Guelf-Ghibelline feud in Florence began over a family quarrel in which Mosca played a key role. Buondelmonte de' Buondelmonti, betrothed to a girl of the Amidei family, rejected her for one of the Donati. Her family was debating how best to avenge her insult, when this Mosca said: "A thing done has an end": Buondelmonte should be killed (28:107). Thus Buondelmonte was murdered and the city of Florence took sides. This event was considered the beginning of the rivalry between the two factions.

4. To illustrate the type of schismatic who divides a family, the poet has chosen another poet, Bertrand de Born, and paints in this last section of the canto (28:118–42) one of the most awesome pictures of the *Inferno*. Bertrand was a noble, the Lord of Hautefort. He was also a Provençal troubadour, most of whose poetry is of a political nature. His most anthologized piece is a song of lamentation on the death of the "young king" (*re giovane*, 28:135) Prince Henry, son of Henry II of England. Bertrand de Born is in Hell because he caused Prince Henry to rebel against his father. He has been decapitated because the act of separating father and son is comparable to severing the head from the body.

Dante, who praises Bertrand de Born in *De vulgari eloquentia* (2:2, 9) for his generosity and for the beauty of his war poems, describes him in canto 28 as carrying his head before him like a lantern. He compares Bertrand's evil counsel to that of Achitophel, who provoked Absalom's rebellion against David, his father and king (2 Samuel 15–17). The severed head speaks as Bertrand condemns his fault and his plight. The last word of the

canto, spoken by the Provençal poet (*lo contrapasso*, "retaliation" or "retribution"), summarizes the principle on which
Dante has built his poem:

> Così s'osserva in me lo contrapasso [28:142]
> [Thus the contrapasso is observed in me.]

Everywhere throughout the *Inferno* the law of divine retribution
is at work.

The *contrapasso* is the biblical *lex talionis*, the law of the
"talion," which adjusts the severity of the reparation to the gravity of the crime. The opening lines of the canto (28:1–21) describe the hideous condition of the "sowers of discord," and the
final word of the canto names the law that controls such a condition.

We are to understand that such sinners as Ulysses and Guido
de Montefeltro in the eighth *bolgia* derived perverse delight
from their lies and deceits. The schismatics of the ninth *bolgia*,
on the other hand, are those who worked deliberately to reach
specific results by sowing discord, war, devastation, religious
schism. The four conspicuous figures of canto 28 did all that:
Mohammed, Curio, Mosca, and Bertrand de Born. The law of
retribution (*la loi du talion*) rules over Dante's *Inferno* and *Purgatorio*. Canto 28, along with cantos 27 and 32, are those most
full of history, perhaps in order to soften the horrors of the
punishment.

Today they might possibly be called anarchists, or terrorists,
these men who set out with deliberate plotting to destroy all
good in social life. In Dante's portrayal of the schismatics, their
own wretchedness is not enough. They are impelled by a need to
relate present, past, and future strifes. Mohammed prophesies
the death of Fra Dolcino, Pier da Medicina speaks of a double
murder on the open sea. Mosca lifts the bleeding stumps of his
arms until Dante hurls a curse at him. Bertrand de Born, by
holding out his head like a lantern, experiences both guilt and
pleasure.

It is often pointed out by Italian commentators that canto 28
and the four cantos surrounding it (26, 27, 29, and 30), have the
tone of epic poetry, a studied rhetorical style that is close to the
style of tragedy. The opening line, in fact the opening word, sets
this tone:

> Chi poria mai pur con parole sciolte
> [who could ever even with words set free]

The gestures are grave and slow—Mohammed lifts one foot to move away and then stretches it out—and Dante among the sad mutilated souls (*tra l'ombre triste smozzicate*, 29:6) is so affected that he pities the *contrapasso*. Three times in canto 28 he uses the adjective *triste* (28:26, 111, 120) and once at the beginning of canto 29 (29:66). He claims that the horror of the subject matter goes beyond his powers as a poet. The canto is eloquent but it is also cruelly realistic. Virgil's role is reduced here: the focus is first on the sinners and then on Dante—on his pity, his memories, his hopes as a man of his party. Dante, who weeps throughout the canto, is quite literally suffering Hell.

Principal Signs and Symbols

1. At the cutting of the sword (*al taglio della spada*, 28:38): this image pervades the canto in the action of the religious schismatics, the civil destroyers, and those who disunited a family. All of them are presented as fanatics who ripped society apart to satisfy some sectarianism.

2. *Apulia:* in southeast Italy, where all the battles referred to in this canto took place.

3. *Mohammed* (28:22–63): held by Dante as the initiator of the schism between the Christian Church and Islam. In Dante's time it was believed that Mohammed was originally a Christian and a cardinal eager to become pope.

4. *Ali* (28:32): he married Mohammed's daughter Fatima. He occupied the Caliphate from 656 until his assassination in 661.

5. *Fra Dolcino* (28:56–60): he headed a sect banned by Pope Clement V in 1305. Dolcino and his followers retreated to the hills near Novara. He was burned at the stake in 1307.

6. *Pier da Medicina* (28:64–75): by intrigue he set the houses of Polenta and Malatesta against each other.

7. *Malatestino* of Rimini (28:76–90): treacherously drowned two leading citizens of the town of Fano, Guido del Cassero and Angiolello da Carignano. This took place off the headland of Focara, notorious for its strong winds.

8. *Curio* (28:94–102): he advised Julius Caesar to cross the Rubicon near Rimini, Caesar then declared war on the Republic.

9. *Mosca* (28:106–8): he instigated the Guelf-Ghibelline feud in Florence.

10. *Achitophel* (28:137–38): provoked Absalom's revolt against David, his father and king (2 Samuel 15–17).

11. *Bertrand de Born* (28:118–42): the decapitated figure of this warrior-troubadour illustrates the *contrapasso*. He helped to bring about the quarrel between Henry II of England and his son Prince Henry.

CANTO

29

Falsifiers of Every Sort (Tenth *Bolgia*)

THE LAST SCENE of the ninth *bolgia* is a conversation between Dante and Virgil. Since time is pressing and Dante seems engrossed in watching the schismatics, Virgil reproves him: "Why are you spending more time here than elsewhere?" Dante replies that he is looking for a relative. Virgil noticed this man, Geri del Bello, a first cousin of Dante's father, while Dante's attention was fixed on Bertrand de Born. What is said about this relative is not very clear, and no special punishment is assigned him. He passes by and vanishes, after threatening with his finger. It was believed that he had been murdered by a member of the Sachetti family, which he had divided. The customary vendetta for his death was probably not carried out, at least not before 1300.

Why is Dante so absorbed by the grim apparition of Bertrand de Born? Possibly because the Provençal poet had been a good man and a distinguished writer. He is another of those whose one sin has placed him in Hell.

Beginning with line 40 and continuing through the canto and all of canto 30, we are in the tenth and last ditch of the eighth circle. Here four kinds of falsifiers are punished. They are the sinners who perverted the physical world by means of fraud, and with it the moral world. These two cantos seem to establish a correspondence with the violence done to nature, God, and art in the third *girone* of the seventh circle.

The dominant motif in this last ditch is disease, demonstrating the inner disintegration and perversion of the physical body of the man who has perverted the physical processes and order of nature. Whereas in the ninth *bolgia* the human organism is seen as rent and cut, in the tenth *bolgia* it is seen as sick and destroyed from within. Dante appears almost as a physician in these last two ditches: as a surgeon on the battlefields in the ninth ditch, and as a pathologist in the tenth, where the scene shifts to the hospital. Hospitals in three places are mentioned (29:47, 48): in Valdichiana, a swampy malarial district of central Tuscany; in Maremma, also in Tuscany; and on the island of Sardinia.

The Italian word for these sinners appears in line 57: *i falsador,* and at the beginning of the new scene Dante, in a classical allusion, compares the falsifiers of the tenth *bolgia* to the victims of a plague on the island of Aegina in the Saronic Gulf. According to this story, told by Ovid in the *Metamorphoses* (7:523–57), the plague, sent by Juno, killed all the inhabitants except Aeacus. When Aeacus prayed to Jupiter to repopulate the island, the god did so by turning ants into men.

The first falsifiers are the alchemists, falsifiers of metals. These sinners caused the substances they worked with to become scabrous and corrupt, thus usurping and perverting nature. Since their work was a fraud—the gold they produced was not real—in Hell their bodies are alchemized and diseased.

The canto is made up of curious notations, nuances of feeling on the part of Dante, a rehearsal almost of the various moods and tempi we have witnessed throughout the *Inferno.* The poet has just been softened by a personal remembrance. His sympathy has perhaps drawn him nearer than was wise to these desperate sinners. What seems clearest in this tenth ditch is the slackening of Dante's moral tension. He moves easily into conversation with the sinners, makes jokes with them, for example, over the foolishness of the Sienese, expressing a growing inquisitiveness, and seems to take pleasure in their replies to him and in their quarrelling. Is he running the risk of being contaminated by the polluted air of the tenth *bolgia?*

Throughout the first part of the canto, Dante accentuates, more than is his custom, the stench (*puzzo,* 29:50) of the tenth ditch, the groanings (*lamenti,* 29:43) of the souls as he sees them crawl and shift, scratch themselves, bite, and howl. He accentuates especially the darkness of the place. At the head of the description is "the other valley" (*l'altra valle,* 29:38), immediately recast as "the last cloister of *Malebolge*" (*l'ultima chiostra / di Malebolge,* 29:40–41), and, a few lines later, ominously named "that dim valley" (*quella oscura valle,* 29:65), which sends us back to the second line of canto 1, to the *selva oscura,* from which

Dante could not escape without going through all of Hell. The physical horror and the insatiate cravings of the she-wolf (1:49) are here demonstrated long after the first appearance of the beast on the hillside.

Two of the shades talk to Dante: Griffolino da Arezzo and Capocchio. They are sitting back to back, scratching their leprous sores. Griffolino was a physicist who extracted money from a foolish young man Albero, supposed to be the son of the bishop of Siena, by promising to teach him how to fly. The reference to Albero as the bishop's "son" (29:117), could mean the bishop was Albero's father or more simply his protector. Griffolino was burned for being an alchemist or sorcerer. The silliness of the Sienese (29:122) is a reference to the habit of the Florentines of making the citizens of Siena, their rival city, the butt of jokes.

The other leper, who at the end of the canto reveals himself to be Capocchio, then gives the names of four men, members of the *Brigata spendereccia* (the "Spendthrifts' Club"), wealthy young Sienese who vied with one another in squandering their money on riotous living. Line 127 refers to some new expensive dish prepared with cloves, a spice imported from the east. Lines 127–29 are called the "clove tercet," and the precise extravagance they allude to is still unknown. D. da Imola contends that it was the roasting of pheasants and capons over a fire made of cloves. The "orchard" (*orto*, 29:129) in the tercet would seem to be Siena.

Capocchio is the name of a man who in 1294 was burned for alchemy. It would appear that Dante knew him in their student days. He was probably a Florentine. Somewhat mysteriously, Capocchio calls himself in the last line of the canto a "good ape of nature" (*di natura buona scimia*, 29:139). This might be explained by his skill as a draughtsman or mimic.

Familiar tones and themes are echoed in canto 29: the grotesque humor of the barrators in cantos 21 and 22; the low sarcasm of Capocchio's speech; Virgil's recapitulation of the purpose of Dante's journey through Hell (29:94–96). The alchemists are only the first category of falsifiers. The other three form the subject matter of the next canto.

Principal Signs and Symbols

1. *Falsifiers:* the tenth *bolgia* marks the end of *Malebolge*, which began in canto 18. We will see examples of those who

falsified things, words, money, and persons. Dishonesty pervades every category. Canto 29 accounts for the falsifiers of things, the representative sin being alchemy, whereby metals are altered.

2. *I was of Arezzo* (*Io fui d'Arezzo*, 29:109): probably Griffolino of Arezzo, who obtained money from Albero of Siena by pretending he could teach him how to fly. Albero, when he discovered he was tricked, had Griffolino burned as an alchemist.

3. *Capocchio* (29:136): also burned for practicing alchemy. He was probably a Florentine and a friend of Dante.

CANTO

30

Virgil Reproves Dante (Tenth *Bolgia*)

THERE IS NO BREAK between cantos 29 and 30. After the falsifiers
of metals we see the falsifiers of persons (impersonators), illustrated in the character of Myrrha. Then come the falsifiers of
coins, the counterfeiters. The last are the falsifiers of words,
among whom Potiphar's wife appears. These sinners are somewhat related to the hypocrites and evil counselors, and the ditches
begin to duplicate one another.

Dante seems to present the miscellaneous sins of the falsifiers
in their most extreme aspects. The suffering of these sinners is
not caused by something outside of them, but by a disease within
them, either a mental disease as with the impersonators, who are
mad, or by a physical disease as with the counterfeiters, who are
afflicted with dropsy. The ending of the canto contains one of
Virgil's strongest rebukes to Dante during the course of the journey through Hell.

In earlier *bolge* we saw how everything is bought and sold:
sex, for example, with the procurers; religion in the activities of
the simonists; government in the manipulations of the barrators.
In the tenth *bolgia*, the coin itself is corrupt and thus the currency is debased. This is the fraud revealed in canto 29 as disease, which might be interpreted as the last stage of a sickness
that condemns the entire city.

In the psychological sense, this fraud of the tenth *bolgia* represents a split personality, quite literally the forging of another self.
It is that form of schizophrenia that grows through the desire to
accommodate to a false self, to a false situation. It is the "you and

I" of *Prufrock*, the determination "to prepare a face to meet the faces." All the great poets have known this fundamental fraud of human nature, and their poems have been composed as strategies for remaining sane. The image of the poem may be that of a division in personality, as in so many poems of Emily Dickinson, but the creation of the image is a victory.

The word *persona* has come to mean in literary study a fictional character in a novel or play. In the psychological sense, Jung uses *persona* to designate the social front an individual plays and which results in a divided self. In opposition to *persona*, Jung names the *anima* as the true self, the self responsible for the archetypal ideals of conduct.

Capocchio and Griffolino, the two falsifiers of metals, are still present at the opening of canto 30. Then two falsifiers of persons, or impersonators, both of whom are mad, appear, and one of them attacks Capocchio. These are the only characters in Dante's poem who are insane, and in order to present their particular form of suffering Dante goes to great pains to recall for his readers two famous examples of mental derangement in classical mythology.

The homicidal madness of Athamas was caused by Juno, whose wrath was provoked by Athamas' affair with Ino, his wife's sister. The second victim of madness is Hecuba, wife of Priam king of Troy. After the fall of Troy she was carried off as a slave to Greece. On the way, the sacrifice of her daughter and the sight of her son's murdered body drove her insane, causing her to bark like a dog.

Griffolino d'Arezzo, called here the Aretine, points out two mad spirits to Dante. The first, Gianni Schicchi, was famous in Florence for his skill in mimicry and once impersonated a man's deceased father (Buoso Donati) in order to change the dead man's will. In doing this, he willed to himself a considerable fortune as well as a prize mare, *la donna della torma*, ("the lady of the troop" or "queen of studs," 30:43).

The other figure appearing with Gianni Schicchi in this *bolgia* is the shade of the depraved Myrrha:

> l'anima antica
> di Mirra scellerata [30:37–38]

Her story is told in the tenth book of Ovid's *Metamorphoses*. Lusting after her father, the king of Cyprus, Myrrha disguised herself in order to make love with him. Discovering the trick, the king planned to have her killed, but she escaped and wandered about until the gods transformed her into a myrrh tree. Her son Adonis, conceived in incest, was born from the tree.

The third type of falsifier is the counterfeiter. Adamo di Brescia is the representative sinner, a man who was induced by the Conti Guidi of Romena to counterfeit the Florentine golden florin, the coin "stamped with the Baptist," (30:73), the patron saint of Florence. He was burned to death for his crime in 1281.

In Hell he suffers from dropsy, which supposedly resulted from the accumulation and corruption of phlegmatic humors. These shades swell up to an abnormal size. Here they suffer from intense thirst as once they thirsted for money. In line 49 Dante compares Master Adam to a lute in order to describe his swollen body.

In Adamo's long narrative (30:58–90) he speaks of craving "one little drop of water." His memories of the cool streams coming down from the green hills of Casentino into the Arno add to his torment. "Brenda's fountain," named in line 78, is a spring that once flowed near Romena.

Thus we observe a different treatment for alchemists and counterfeiters. Alchemists, suffering from skin irritation, and counterfeiters, suffering from dropsy, both represent public fraud. In the fifth book of the *Ethics*, Aristotle states that money was invented for common utility and common benefit. Dante, in keeping with Aristotle, claims that forgery of any kind is a crime that disturbs the social order and commerce of the city.

The final group of falsifiers occupies much of the remaining part of the canto (30:91–148). These sinners might be called falsifiers of words. In life they feigned innocence, honesty, or virtue. Their sin might be called hypocrisy, and in the case of Sinon, who speaks to Master Adam, the sin might be classified as evil counsel. As we have already seen, the ditches of *Malebolge* are beginning to overlap.

Dante asks Adamo about two sinners nearby who suffer from a raging fever. He learns that one is Potiphar's wife who in the book of Genesis (chapter 29) accused Joseph of trying to seduce her, whereas it was she who had made amorous advances to the young Joseph. The other figure is the Greek Sinon, who allowed the Trojans to take him prisoner and then persuaded them to admit the wooden horse into Troy.

A quarrel breaks out between Adamo and Sinon. Each hurls disgusting recriminations at the other while Dante listens to the

scene and watches it with such eager interest that Virgil inter-
venes with a strong reproof, bringing to an end not only the canto
but the entire eighth circle. The timing of the rebuke emphasizes
its importance.

Virgil says:

Or pur mira,
che per poco che teco non mi risso! [30:131–32]
[Now keep looking
and soon I will quarrel with you.]

Dante instantly feels shame and silently composes an extremely
complicated reply (30:136–41) to the effect that he wishes to
excuse himself, although he is unable to articulate a cogent excuse. Virgil is touched by Dante's obvious sincerity and pardons
him, reminding his pupil that he will at all times be at his side.

Then, in highly elliptical language, Virgil summarizes the
misdemeanor ("that" is the dialogue between Adamo and Sinon):

ché voler ciò udire è bassa voglia [30:148]
[to desire to hear that is a low wish]

This is the strongest formulation of a warning that has often
been in the mind and words of Virgil. Dante's attentiveness to
the various scenes in Hell is often on the verge of degenerating
into mere curiosity or even a morbid curiosity or a perverse delight, which seems to be the case in canto 30. Virgil is always
more attentive to Dante than to activities of the spirits and their
tormentors. Here he divines a possible evil inclination in Dante
and warns him with the very strong words *bassa voglia:* "vulgar"
or "low desires." Especially in this lowest part of Hell, sympathy
is out of place. The hint of Dante's sympathy at the beginning of
canto 29 has now turned into something more serious, and Virgil
realizes that Dante's moral tension has slackened. In this tenth
bolgia, full of disease and polluted air, Dante seems to be taking
pleasure in the chatter and quarrelling of the spirits.

The diversity of so many types has perhaps dazzled Dante:
alchemists, counterfeiters, forgers of wills, the incestuous
Myrrha, Potiphar's wife, Sinon. The fury is swinish here: Myrrha
and Gianni Schicchi bite, run, and scream. It is a picture of vile-
ness with no trace of intelligence or nobility. Because of the
disease in these spirits, the fever and hydrophobia in their
bodies, they may lose the full consciousness of their guilt. Hence
they insult, berate, and trick one another. Dante does linger here

a bit too long. He is castigated by Virgil and feels shame. For one brief moment psychological curiosity in Dante wins over his sense of morality. This presents to the readers of the *Inferno* as well as to Dante himself the real peril of the poem.

Principal Signs and Symbols

1. *Falsifiers* of three kinds figure in this canto: (a) Gianni Schicchi (of Florence) and Myrrha counterfeited the persons of others for wicked purposes; (b) Master Adamo counterfeited money; (c) Sinon and Potiphar's wife counterfeited their words.

2. *Sinon* of Troy: a Greek spy who persuaded the Trojans to bring the wooden horse into Troy.

3. *Gianni Schicchi:* of the Cavalcanti family, a famous mimic.

4. *Myrrha:* her story of incest is told by Ovid in the tenth book of the *Metamorphoses*.

5. *Master Adam of Brescia:* he counterfeited the golden florins of Florence. He was burned in 1281. The currency of Florence was affected by his counterfeiting.

6. *The alloy sealed with the Baptist's image (la lega sugillata del Batista*, 30:74): the Florentine florin bore the image of Saint John the Baptist, patron saint of the city, on one side, and a lily on the other.

7. *Potiphar's wife (la falsa ch'accusò Giaseppo*, "the false wife who accused Joseph," 30:97): the story is in Genesis, chapter 39.

8. The sinners in this tenth *bolgia* all suffer from some disease: the *alchemists* suffer from leprosy; the *impersonators* suffer from madness; the *counterfeiters* suffer from dropsy; the *liars* suffer from a fever that causes them to stink.

HELL Canto 31

CANTO

31

The Giants (Ninth Circle)

THE DESCENT to the last circle marks a startling change in both the appearance of the sinners and in the setting. After the writhings and convulsions of the diseased spirits, we come to a scene of petrification, immobility, stolidity, and of freezing cold. Nature is benumbed with ice and the frozen souls are almost dead. We know that Lúcifer is at the end of the journey, at the very bottom of Hell.

The ninth circle is composed of four zones, which are not distinct but merge with one another. At the beginning, where all is ice, stand the giants, ghostlike guards, so massive that to Dante's eyes they appear as towers. In the cold darkness Dante's sight is impaired and his impressions remain vague. A high pitched horn strikes his ears, much louder than thunder, much louder than the horn Roland blew after the defeat of his army at Roncevaux when he called for help from Charlemagne.

Before the apparitions and the horn-blast, Dante relates what took place at the end of the previous canto. In the first six lines, Virgil's tongue is compared to Achilles' lance, which was able both to produce a wound and to heal it. The remedy for the thrust of the lance was to sprinkle on the wound rust scraped from the lance's point. At first Virgil's tongue (the lance) was a sad gift but then it became a kind gift for healing:

> prima di trista e poi di buona mancia. [31:6]

After Virgil's words of reproof for Dante's curiosity in listening to the squabble between Adamo and Sinon, he pardons his pupil.

The word *mancia* in line 6 means any kind of gift. It is the key word in the passage bridging the two circles. Virgil's tongue first caused pain and then served as its anodyne. The *Inferno,* even here in the lowest part of Hell, suggests the remedial nature of all punishment.

In silence Virgil and Dante cross the bank that leads them away from the valley of the tenth *bolgia.* Behind them lie the two most complex circles of Hell: the seventh circle of violence and the eighth circle of fraud and malice. Ahead of them lies the ninth and last circle, that of treachery. The giants, whom Dante mistakes for the towers of some town, are the prelude to Satan, whose body is also of stupendous size.

Two traits in particular are ascribed to the giants: their heaven-defying strength and their malice. They are also stupid because God, the source of intelligence, is no longer with them. In this ultimate circle Dante draws upon his three principal sources: Hebraic, Greek, and Teutonic. The northern ice and fog recall the Niebelungen or fog-folk. As so often in earlier parts of the *Inferno,* Dante here gothicizes the Hellenic and Hebraic worlds. Giants are found in the lore of all three civilizations; frequently they are depicted as the enemies of the gods. Dante presents his giants as bodies and souls that are mysterious and unintelligible.

The blast of a horn, louder than Roland's, at the beginning of canto 31 is an echo of popular fiction in Dante's time. When Dante asks about the towers he believes he sees, Virgil replies:

> sappi che non son torri, ma giganti [31:31]
> [know that they are not towers, but giants]

Then as the fog clears, the man from the south sees the giants held fast in the bank up to the navel, standing in a circle round the pit like the battlements of Montereggioni, a castle near Siena.

Nimrod (Nembrotto) is described first in a fairly long passage (31:46–81). Although Scripture does not state that he was a giant or that he built the tower of Babel (Genesis 10 and 11), he did come from Babel and he is referred to as a "mighty hunter." Dante accepts the tradition that Nimrod began, as a gesture of pride, to build a tower to heaven. This act was a primordial sin, the attempt to reach God by physical means. Nimrod, whose name means rebel, is associated with the confusion of tongues, and here his savage mouth speaks gibberish.

Genesis 6:4 refers to a race of giants outside the divine succession of Israel: "There were giants in those days." This has been a troublesome genealogy to biblical scholars. God sent the flood in order to end the race of giants, but they reappear in Job 26:5. Nimrod, chosen by Dante as a prominent giant, comes from a race different from the giants who appear later in the Bible, figures like Goliath and Samson, who were merely men of unusual size and strength. The poet points out the difference between huge animals (whales and elephants) which nature allows to exist because they have no rational faculty, and giants, who possess an evil will and can therefore cause great harm.

The second giant in canto 31, Ephialtes (31:84–96), is from Greek mythology, and was a son of Neptune who warred against the gods of Olympus. Ephialtes, who "tried his power against high Jove," is a fiercer, cruder giant than Nimrod, and larger. He is fixed in the earth and his arms are chained. When on the earth, he attempted to pile mountain on mountain in order to reach Jove. The stories of Nimrod and Ephialtes are two fables stemming possibly from the same tradition. The building of a tower and the piling of mountain on mountain are similar acts of defiance.

Briareus (31:97–111) is another of the giants who defied the gods of Olympus. He is used by Dante principally to introduce Antaeus, the giant who concludes the canto (31:112–45), and who appears unfettered, probably because he did not participate in the war of the giants against the gods. In a speech to Antaeus full of biographical details, Virgil orders the Titan to set him and Dante down in the last circle.

Antaeus appears far more tractable than the guards of the other circles, Charon, for example, or Phlegyas, Nessus, and Geryon. Virgil uses flattery in speaking to him and points out that Dante, who is still alive, can restore fame to the giants on earth. Antaeus, the son of Neptune and Gaea (the Earth), derived his strength from his contact with the earth. He once wrestled with Hercules who, by lifting Antaeus off the ground, killed him. As soon as Antaeus sets Dante and Virgil down on the bottom of the pit (*pozzo*), he raised himself up like a mast in a ship:

> e come albero in nave si levò. [31:145]

The Greek giants (besides the three described, two are referred to in line 124, Tityos and Typhon) appear in the writings of Hesiod and Homer, and in the Roman poets Virgil and Ovid. Dante's versions principally follow Lucan's *Pharsalia*. Most

commentators see in the giants the emblems of that pride by
which the rebel angels fell. In the *Inferno* we pass from the
lightest sins, such as carnality, to the blackest crimes. Rebellion
against God is the gravest of all: it is the sin of the giants and of
Lucifer who lies in the lowest pit. (The reverse order rules in the
Purgatorio, where the progression moves from the darkest sins to
the lightest, and where carnality is the last to be purged.)

Thus in Purgatory pride is classified as the most serious of all
sins. In Hell no specific place is reserved for the punishment of
pride. Dante may have considered it the basic element in all the
sins, or he may have planned to allocate pride to the very center
of the earth, with Lucifer as its sole representative. Some inter-
preters believe that pride is punished among those who committed violence against God, represented by Capaneus in canto
120. The giants of the ninth circle appear surrounding their
leader, as if they were body guards. They remind us of the Furies
over the gates of Dis, and their formation will be recast as the
heavenly choirs of angels surrounding the throne of God in the
Paradiso.

In all mythologies one finds the story of a primeval contest
with God. It is the endless struggle between Earth and Heaven.
The gigantic figures in canto 31 represent this assault on the
divine order. Even Antaeus, who is overruled and made to obey
Virgil, is still in rebellion. Throughout the eighth circle we saw
countless examples of men attacking human order and society by
means of fraud, and here in the ninth circle we may ask the
question: Is it pride that is being punished here or treachery,
which involves a special relation between the individual and his
own heart? This lowest level of degradation coincides with the
death of the soul and a congealment of nature. All the giants here
have been subdued. Their acts of heroism are behind them and
now they stand as memorials to the past.

In terms of the poem's action, they provide for Virgil and
Dante a means of transport from *Malebolge* to the bottom of the
well. They also provide for the reader a transition, a relief from
the final loathsome scenes of the eighth circle, an almost necessary interval of comparative quiet before the reader comes to the
new horrors of the ninth circle. The pride of Ephialtes in his
rebellion against Jove prepares the final picture of the pride of
Satan who rebelled against God.

The appearance of the giants is part of the all pervading theme
of the grotesque in Dante's *Inferno*. The monstrous throughout

the work is not comic in the sense of Aristophanean of Shake-
spearean comedy. It is quite simply grotesque, with a strong
ethical significance as well (as in the "gigantic" nature of pride.)
The grotesque is indeed one of the distinctive qualities of
medieval art as seen in the gargoyles of the cathedrals and in the
miracle plays: it emphasizes the absurdity of evil. Satan can be
seen as the clown of the universe, a fool in the eyes of God.

Principal Signs and Symbols

1. *Nimrod* (31:7): associated with the city of Babel. In Genesis
10 we read "the beginning of his kindgom was Babel." The following chapter relates the building of Babel and the confusion of
tongues. Saint Augustine saw Nimrod as a giant (*De Civ. Dei*, 16)
and Dante doubtless follows him. Since he was "a mighty hunter
before the Lord," he has a horn.

2. *Ephialtes* (31:94): a son of Neptune in Greek mythology. He
was one of the more violent giants, threatening to pile mountain
on mountain to reach the heavens.

3. *Briareus* (31:99): referred to in Homer, Virgil, Statius, and
Lucan.

4. *Antaeus* (31:101–2): a giant invincible as long as he was in
contact with his mother Earth (Gaea). Dante depicts him without
chains because he did not rebel against the gods. Antaeus provides the means of transport for Virgil and Dante from *Malebolge*
to the depths of the *pozzo* (well), and, aesthetically, the scene of
the giants provides a relief between the diseased figures of the
tenth *bolgia*, and the horrors to come in the pit of the traitors.

CANTO

32

Cocytus: The Zones of Caina and Antenora

THERE IS A PAUSE in the opening of the new canto during which Dante expresses his fear that he will be unable to put in words what he witnessed in the last of the circles. In the most classical of traditions, he invokes the Muses (*quelle donne*, 32:10) for their help as he attempts to describe the bottom of Hell. When Amphion played on his lyre in trying to bewitch the Muses, the stones of Mount Cithaeron approached in order to hear him and formed themselves the walls of Thebes. A comparable miracle will be necessary for the Italian poet with his human speech accustomed to express only ordinary things. Dante is asking whether language is able to transcribe the power of the imagination; it almost seems that Dante is beginning a new poem at this point.

Cocytus is the eternally frozen lake on which Virgil and Dante have been set down by the giant Antaeus. It lies at the bottom of the lost city of Dis below all the circlings the two travelers have taken. We are at the beginning of one of the greatest images in the *Inferno*, the place called Caina, named for Cain who slew his brother (Genesis 4). Caina was first mentioned by Francesca in canto 5 (line 107), as being that place in Hell where the worst sin is punished, the sin of treachery, which is also cruelty. Strong feelings of hatred and destruction are here in Cocytus, the fourth of the infernal rivers. This is Dante's stupendous image of the final state of sin.

Caina, then, contains those sinners who did violence to their own kindred. When they raise their heads, Dante can see hot tears freezing and dropping into icicles as they seal the eyes. The hot blood of the Phlegethon has now turned to ice, designating cold-blooded murder.

Cain himself is not mentioned by Dante. He was the first murderer and fratricide in the Bible. In calling this first region of the ninth circle Caina, Dante is interpreting the act of Cain as the result not of sudden violence but of treachery. When Cain said to Abel, "Come let us go into the field," he was, according to this interpretation, planning to murder his brother. Already in the biblical narrative he was seen to be capable of lying. When the Lord asked him, "Where is thy brother Abel?" he answered, "I do not know."

The first encounter Dante has in Caina (32:40–69), is with two Italian brothers who had slain each other. Pressed together, they butt each other like goats. Another spirit tells Dante that the two brothers are Alessandro and Napoleone, sons of Count Alberto degli Alberti. They killed each other while quarreling over their inheritance.

In describing this act, the spirit refers to Mordred, the traitor who attempted to usurp King Arthur's throne. Arthur struck him so fiercely that when the lance was withdrawn, the sun shone through the wound. A few other traitors are named by the spirit, who finally names himself at the end of the speech. He is Camicion de' Pazzi, of Valdarno, who murdered his kinsman Albertino. The traitors are reticent and sullen about being identified themselves, but are eager to denounce one another and provide names without being asked.

Without any clear demarcation being indicated, Dante moves into the second part of the ninth circle which is called Antenora in line 88. According to a medieval tradition, Antenor was the Trojan who betrayed his city to the Greeks. It is a curious transmigration from Homer to Dante's ice. Here, where Dante sees thousands of faces made doggish by the cold, the sinners are plunged more deeply into the ice.

As Dante steps among the heads, his foot kicks against one of the faces. The spirit screams at the poet, who asks his name. When the spirit refuses to answer, Dante grabs him by the hair and threatens him. Another spirit yells out that he is Bocca degli Abati, a Ghibelline who sided with the Florentine Guelfs. In the battle of Montaperti, he fought on the Guelf side, and at one

point cut off the hand of the standard-bearer of the Florentine
cavalry. The standard fell, which threw the Florentines into a
panic and lost them the day.

Thus, in this brief episode Dante obtains the name he wants
through the treachery of a suffering companion of the spirit.
These spirits appear as demons punishing one another, and
Dante himself is close to being a demon. In his cruel gesture, it
would seem that he is becoming more and more obsessed by the
scenes he is observing. Between line 112 and the end of the
canto (line 139), several traitors are named, both mythical and
historical figures that mean very little today. The last sixteen
lines introduce the tale of Ugolino, one of the most demonic
figures in Dante's Hell.

Antenor himself does not appear in Antenora, just as Cain did
not appear in Caina, but the reader must suppose that both are
present. In the cold of these regions there is only one sound: the
chattering of teeth, compared to the noise that storks make with
their bills.

The traitor is cruel. This characteristic is emphasized in all
four parts of this final circle. And in all four cases, treachery
involves murder: betrayal of family (Caina), of country (Antenora), of guests (Ptolomea) and of lords and benefactors (Judecca).
In all the scenes the vile dispositions of the traitors are un-
changed. All are eager to betray one another.

The end of canto 32 and two-thirds of canto 33 are given over to
the story of Ugolino. He is not named in 32 and his silence during
the first picture we get of him arouses our curiosity. It is an
arresting introduction to one of the most illustrious episodes of
the *Commedia*. The hardest part to read, the most disgusting, is
here in canto 32. Two heads are frozen together in the ice, one
above the other. One head is a cap to the other (*l'un capo a l'altro
era cappello*, 32:126). The upper head gnaws the scalp of the
lower "where the brain joins with the nape" (32:129). Dante
compares this act to an incident related by Statius in the eighth
book of the *Thebaid*. In the war of the Seven against Thebes,
Tydeus, although mortally wounded by Menalippius, was still
able to kill his adversary, whose head, when it was brought to
him, he began to gnaw in a frenzy of rage.

This brief passage is a mixture of horror and erudition, and
although the horror continues in the next canto, it is joined with
pathos. The episodes of Count Ugolino is one of the most inhuman and at the same time one of the most human. In the last

lines of canto 32 Dante invites the sinner to speak and to accuse his enemies. The poet then promises to repeat the truth on the earth.

This promise made to Ugolino is dependent on the power of poetry. From the initial silence of the ice and the opening vision of the two brothers butting each other like goats, we have come through a series of ever-growing contrasts and images of violence to Ugolino, who in the next canto will reveal a story of utter pathos. To this is added Dante's belief in the power of his art and his offer to tell the story "unless my tongue dry up before I die" (32:139). At the beginning of canto 31 reference is made to Virgil's tongue, which reproves and pardons at the same time. At the end of canto 32, Dante's tongue serves as the writer's introduction to his following canto. Nimrod, whose speech is gibberish in canto 31 is the gigantic symbol of the confusion of tongues.

Principal Signs and Symbols

1. *Cocytus* (*Cocito*): the fourth river of Hell, turned to ice by the flapping of Satan's wings, located at the bottom of the city of Dis at the farthest point from the source of light and heat. In this canto we find the first two regions or zones of Cocytus: Caina, where treachery to a relative is punished; and Antenora, for the betrayal of one's city or country. Here in these two zones Dante finds many countrymen, both Guelfs and Ghibellines.

2. *The story of Mordred* (32:61–62): this is told in the Old French text *Lancelot du Lac*, the book Francesca and Paolo read in canto 5.

3. *Ganelon* (32:122–23): the knight who betrayed Roland to the Saracens in *La Chanson de Roland*.

CANTO

33

Antenora (Ugolino); Ptolomea

CANTO 33 CONTINUES canto 32 without interruption or a new beginning. We are still on Cocytus, at the bottom of the universe, in the hollow center of the earth, at the point where all gravitation (*gravezza*) converges. There will be no more movement downward. Love aspires upward, and that will be the experience of Purgatory. The farther one proceeds on Cocytus, from Antenora to Ptolomea, the deeper the sinners are in ice. Finally, at the beginning of canto 34, they appear as only pieces of straw in glass.

All the sinners are imprisoned in a glassy sea and one marvels that here among the frozen sinners we hear the narrative of the most eloquent character of the entire *Divine Comedy*. In his poem Dante presents Ugolino as a man betrayed. But he was a traitor himself, and that of course is why he appears in Antenora. In 1288 the Guelfs were in power in Pisa, but they were divided into two parties, one led by Count Ugolino della Gherardesca, the other by his grandson, Nino dei Visconti. The Archbishop of Pisa, Ruggieri degli Ubaldini, was head of the Ghibellines. To get rid of Nino, Ugolino allied himself with Ruggieri. When the archbishop saw the Guelfs weakened, he turned on Ugolino and imprisoned him along with four of his sons and grandsons (older than the boys in Dante's version) in a tower, subsequently named "the tower of famine" (*la torre della fame*). In March of the following year, Ruggieri ordered the tower to be locked and the keys thrown into the river. After eight days the tower was opened and Ugolino and the four young men were found dead of starvation.

Ugolino does not tell his story, but Dante knew it well since he was twenty-three years old in 1288, and assumes his readers would know it. Thus Ugolino makes no allusion to his crime as he speaks to Dante. With teeth fastened to the skull of Ruggieri, he is the witness to the crime of the archbishop. The head under his teeth is that of a traitor who, motionless and silent, is the model of petrified humanity.

This is another supreme example of the *contrapasso*, the law of the talion made so explicit in the case of Bertrand de Born in canto 28. Ruggieri is the *fiero pasto* (the "savage meal" of line 1) of the man he caused to die of starvation. But Ugolino's grief is not assuaged by the vengeance he carries out in Hell. Dante presents him as a man whose grief is infinite, wilder than the deed he committed on earth.

Because of the phrases he uses and because of the situation, Dante deliberately indicates a parallel between Francesca and Paolo in canto 5 and Ugolino and Ruggieri in canto 33. When Ugolino says

> parlare e lagrimar vedrai insieme [33:9]
> [you will see me speak and weep at the same time]

we remember from canto 5

> dirò come colui che piange e dice. [5:126]
> [I will speak as one who weeps and tells]

These lines that introduce the stories are taken from the same passage in Virgil (*Aeneid* 2:10, 12–13). Both Francesca and Ugolino recall the past with grief, both yield to Dante's request, and both weep and speak at the same time.

There is, however, a major difference: Francesca's past was voluptuous and joyful, and in Hell it is one with her misery. Ugolino's past and present are the same, tormented with grief, rage, and hatred, as the victim on earth plays the role of executioner in Hell. He is a complex character who in his narrative reveals the tragic richness of his inner life, despairing because he can devise no vengeance to pay adequately for his injury. He relives the horror of watching his children die while crunching the bones of Ruggieri with his teeth.

Ugolino's narrative begins with his life as a prisoner. Months went by since he was placed in the dungeon. Light came through a "narrow hole in the mew":

> Breve pertugio dentro da la Muda [33:22]

Muda means "molting" or "mew," a cage for hawks when they are molting.

After this brief introduction Ugolino speaks of an evil dream he had in which the future is revealed to him. He sees Ruggieri and three other men hunting a wolf and its whelps (*il lupo e ' lupicini*, 33:29). The animals are, of course, himself and his children. He wakes up and hears his sons, who also have been dreaming. They are crying and asking for bread. The scene is thus set in this first part of the narrative. In what follows, we realize that all the drama comes from the presence of the children in the father's cell. Ugolino is destined to suffer not only his own death but also that of his sons.

The second part begins when Ugolino hears the door of the cell being nailed up:

> e io senti' chiavar l'uscio di sotto
> a l'orribile torre [33:46–47]
> [and below I heard the outlet of the
> horrible tower locked up]

Ugolino's first impulse was to look up at the boys' faces. Evidently they heard nothing. This is not explicit in the text but the reader understands from what follows that this is the case. The father knows his fate, but the boys do not.

Life is drained from Ugolino. He is unable to weep and inwardly he is being turned to stone:

> Io non piangëa, sì dentro impetrai [33:49]

But his sons cry, and little Anselm notices the strange look on his father's face:

> Anselmuccio mio
> disse: 'Tu guardi sì, padre! che hai?' [33:50–51]
> [My little Anselm said:
> You look so, father, what is the matter?]

The father's love for his son is expressed in the diminutive: *Anselmuccio mio*.

Ugolino is unable to speak until the next day. His silence for a day and night is the expression of total despair. Then with daylight Ugolino changes from a statue back into a man who gives vent to his feelings. When a small ray of light enters the prison, he sees the figure of stone he resembles reflected in the four faces of his sons. And through grief he bites both of his hands:

ambo le man per lo dolor mi morsi [33:58]

The boys interpret this act as hunger (*per voglia / di manicar*,
33:59–60), and they offer themselves to their father as food, even
though they themselves are dying of starvation. They' make an
offer of filial devotion and at the same time a prayer to end their
agony. Their words are totally simple and as deeply moving as
can be found in the *Commedia:*

> 'Padre, assai ci fia men doglia
> se tu mangi di noi.'[33:61–62]
> [Father, it will be less painful to us if you eat of us.]

(The reader cannot forget, as he reads this part of the narrative,
that Ugolino, as he tells his story, has his teeth deep in the skull
of his enemy.)

Then once again Ugolino turns to stone. All quiets down in the
cell until the father utters a cry for the earth to open up, a cry for
death:

> ahi dura terra, perché non t'apristi? [33:66]

The tragedy deepens on the fourth day when Gaddo cries out
for help:

> 'Padre mio, ché non m'aiuti?' [33:69]
> [Father, why don't you help me?]

The poignancy is in the phrasing of the question. Gaddo seems to
be saying: "You could help me and you don't want to." The boy
dies at the moment of asking his question, and then begins
Ugolino's hardest trial as he sees the other three boys die one
after the other between the fifth and the sixth days. Death is
repeated four times at long intervals.

Then in the last tercet (33:73–75) Ugolino, blind as the result of
starvation, gropes over the dead bodies of his sons and calls them
for two days. The father ends his narrative with the pathetic line:

> Poscia, più che 'l dolor, poté 'l digiuno. [33:75]
> [Then, hunger proved more powerful than grief.]

As so often in Dante's text, the reader's imagination has to interpret this line. Is Ugolino confessing here that he literally ate the
flesh of his sons? Or is he saying that the cause of his death was
starvation rather than grief? The picture of Ugolino chewing on
the skull of Ruggieri with both figures are frozen in the lake of

Cocytus has led some commentators to conclude that he performed an act of cannibalism in his tower cell.

It is impossible for the poet to say all that he might have said about any of these major episodes. Here in Ugolino's story, he does not point out that the traitor was denied a confessor. In the thirteenth century this would have been the most terrible of punishments.

At the end of the story, Dante's wrath against Pisa explodes as he describes a way in which the city can be destroyed: let the Arno be stopped up and drown every living soul. For a moment one can almost believe that Dante himself has been demonized as he sentences to death an entire city in order to avenge four innocent boys. Is this an example of biblical wrath following the complex contradictory picture of Ugolino?

Out of the background of a gigantic nature emerges the dramatic, realistic life scene of Ugolino's death. He first appears to us (in canto 32) as an unnamed figure of hatred, eternally ravenous. Then he appears as a father with his children. In this scene he weeps, bites both his hands, and shows an expressive anguished face. Then at the conclusion of his story, he sets his teeth again into Ruggieri's skull (33:77). Dante here depicts an eternity of hatred. In the prison scene the boys by their presence act as Ugolino's tormentors. Similarly, Paolo, by his continuous presence, acts as Francesca's tormentor in canto 5. The situation is the same in Beckett's play *Endgame,* in which the father-son pair, Hamm and Clov, are unable to separate or to cease tormenting each other.

Dante has now experienced all of Hell, save for the final region of Judecca. At the beginning, in the second circle, Francesca's story moved Dante to pity, but at the end, in Antenora of the ninth circle, he is moved to wrath by Ugolino's story. He observes two beings, hateful to each other, doomed to stay forever united in hate, as in the previous zone of Caina he observed two hostile brothers forever unable to separate from each other.

The third region of the ninth circle is called Ptolomea in line 124 (*questa Tolomea*), where treachery to a friend or to a guest is punished. This is a more serious sin than the sins of Caina and Antenora because the element of choice or free will plays a large role. A man cannot choose his brother (Caina) but he can choose a friend (Ptolomea). A man cannot choose his native country (Antenora), but he can choose a spiritual master (Judecca). In treachery perpetrated on a friend or on a benefactor, there is a deeper responsibility, a deeper guilt. The first two regions are concerned with natural relationships: family and state. The last two are voluntary relationships: guests, friends, or even God.

The origin of the name Ptolomea is not explained by Dante, and there is no Ptolemy punished here, as there has been no Cain or Antenor. In all likelihood, the name is based on Ptolemy, captain of Jericho who invited "Simon and two of his sons into his castle, and there treacherously murdered them" (1 Maccabees 16:11–17). Another possibility is Ptolemy XII, the Egyptian king who, after welcoming Pompey to his realm, slew him. Each of these sources is the story of the betrayal of guests.

The traitors to hospitality are denied the ability to weep. They are almost sealed off from humanity because their faces are not simply turned down, but are wholly reversed. The tear drops freeze and turn inward to increase their agony.

> Lo pianto stesso lì pianger non lascia [33:94]
> [the very weeping there does not allow them to weep]

Dante feels a wind and Virgil promises that soon he will find the cause of the wind that blows over Cocytus and freezes it.

The canto ends with another scene of some length (33:109–57) in which Dante is the chief actor, and which is a counterpart to the comparable scene in canto 32.

A spirit cries out requesting Dante to remove the ice ("the hard veils") from his eyes, so that he can give vent to his grief. Dante asks his name and promises to relieve him. The spirit then reveals his name. He is Fra Alberigo of the Manfredi family of Faenza. In the course of a dispute his younger brother Manfred struck him in the face. Alberigo pretended to forgive him, and later invited Manfred and one of his sons to a dinner. At dessert time, he called out "bring on the fruit," a signal for servants to rush in and kill Manfred and his son. In line 119 the "fruits of the ill garden" is probably an allusion to this episode. "To receive dates for one's figs" (33:120) is a Tuscan expression meaning to pay off with interest. The fig is the cheapest of Tuscan fruits; the date is imported and more costly.

Ptolomea has a special privilege (vantaggio, 33:124) which accords with Church doctrine and which is referred to by Alberigo. Through an act of treachery, a man may lose his soul before he dies (before Antropos sends it off by cutting the thread of life) and then, on earth, a devil inhabits the body until its natural death. The example here pointed out by Alberigo is Branca d'Oria, who murdered his father-in-law, Michele Zanche, after having invited him to dine with him. The soul of Branca fell into Ptolomea in 1275, long before he actually died in 1325. Thus the real Hell of Dante's conception is a hell for the living.

Again, Alberigo pleads with Dante to open his eyes (aprimi li occhi, 33:149) and now Dante refuses by saying: "To be rude to him was courtesy." An ominous change is taking place in Dante. His hate of treachery is turning into treachery. His love of justice is forcing him into the role of torturer: here Dante is the devil to the sinner. The Malebranche fiends were not more guilty of fraud in the eighth circle than Dante is in the ninth. The first signs of this attitude in Dante were apparent in canto 8 when he crossed the Styx and wrathfully denounced the wrathful Filippo Argenti. Here in canto 33 Dante's cruelty is at its worst, and he concludes the canto, which is in many eyes the most terrifying of the Inferno, with a denunciation of the Genoese, since Branca d'Oria was a Ghibelline of Genoa.

Principal Signs and Symbols

1. Ugolino and Ruggieri: the last scene demonstrating partnership in sin, following that of Francesca and Paolo (canto 5) and that of Ulysses and Diomedes (canto 26). We hear only one speaker in each scene. The evident correspondences between Francesca-Paolo and Ugolino-Ruggieri emphasize the development from sensuality in love to the last stage of corruption of love, or the corruption of every passion that is directed against the order of the city, and that bears the seeds of treachery. Treachery was in the passion of Francesca and Paolo as well as in the strife between Ugolino and Ruggieri.

2. In the ice of Ptolomea (33:91–157), lie traiters to hospitality, one of the oldest human institutions. They are unable to weep.

3. Fra Alberigo (33:110–35) believes Virgil and Dante to be damned souls on their way to Judecca, and asks them to remove the "hard veils" (i duri veli, 33:112) from his face. Through him we learn that these sinners live on earth when they are dead to humanity. The man in them is in Ptolomea while a devil inhabits their human form. This explains the words of Branca d'Oria (33:137–41) who had not yet died, and yet is here in Ptolomea. Church doctrine does say that by an act of treachery a man may lose possession of his soul and a devil inhabit his body until his natural death.

CANTO

34

Judecca; Lucifer; the Ascent out of Hell

THE GIANTS introduced the ninth circle, and in this final canto we come to *the* giant, to Lucifer himself as the supreme example of treachery, which is the end of all human values, the freezing of all human conceptions. Here the final ties that bind one person to another are broken and we reach the culmination of the ninth circle which is the culmination of the *Inferno*.

Betrayal of the ties of kindred (Caina) and of country (Antenora) is less serious because we are born into them. Yet even if we do not choose them, we are bound by them, and Dante allows room in these first two realms for a little remorse. The tears of the sinners may flow if they keep their faces down.

Then, in the third realm (Ptolomea), we see those sinners who betrayed an invited guest. This is presented by Dante as a lower form of treachery because the traitor chooses his guests and his friends. Here the suffering is greater because the tears are frozen into the masks of ice.

The fourth division of the circle, Judecca, is the region of the traitors to sworn allegiance. It is obviously named after Judas Iscariot, who betrayed Jesus. Here the sinners lie wholly submerged in the ice and are thus cut off from all contact with one another and from all means of expression.

If we pause before continuing Dante's journey, we can begin to see in retrospect the great change that takes place in the traitors' pit. In the first through fourth circles, the place of incontinence, and in the seventh circle where violence is punished, our attention is focused on great characters and their powerful passions: Francesca (canto 5), Farinata (10), Pier della

Vigna (13), Brunetto Latini (15), and Capaneus (16). Then, in the eighth circle, *Malebolge*, where fraud is punished, we see passion change into vice, and violence change into malice. Vice has become in these lower circles a deep-rooted habit, not far removed from the bestial. Vanni Fucci, the thief, is the typical figure here, and he says of himself he was a beast on earth in his city of Pistoia.

Then in the ninth circle, after watching the change from man to beast, we see the change from man to ice or stone (*pietra, ghiaccia*). In Judecca, where the souls are completely enclosed, the fallen spirit has gone the whole way. (The word *cammino*, "way," is in the opening line of the poem, and it is recalled in the seventh line from the end of the poem: *quel cammino ascoso*, 34:133, "that hidden road.") Here in Judecca, where treachery and cruelty are extreme, no one speaks, no one hears. Instead of speech, Dante hears the wind. The cold is eternal.

The last canto opens with the first words of a Latin hymn, one of the Passion hymns of the Roman Church in praise of the cross, which is traditionally sung on Monday in Holy Week at Vespers and at the feast of the exaltation of the cross:

> Vexilla regis prodeunt [34:1]
> [the banners of the king advance]

Dante changes "king" to "infernal king" (*regis inferni*), and thereby changes the reference from Christ to Lucifer. Thus he infernalizes the hymn composed in the sixth century by Fortunatus, an Italian bishop of Poitiers.

These parodied words are spoken by Virgil as he prepares Dante for the sight of Lucifer. The "banners" or "standards" are Lucifer's wings. When sung on Good Friday, Fortunatus' hymn immediately precedes the unveiling of the cross. The added word *inferni* recalls to us the reality of Hell and the presence of Lucifer. In the silence reigning over Judecca, Dante observes the sinners fixed in the ice in various postures. They seem like straw in glass. The unclear shade of Lucifer appears to Dante first as a windmill, and before Virgil's words of explanation there is a reference to the mythic Lucifer:

> la creatura ch'ebbe il bel sembiante [34:18]
> [the creature who once was so beautiful]

Lucifer: the light-bearing seraph, was the most beautiful of all angelic creatures. In the verb *ebbe*, "he had," we can feel the form of the past absolute. His present ugliness is contrasted with his former beauty.

Virgil, very much in his role as guide, makes Dante stop and again speaks briefly: *Ecco Dite*("Behold Dis"). The classical poet uses the name Dis or Pluto, king of the underworld, but to Dante he is Lucifer (or Satan or the Devil or Beelzebub). Dante becomes chilled and hoarse as he faces Lucifer for the first time. He describes this intense experience in very few words:

> Io non mori', e non rimasi vivo [34:25]
> [I did not die, and did not remain alive]

Lucifer, fixed in the center of the earth, at the last point of Hell, does not change his place as others do in the *Inferno*. He freezes Cocytus by flapping his huge wings. The description of him begins with a solemn line, full of the long "o" sound:

> Lo 'mperador del doloroso regno [34:28]
> [the emperor of the dolorous realm]

The grotesqueness of the scene reaches its culmination when Dante sees the three faces of Lucifer and realizes that the giant is champing and tearing three archtraitors in his three mouths: Judas, who betrayed Christ, and Brutus and Cassius, who betrayed Caesar. (Although Caesar was never emperor in the literal sense, he was the founder of the Roman Empire, and therefore he is the image of that institution which for Dante was divinely appointed to govern the world.)

The poet avoids any attempt to dramatize the story of Lucifer or to make him into a character as Milton does in *Paradise Lost*. Dante is content in canto 34 to give us just the notion of the first and the greatest sinner. The color symbolism of the three faces (yellow, red, and black) is not certain. One interpretation would make them representative of hatred, impotence, and ignorance, the opposing qualities of the Holy Trinity (love, power, and wisdom). In seeing Lucifer, Dante sees the opposite of God. At the height of Paradise he will see God in his triune shape, in the form of three circles of light. Thus the extremes of Hell and Paradise are determined by the Trinity. The Holy Trinity (Father, Son, and Holy Spirit) is often looked upon as the deepest speculative mystery of the Christian Church. Dante is presenting God and Satan as the positive and negative Trinity, the two opposite limits of *The Divine Comedy*.

Why were these three men selected by Dante to be eternally

punished by Satan? According to Dante's view they betrayed the two heroes of the human race: Julius Caesar, who founded the secular branch of the new order; and Christ, who founded the ecclesiastical branch of the new order. The treachery of the sinners in Judecca is directed against the world order because it harms the benefactors of mankind.

With Virgil's naming of the three traitors, we are midway in the canto, and the master (*il maestro*) tells Dante it is time to depart, that "all has been seen" (34:69). The ascent begins as Virgil and Dante climb down the shaggy body of Satan. A medieval convention described Satan's body as shaggy like that of a satyr. The poets clamber down feet first, as if they were climbing down a ladder, when suddenly (34:79) they turn upside down and begin to go up head first.

The point they had reached at this reversal was the center of gravity, situated at Satan's navel. It is a physical turning point but also a spiritual transition. When Dante sees Satan's legs turned upward, he is understandably confused, and Virgil explains patiently the changes that are taking place. The time is halfway between the canonical hours of prime and terce, or approximately 7:30 A.M. on Saturday morning. Having passed the center of the earth, they are now in the southern hemisphere, and since they are in southern time, day and night are reversed. Purgatory stands on the meridian opposite to Jerusalem, and thus Purgatory time is twelve hours behind Jerusalem time.

Dante tells very little of Satan's fall (that will be left for Milton, who shows Satan moving from defeat in Heaven to victory on earth). Dante, in just these few lines of canto 34, portrays him undone by God and mastered by man. Satan, almost as if he were a stage prop, serves as Dante's ladder up which he climbs out of Hell.

The drama of the ninth circle is projected as an ever-increasing development in size and space. It began with the giants and then moved to Lucifer, the biggest of the giants, whose head is at the center of the earth and whose legs are in the southern hemisphere. As Dante looks back he sees the earth, and as he looks up, at the very end of the canto, he sees the cosmos.

When Lucifer fell from Heaven, his head bored through the earth's center. Before he fell, the southern hemisphere was covered with land, but after his plunge, the land sank below the sea and shifted to the northern hemisphere (*emisperio nostro*, 34:124, "our hemisphere"). At the center of the earth, the land rushed upward, leaving an empty space and forming the mountain of Purgatory, the only land in the southern hemisphere according to Dante.

Through the empty space a stream passes. This is probably the Lethe, the river of oblivion. Dante and Virgil will climb through this space in order to reach the base of the mountain. "A space down there" (*Luogo è laggiù*, 34:127), as far from Lucifer as the limit of his tomb, serves as an entrance to the passage from the earth's center to its circumference, created by Lucifer in his fall from Heaven to Hell. Denied their sight for so long, Dante can now look up and see the stars in the heavens.

This is the last line of the poem:

> E quindi uscimmo a riveder le stelle. [34:
> [And thence we came out to see once again the stars.]

The word *stelle* closes each of the three parts of the *Commedia*. From this point on, the direction of Dante's journey is upward. The word *stelle* underscores the concept of the movement toward God.

There is scriptural authority for the fall of Lucifer in the fourteenth chapter of Isaiah (12–15):

> How art thou fallen from heaven, O Lucifer, son of the morning! . . . For thou hast said in thine heart, I will ascend into heaven, I will exalt my throne above the stars of God. . . . Yet thou shalt be brought down to hell, to the sides of the pit.

In Luke 10:18 we read "I beheld Satan as lightning fall from heaven."

The fathers of the Church maintained that "Lucifer" is not the proper name of the Devil, but a word denoting the state from which he fell. Saint Thomas Aquinas taught that Satan sinned by desiring to be as God. There is sin only when this desire is inordinate, namely the sin of pride. The vision that Dante has of Lucifer as an almost inert natural phenomenon is only one of the many notable matters in this canto.

The way out of Hell (or out of punishment) has brought Dante and Virgil to the realm of purification. Except for the introductory canto, and possibly the narration of Ulysses (canto 26), there has been no allusion to Purgatory. Hell is an eternal independent world. In this sense, the *Inferno* is a more complete and more closed poem than the *Purgatorio* and *Paradiso*. After the opening canto, the unity of the thirty-three cantos is in the underlying ethical keynote and the effect of the ethical meaning of each circle on the traveler.

There is a definite change in Dante's mood about the middle of the eighth circle, after the comic scenes of the barrators (cantos 21 and 22). At that point his ethical hatred becomes clear and he almost takes delight in the penalties, as he sees the city being betrayed in every possible way. Then, with considerable effort, he forces himself to turn away from the attraction of sin. He literally turns his back on it, with the help of Virgil and the power of reason that Virgil represents.

He is able now to climb out from Hell because he has explored all the manifestations of sin. *Ecco Dite*, Virgil said in line 20. "Behold Dis." Twice Virgil used the name of "Dis" to designate lower Hell (11:65, 12:39). In the *Aeneid* (6:127) Virgil used "Dis" for Pluto, god of the underworld. And here at the heart of the Infernal City we see Dis himself, Lucifer, chief of devils, whose sin was the desire to be as God.

Thus we understand that the ethical cause of the *Inferno* was Lucifer's primordial revolt in Heaven. Here, for Dante the poet, the ethical joins with the mythical. The primitive dualism between God and Lucifer made Hell, both physically and ethically. The *Inferno* ends with two images: that of Lucifer falling downward in his flight, and that of Dante climbing upwards along the path of that primordial fall.

This final colossal figure, in his total alienation from God, turns all of Hell into one circle of which Lucifer is the center, the lost soul at the heart of the universe. The original lapse from God is now seen to be the source of all other lapses. Once an angelic soul in harmony with God, Lucifer is now demonic. The end of Hell is the picture of the primal cosmic fact of the fall.

Principal Signs and Symbols

1. *Judecca* (*Giudecca*): the last zone of Cocytus where the traitors to benefactors are wholly submerged in the ice and have no means of expression.

2. *Judas:* illustrates the betrayal of God (*Giuda Scariotto*, 34: 62). *Brutus* and *Cassius* (*Bruto*, 34:65; *Cassio*, 34:67) betrayed Julius Caesar (who is in limbo, 4:123). Caesar was never emperor but Dante considers him the founder of the Roman Empire and

thus divinely apppointed to govern the world. Therefore, in the most significant sense, Brutus and Cassius betrayed the world-order.

3. *Behold Dis (Ecco Dite,* 34:20): for Virgil, Dis is the king of the underworld, but for Dante he is Lucifer.

4. *The three faces (tre facce,* 34:38): are they the three races (the red European race of Japhet, the yellow Asiatic race of Shem, and the black African race of Ham)? Or are they simply the opposite of the Blessed Trinity?

5. *Terce:* first of the four canonical divisions of the day, from sunrise to 9 A.M. Mid-terce would be about 7:30 A.M. (*mezza terza,* 34:96).

Note on Reading Dante Today

WITH EVERY READING of the *Inferno*—and especially, because of my profession, with every biannual effort to teach the poem—I ask myself the same question: how can I understand a text so distant as the *Commedia?* Can I ever hope to know today, almost six hundred years after the poem was written, what it is really saying? Is it possible to make a purely literary approach to a work whose ever present subject is eternal damnation? Will Santayana's statement, "the damned are damned for the glory of God," help with such a problem? Would it be better simply, through the reading, to enter into an alien "historical" world? Or is it more advisable to try to translate Dante into the language of psychology?

The world looks upon *The Divine Comedy* as a religious poem, as, in fact, the greatest religious poem in our tradition. Such an acknowledgment should be a help in the dilemma I often experience. And then, to offset such reassurance, I remember T. S. Eliot's admonition: "you are not called upon to believe what Dante believed." I am no longer sure that such a claim is true. My mind is no longer relieved by it. If we must be converted in order to read Dante, might we call the conversion that of the imagination?

On the one hand, we read in the *Inferno* many facts about individual people, men and women who are historical or legendary, and many facts about cities, towns, and events: wars, encounters, occurrences of all kinds. Then, on the other hand, we become fascinated by modes of thought and feeling that are as current as they were in Dante's age. We think first: how the world is changed! And then we begin to realize that there has been little change. Little change, that is, in the ability of the human heart to sustain great evil or great good.

A world unfolds before us, with its various societies, its stratifications of classes; and history unfolds with its dates, its achievements, its disasters. But not until we are really under the spell of Dante's verse do we realize that the poet is showing us how God is above and behind it all, how all the things of this world are his handiwork. The patterns of Dante's poem are those of the Christian mind and the Christian imagination. This might be rephrased more simply by saying that this world is a place of transit, and that the Christian is a pilgrim.

Because of the breadth and intensity of Dante's poem, I believe that a purely aesthetic response, a poetic assent such as Coleridge describes, is inadequate. To read Dante as he deserves to be read, we have to bring to the work not only all our knowledge of literature and all our experience of life, we also have to draw up within us all the beliefs we have held, juvenile and mature, and all the metaphysical doubts that have both flattered and tormented us. A text such as Dante's does not have a timeless, unchanging identity. It is nothing when it is not being read, and when it is being read, it bends and adapts itself to the understanding of the reader, to his limitations and dreams, to the life he has already led and to the life he hopes to lead.

A modern reader tends to read the *Inferno* as a series of great human encounters, and thus tends to diminish the importance of the theological framework, and even to consider this framework irrelevant. It seems to me now far too easy a solution, far too unjust, to look upon Dante's Hell as a mere metaphor for alienation or for the loss of the good in a man's soul. No, Hell is an ordered world, meaningful from top to bottom. There is no place in it for an element of chance. In this sense of an ordered world, the *Commedia* is the fourteenth-century model for the modern novel—that form of literary art that comes closest to presenting a world in which every encounter, ever desire, every suicide is preordained, announced and explained before it occurs. *Le rouge et le noir, Madame Bovary, Ulysses, A la recherche du temps perdu*, and, to a lesser degree, the luminous stories and novels of Flannery O'Connor and Iris Murdoch: the relations are all there, plotted in advance; each one timeless and each firmly attached to a tradition in time and history.

Hell is the image of the evil of which man is capable. With Virgil at his side, Dante is permitted to see this image, or series of images, and he reacts to each in a slightly different way. At every turn of the long road which leads him to the center of the earth, he faces sign after sign of the ultimate cruelty of man to man, and of man's disobedience to God.

This extraordinary permission to witness the cruelty of Hell was granted by Heaven, first at the beginning of the poem by the intervention of Mary, who urged Beatrice to solicit Virgil's help, and then, at the entrance to Dis, which contains the most extreme pictures of cruelty, this far more difficult passage is opened up by an angel. It is a moment of ritual that follows the lesser horrors of Hell and precedes the greater ones, when all Dante's attention and ours is fixed on this solitary figure moving swiftly to the gate of Dis. The angelic figure appears preoccupied and scornful of the place and of the threats of the fallen angels and the Furies. His wand, like the golden bough that secures for Aeneas the way to the underworld, performs a rescue that is both ritualistic and real. The angel's wand opens the gate of Dis and Dante thus is able to leave the darkness that enveloped the incontinent, and descend into the deeper gloom where the fraudulent suffer. The power of renewal in vegetation, symbolized by the golden bough, is comparable to the effective rescue by the angel in canto 9. Renewal, rebirth, restoration: these are necessary moments in the life of every man, and they are parts of the general pattern of the *Aeneid* and the *Commedia*.

The horror of Hell is made bearable by Dante's momentary vision of the angel and by the poet's encounters with certain figures who remind us more of their greatness than of their damnation: the Promethean figure of Farinata, so defiant of his eternal fate; Ulysses, whose evil counsel is transcribed by the poet as the will to gain experience of the world and of human worth and vice. Dante's Ulysses is appallingly modern in his basic drives. The passion for defiance is in him. Francesca, too, has greatness in her soul. Her loveliness and her courtesy are made clear by Dante, and the pathos of her fate is made clear in the line that always seems to me the most poignant. She points out in her narrative that she and Paolo cannot be friends of the king of heaven.

But Francesca, in that early circle where the sin of carnality is punished less than other sins, is the figure of woman, bearing in her that strange power to lead, to restore, and to give birth. She is an individual soul, but she is woman too: Beatrice, Virgil's Dido, Goethe's Margaret, who had sinned as Francesca had, and who represents the immortality of woman in the last lines of *Faust:*

> Das Ewig-Weibliche
> Zieht uns hinan.

We have the right and even the obligation to ask of any artist of Dante's stature, what he thinks of the world. Such a question may move us closer to understanding the difference between Dante's world, or what Dante believed the world to be, and the newer world that was soon to be described or redescribed by Galileo, and which has grown to be our world.

Dante believed that he lived in a created world. He believed that the creator of the world was God and that everything in the creation pointed toward God. This relationship between the world and its creator, between every aspect of life and the prime mover of life, is symbolic in the most religious sense of the word. Even if Galileo in his private life accepted the dogmas of the Christian Church, as a scientist he drove medieval symbolism out of the natural world. In his role as scientist he eliminated from his study any possible intervention of God in the natural world and in human affairs.

Galileo did not deny God, but he relegated him to such a distance from man, that the new man of the new age we call the Renaissance began to depend solely upon himself for his accomplishments in life. Humanism is the history of man's independence, of the awareness of his power and his potential, and it has dominated our thought ever since the sixteenth century. *The Divine Comedy* was the last work to illustrate a different view, a different philosophy of man.

The medieval world cultivated and protected a sense of mystery. The spirit of the Renaissance has done its best ever since the time of Galileo to rid the world of any sense of mystery. Coleridge claimed that the reading of a poem such as Dante's entails "a willing suspension of disbelief," and Nietzsche explained the birth of tragedy and announced its death in the modern world. Galileo was one of the first to train man to look far beyond himself into a universe that was not a forbidden mystery, but one that could be opened by humanly devised instruments.

The history of Dante's commentators might appear as the history of man's approach to literature, to its meaning and worth. In the fourteenth century Boccaccio was one of the very first, in his

Il comento alla Divina Commedia, to stress the double aspect of the poem in its literal sense (the state of souls after the death of the body) and its allegorical sense (the way in which a man in the practice of his free will is finally rewarded or punished in accordance with justice).

It was Boccaccio who added to Dante's title *Commedia* (which he uses in canto 21 of the *Inferno*) the adjective *divina,* in order to distinguish Dante's work from the usual meaning of comedy as "rural song," and emphasize the larger significance of the work. Boccaccio also points out that the name "Dante" means "giving," and is used twice in the *Commedia:* in the thirtieth canto of the *Purgatorio,* where Beatrice takes over the role of Virgil,

> Dante, perchè Virgilio se ne vada [30:55]
> [Dante, because Virgil leaves you]

and in the twenty-sixth canto of the *Paradiso,* where Adam speaks to Dante:

> Dante, la voglia tua discerno meglio [26:104]
> [Dante, I see better your wish]

(the preferred reading today of line 104, however, is *da te, la volgia,* which means that the poet uses his name only once in the *Commedia*).

In the eighteenth century, Giambattisto Vico, in his *Discoverta del vero Dante,* emphasized the loftiness of Dante's mind, a mind nurtured on the public virtues of magnanimity and justice. Vico theorized that since Dante was born during the period of Italy's expiring barbarism, he brought into focus the best of medieval thought.

Coleridge, lecturing on Dante in the early nineteenth century, saw him as the poet who presented in his work the drama of Providence. In painting the picture of his age, Dante forged a link between religion and philosophy. Dante's style is extolled for its vividness and strength. His images, so often taken from nature, are all intelligible. Coleridge cites the famous example of the flowers closed by the night's frost and opened by the morning sun:

> Quali fioretti dal notturno gelo
> chinati e chiusi, poi che 'l sol li 'mbianca [2:127–28]

After discussing style and images, Coleridge comments on the "profoundness" of Dante's poem, citing the inscription over the gate of Hell at the beginning of canto 3 as a passage that reveals the true nature of religion.

In the latter nineteenth century the Italian writer Carducci lectured on the universality of Dante and called him the poet of all times. He identified the three participants of the poem as Beatrice, representing the cult of woman; Virgil, representing the civilization of antiquity; and Dante Alighieri as man going his way through life. Following the strong Italian tradition, Carducci emphasized the significance, both real and mystical, of the number three. He sees the three *cantiche* as three states of the soul: the *Inferno* is sin; the *Purgatorio* is conversion; the *Paradiso* is virtue. Three and nine govern the whole vision and poetry of the *Commedia:* three realms, thirty-three cantos form each realm, the three-line stanza used throughout, and the sum of the cantos is ninety-nine, plus one introductory canto.

Again, as an Italian, Carducci is sensitive to the effort Dante made to write a popular work, in the language of the Italian people, work closer to popular fiction than to its models in antiquity. All possible sources—Hellenic, Italian, Semitic, Nordic—are drawn into the *Commedia* to assure its appeal to as vast an audience as possible. Carducci speaks of the Etruscan lines visible in Dante's face, Dante who boasted of Roman and German blood. The very intensity of the poem, coming from its colors and sounds, from its grotesque elements and its hillscapes of Tuscany, makes it a darkened ending for the Middle Ages and a half-visible new light for the Renaissance.

Among twentieth-century commentators, Philip Wicksteed has discussed more persistently than others the state of the damned in the *Inferno*. He reminds us that both Aquinas and Dante speak of the damned as being impenitent. Wicksteed considers the essential feature of Dante's Hell the absence of any change in the sinners' sense of moral values. They do not repent. They chose and Divine Justice gave them what they asked for. This principle explains the congruity between the choice of the sinner and his eternal fate. There is no indication that the sinner wants to escape from his circle.

This is the lesson which Dante as pilgrim-protagonist has to learn in his journey through the world beyond death. The pilgrim is also a learner, and this trait caused Croce, for example, to ask whether the *Commedia* is a poem or a demonstration. The answer to this perfectly reasonable question may lie in the relevance of the major scenes to the overall scheme of the work.

Francesca, first, because her canto, the fifth, is the first division of Hell in which the sinner's error is clearly defined as sin. Despite the reader's inevitable identification with Francesca, she is nevertheless a soul in Hell. In the canto Dante is all compassion with no sense of judgment, but this stance is impossible for the reader. We are conscious of the circle's punishment, and know that this loving woman is impenitent, and we may even question Dante's deeply felt sentiment when he is overcome and falls to the ground at the end of the dialogue.

As an introduction to Dante's dialogue with Francesca, we hear a list of great lovers: Dido, Semiramis, Cleopatra, Paris, Tristan. But Francesca is the one chosen to illustrate all these victims of pure feeling. Not until we know the entire *Commedia* can we read Francesca's canto as it should be read within the context of Dante's love for Beatrice. Behind Francesca's story of the day that she and Paolo read of the kiss that Lancelot gave to Guenivere, when the book became the pander of their love, we have to imagine many meetings between the two young people, in a quiet spot in a medieval castle where they read together other books, presumably, before reading the story of Lancelot.

Farinata's canto (10), the second encounter with an imposing figure, provides another instance in which a casual reading will throw into promimence the power of the character's personality and tend to make the reader forget that the pain of Hell is the pain of sin. Farinata proudly defies his habitation (the burning tomb) as well as his suffering. We see this in his posture and hear it in his speech. He is the political partisan representing the overbearing spirit of faction. And Farinata the Ghibelline leader is Dante's adversary. Both men are citizens of Florence and are joined by a love of their city. Yet Farinata's love for Florence was not as strong as his love for the Ghibelline party.

But Farinata, like Francesca, cannot be separated from the significance of the scene that represents his sin and its punishment. A close reading of the text will make us realize that the proud Ghibelline is in a tomb for the Epicureans, those men who rejected all belief in immortality and who thus buried their own souls. In his admiration for his rival Farinata, Dante may have wished to exonerate him, but the scene he depicts of the burning tombs, just below the four circles of the incontinent and just above the sins of violence and fraud, makes any pardon invalid.

How perfectly does this scene in canto 10 demonstrate the nature of error! In heresy the individual clings to one part of the whole. His short-sightedness forces him into a position of isolation, hence the tomb of pride where we see Farinata. His love of party rather than love of country was partisanship; his seeming spirit of arrogance is in reality the spirit of faction dividing the city. The scene, which Dante shares with Farinata, is at once allusion, synecdoche, metonomy, and metaphor.

We should remember, as we read canto 13, that the desire of the suicide is to be alive no longer, to quit the place where he normally lives, to be absent. This desire is dramatically realized by Dante in the appearance of the suicides not as men but as trees. The personal pride of Pier della Vigna made him unable to live in prison because of his love for Frederick II, who had condemned him to prison. He is an eternally immobilized soul, wholly unrecognizable because he denied the mobility of his God-given body and all of his human features. A tree is blind and has no means of expressing the violence of his soul that led him to take his life. Dante's Hell makes perfectly concrete the state of mind of the sinner when he committed his sin. Pier della Vigna, as the leading suicide of canto 13, willed his blindness to his world and to his life, and the qualities he displays in Hell are those of a rigid shrub, although he is still conscious of his role as courtier-chancellor to his emperor.

In canto 15 Dante and Virgil come upon the sodomites, spirits who are continuously running and trying to ward off flakes of fire that fall on their naked bodies. Here an extraordinary meeting takes place between Dante and a fellow Florentine, Brunetto Latini. Brunetto had been a scholar, a notary, a poet, and possibly a teacher of Dante.

When Brunetto recognizes Dante and cries out *"Qual maraviglia!"* Dante looks down at the scorched features of his old teacher, and he, too, recognizes the man and utters the question that T. S. Eliot uses in "Little Gidding":

> Siete voi qui, ser Brunetto? [15:
> [Are you here?]

Dante's first impulse is to stop and talk, but Brunetto tells him he must keep moving. As the two walk together, one safe above on the bank, the other below on the fiery plain, there is a fervent exchange of thoughts about Florence, and finally (in a moment that resembles an epiphany) Dante's recognition of what he owes to Brunetto Latini: "You taught me hour by hour in the world how man makes himself eternal."

These are two poets talking. Brunetto refers to one of his works by its title, and he promises glory to Dante because spirits can foresee the future. Dante's acknowledgment to Brunetto is strong. He is saying, "From you I have understood something concerning eternity." If he were speaking to Beatrice, he would doubtless mean by "eternity" spiritual salvation. But he is speaking to Brunetto, and seems to imply that a successful work is immortal. Dante Alighieri is continuing the mission of the writer taught him by Brunetto and by all the masters he has studied. In the twentieth century Eliot will acknowledge the same debt when in his scene copied from this canto he says that he is one and many. All poets are in him. Dante needed to see and experience the eternity of Hell in order to comprehend the poet's eternity.

This death of a master in the *Inferno* often reminds me of Bergotte's death in Proust's novel. Bergotte, the novelist in the novel, has been ill for some time when he appears in *La pris-onnière*. A critic, in speaking of Vermeer's painting *Vue de Delft*, on loan exhibit in Paris, had praised the beauty of a little patch of yellow wall which Bergotte could not remember, although he thought he knew the painting very well. He decides to disobey his doctors and goes to the gallery. There, thanks to the critic, he marvels at *"le petit pan de mur jaune,"* as well as a few other details on the large canvas.

His last thoughts in his life are about the little patch of yellow wall, and he says: "that is the way I should have written" (*"C'est ainsi que j'aurais dû écrire"*). As he repeats the phrase *"petit pan de mur jaune,"* he sits down on a divan, falls onto the floor, and dies.

For Proust, the narrative here is very simple and direct. There is almost no commentary except the phrases: *"mort à jamais? qui peut le dire?"* Two brief questions: "Has Bergotte died forever? who can say?" The night before his burial, his books, arranged in threes, watch over him as if they were angels. The Vermeer painting, a symbol of artistic perfection, is closely allied to the absolute of death.

The scenes from *La prisionnière* and canto 15 touch on death, and specifically on the death of a writer. We witness Bergotte's sudden death in a painting gallery, and we encounter Brunetto Latini undergoing a special form of punishment throughout eternity. Proust raises the question of Bergotte's immortality without answering it directly, but implies indirectly that Bergotte's books will provide him with some other kind of afterlife. Dante recognizes with astonishment his master on the fiery plain of the seventh circle, and pays homage to his learning and example, as he, a living man, expresses his literary debt to the dead soul who lives on in another world.

In each of these two passages the sudden revelation depends on two statements. Bergotte speaks first in almost technical terms concerning his and Vermeer's art: "That is how I should have written my last books." And then, as soon as he dies, a few minutes later, Proust asks, Has Bergotte died forever? Dante himself makes the two statements in the *Commedia* passage: "Is it you I see in this *girone* of the sodomites?" And then, a few lines later, "You taught me the lesson of eternity."

Both passages, one about a man dying and the other about a man already dead, seems to me principally concerned with derivation. Bergotte, who in the novel had never acknowledged any masters or rival in the art of the novel, suddenly, at the moment of his death, sees the work of a master painter and realizes that his writing could have profited from Vermeer's example. Dante, in the midst of his journey through Hell, greets a poet he had known, a master who had taught him the art of poetry, and celebrates him, even as flakes of fire fall on Brunetto Latini's body. Near the beginning of the *Inferno,* in canto 4, in limbo, Dante had met four poets of antiquity (he was already being led by Virgil) and ranks himself as the sixth world poet.

No poet, no writer exists alone. Saint Peter's great sin was his unwillingness to acknowledge his Lord: "I do not know the man." Bergotte, at his death, and Dante in the world of the dead, both proclaim their antecedents. They both realize at a given moment that they are one and many, that their art is not unique but comes from others who preceded them and will be continued in others who come after. Art therefore may be looked upon as one step leading to an understanding of immortality.

In the experience of death, whether the event of death for Bergotte or the eternity of death for Brunetto, both Dante and Bergotte attain a knowledge of their sources, or what should have been their sources. They become aware of derivation, and the mysterious joining of the past and the future.

I would suggest that Proust's question, *"mort à jamais?"*— dead forever?—is often in the minds of Dante's readers as they observe scene after scene, in canto after canto. Is it possible to conceive of the eternity of Hell as we watch Francesca and Paolo buffetted by the wind, or Brunetto Latini running to catch up with his group of companions as if he were one of the runners in the games at Verona, or Ulysses changed forever into a flame that speaks?

Dante's *Inferno* is purely imaginary, but we follow and marvel at the pure realism of each of the nine circles. Proust's *A la recherche* is a remembered world, turned into a literary form that may well have a long life even if he calls it his tomb. Proust's world was real, and Dante makes his infernal world real for us today. But both authors present their worlds as a baffling maze of illusions pierced from time to time by a sudden intuition, so mysterious that we call it an epiphany.

Dante's art, especially as revealed in the *Inferno*, has traits in common with the work of two modern architect novelists: Joyce's *Ulysses* and Proust's *A la recherche du temps perdu*. All three have been revived and revitalized by the critics. Dante has been kept alive during centuries, but especially during the nineteenth and twentieth centuries by a very specialized race of exegetes. This type of exegete has now fixed on Joyce, so determinedly that Anthony Burgess recently asked: "Will the line stretch out to the crack of Bloom?"

The names of these three creative writers, one poet and two novelists, are now juxtaposed by critics eager to see Proust's Paris resembling, not in the social sense but in the structuralist sense, Joyce's Dublin, and, in the close analyses of moral defects, the categories and divisions of the *Inferno*.

Proust makes very few direct references to Dante in *A la recherche*. His references to Virgil are more numerous. But Dante is a distant model for the form of modern fiction (Proust, Kafka, Joyce, Beckett) sometimes called *Bildungsroman*, that is essentially a narrative of search and research. This important relationship is carefully discussed by Walter Strauss in his article "Proust, Giotto, Dante" (*Dante Studies* 96, 1978).

Joyce and Proust are so close to us chronologically, and are so basic to literary fashion, that they have innumerable snobbish readers who talk about the two writers more than they read them. Dante suffers less in this regard. He can't simply be read; he has to be studied, he has to be known intimately. Passages must be learned by heart. He has to be approached in Italian, at least to some degree, and with some partial knowledge of theology. His readers are still today the most fervent and the most satisfied. Readers are more consistently overwhelmed when reading Dante than when reading Joyce and Proust.

All three writers labored under the pressures of design: the intricate structure of Hell; the Homeric pattern imposed on the day's wanderings of Stephen and Bloom; Marcel's experience of all forms of happiness whose disappointments lead him to the final revelation, comparable to the sight of the stars at the end of the *Inferno* and the *yes* of consent that Molly utters at the end of *Ulysses*.

Each of these three masters tells us something about the interdependence of mankind. Each found the bank of a river an appropriate setting for his tale: the Vivonne in Combray, the Liffey in Dublin, and the four rivers of Hell. A river is eternal, and thus designates the permanence of man. A river flows by and is never the same, and thus designates the mutability of man.

But of course there is a fundamental difference among these works, that between poetry and prose. Dante's work is a poem in which each word counts. Each syllable in fact is counted, each line is a unit, each image is all-important for the whole of the canto. And yet Proust and Joyce, among all novelists, come closest to the poets, in the way they write, in their care for each word, in the meaning of a word in its relationship to the whole, in the images and the allusions, in the actual use of other poets in their work. They are in a sense our modern epic poets, with a knowledge of the condensed power of words learned from their study of Dante and Baudelaire and Mallarmé. Thus the bridge joining Dante to Joyce and Proust is not that extensive.

The aesthetic resemblances between Joyce and Proust far outdistance their differences of temperament. Joyce's nature was as antiaristocratic as Proust's was elitist. But both revelled in the gossipy side of human nature: Joyce in the gossip of the Dubliners, Proust in the gossip of Eulalie and aunt Léonie, as well as that of the Baron of Charlus and his sister-in-law, the Duchess of Guermantes. Joyce and Proust remained remote from their worlds only when they were engaged in writing about them. There was no icy aloofness in either one, and Dante expresses at a hundred points in his poem his sympathy with others, his understanding, his warmth of character. Countless examples in all three writers could be listed to prove this democratic willingness to see and comprehend the viewpoint of the other man.

There is, of course, something of the author in every one of their characters, but the miracle of their art is that each of these characters exists by himself, independent of his creator.

In the unfolding of the *Inferno*, of *Ulysses*, and *A la recherche*, one human failing in particular is condemned, one trait that returns over and over again in the pages of the poem and the novels: the human will to power. When a man finds himself in a position of power, he finds at the same time in those people who wait upon and for him both clear and disguised signs of suspicion and hatred. Power inevitably brings about its own collapse. To offset this insidious drive, Dante makes it clear that he needs Virgil, and that Virgil likewise needs Dante. A similar pattern of restriction and control is visible in Joyce's Stephen and Bloom, and in Proust's Marcel and Swann.

With these examples of medieval and modern art, I am trying to point out, as a final homage to Dante, that literature, both its creation and its study, is not an escape from life, but the central expression of life. The poet in the practice of his art is capable of assimilating all the life that surrounds him and then of sending it abroad to all countries of all tongues. Thus the poem written in the Tuscan dialect of the fourteenth century is read six hundred years later at the end of the twentieth century in the United States of America.

The artist needs something greater than himself, something outside himself. This doctrine is illustrated not only in Dante's dependence on Virgil, but also in his meeting with Brunetto Latini in canto 15. It is almost the son's need for fatherhood that we sense in Stephen and Bloom in *Ulysses*, and in Marcel's strong attachment to Swann. Stephen has a real father as well as a mythological father, Daedalus, whom he addresses in the final sentence of *Portrait of the Artist as a Young Man:* "Old father, old artificer, stand me now and ever in good stead."

Daedalus with his skill as artificer built first the labyrinth (to contain the Minotaur), and then the wings that enabled him to escape from Crete. The streets of Dublin are as labyrinthine for Joyce, as are the streets of Paris for Baudelaire, as complex as Eliot's *Wasteland* and Dante's Hell with its vestibule and nine circles. The labyrinth is that place where the artist is trapped. It is made up of his nation, his language, and his religion. It is that complexity out of which he has to escape by means of his art. Daedalus in his flight from Crete is the archetype of Joyce fleeing from Ireland, of Marcel fleeing from Paris to Venice in a key passage near the end of Proust's novel, and of Dante Alighieri in his nineteen-year exile from Florence.

Then, in the transformation that great art brings about, the labyrinth, by which and in which we live, is changed into the circle. The structure of *Ulysses* is cyclical. Bloom leaves home at the beginning and returns home at the end. Dante's journey through Hell is a vindication of Providence. It starts in a dark wood on the surface of the earth and ends with a vision of the stars.

The elements of the cycle—words, myths, and metaphors—are not mere imitations of nature. They are insights into reality.

Selected Bibliography

Italian Editions of "The Divine Comedy"

Alighieri, Dante, *La divina commedia*. Testo critico della Società dantesca italiana; riveduto col commento scartazziniano; rifatto da Giuseppe Vandelli. Milan: 1957 (seventeenth edition).

Alighieri, Dante, *La divina commedia*. Edited and annotated by C. H. Grandgent. D. C. Heath: 1913.

Alighieri, Dante, *La divina commedia*. Edited and annotated by C. H. Grandgent. Revised by Charles S. Singleton. Harvard University Press: 1972.

Bilingual Editions with Commentary

Singleton, Charles S., *Inferno*. Vol. 1 text, vol. 2 commentary. Princeton: 1970.

The Inferno. Translated by J. A. Carlyle. Revised by H. Oelsner. The Temple Classics: 1970.

Dante's Inferno. Translated by John D. Sinclair. Oxford: 1974.

English Translations

The Comedy of Dante Alighieri. Cantica I, *Hell*. Translated by Dorothy L. Sayers. Penguin Books: 1974.

Dante's Inferno. Translated by John Ciardi. Rutgers University Press: 1954.

Dante's Inferno. Translated by Mark Musa. Indiana University Press: 1971.

Commentary and Criticism in English

Auerbach, Erich, *Dante Poet of the Secular World*. Translated by R. Manheim. University of Chicago Press: 1974.

Auerbach, Erich, *Mimesis*. Translated by W. Trask. Doubleday-Anchor: 1957. (See chapter 8, "Farinata and Cavalcante.")

Barbi, Michele, *Life of Dante*. Translated by P. Ruggiers. Cambridge University Press: 1955.

Bergin, Thomas G., *Dante*. Orion Press: 1965.

Brandeis, Irma, editor. *Discussions of The Divine Comedy*. D. C. Heath: 1961.

Brandeis, Irma, *The Ladder of Vision*. Chatto and Windus: 1960.

Charity, A. C., *Events and Their Afterlife: The Dialectics of Typology in the Bible and Dante*. Cambridge: 1966.

Eliot, T. S., "Dante" in *Selected Essays*. Harcourt, Brace: 1932.

Fergusson, Francis, *Dante*. Macmillan: 1966.

Freccero, John, editor. *Dante, A Collection of Critical Essays*. Prentice-Hall: 1965.

Musa, Mark, editor. *Essays on Dante*. Indiana University Press: 1964.

Snider, Denton J., *Dante's Inferno, A Commentary*. William H. Miner: 1892.

Strauss, Walter A., "Proust, Giotto, Dante." *Dante Studies* 96:

Williams, Charles, *The Figure of Beatrice*. Noonday Press: 1961.

Aids to Reading the "Inferno"

Bodkin, Maud, *Archetypal Patterns in Poetry*. Vintage Books: 1958.

Dunbar, H. F., *Symbolism in Medieval Thought*. Oxford: 1929.

Vossler, Karl, *Medieval Culture: An Introduction to Dante and His Times*. Vols. 1 and 2. Harcourt, Brace: 1929.

Index